America in Retreat

Foreign Policy under Donald Trump

Mel Gurtov
Portland State University

ROWMAN & LITTLEFIELD
Lanham • Boulder • New York • London

Executive Editor: Susan McEachern
Assistant Editor: Katelyn Turner
Higher Education Channel Manager: Jonathan Raeder

Credits and acknowledgments for material borrowed from other sources, and reproduced with permission, appear on the appropriate pages within the text.

Published by Rowman & Littlefield
An imprint of The Rowman & Littlefield Publishing Group, Inc.
4501 Forbes Boulevard, Suite 200, Lanham, Maryland 20706
https://rowman.com

6 Tinworth Street, London SE11 5AL, United Kingdom

British Library Cataloguing in Publication Information Available

Library of Congress Cataloging-in-Publication Data
Names: Gurtov, Melvin, author.
Title: America in retreat : foreign policy under Donald Trump / Mel Gurtov, Portland State University.
Other titles: Foreign policy under Donald Trump
Description: Lanham : Rowman & Littlefield, [2021] | Series: World social change | Includes bibliographical references and index.
Identifiers: LCCN 2020013240 (print) | LCCN 2020013241 (ebook) | ISBN 9781538145661 (hardcover) | ISBN 9781538145678 (paperback) | ISBN 9781538145685 (epub)
Subjects: LCSH: United States—Foreign relations—2017- | Trump, Donald, 1946- — Influence.
Classification: LCC E895 .G87 2021 (print) | LCC E895 (ebook) | DDC 973.933—dc23
LC record available at https://lccn.loc.gov/2020013240
LC ebook record available at https://lccn.loc.gov/2020013241

To a Free Press: to its principles and practices,
and to the independent journalists who fight to preserve them against
the real "enemies of the people."

And to Brynn Appel and Gavin Joseph Gabor,
my wonderful grandchildren.

Contents

Preface

Friends laughed when I told them I was writing a book about Donald Trump's foreign policy. Does he *have* a foreign policy, they asked with a smile? A good question, actually, because explaining Trump's foreign policy entails explaining the complexities of Donald Trump himself, and that's no easy task. Still, I take Trump's foray into foreign policy seriously, if for no other reason than that his policies and, equally, his behavior have done serious damage to US diplomacy, the institutions of government, relations with key partners, and the global economy and environment. Trump's tenure, which may not end in January 2021, should serve as a lasting lesson for what future presidents should and should not say or do.

My book is a highly critical account of Trump the person and Trump the chief executive and commander in chief. I confess to sometimes having a hard time being objective about a man who harbors such deep prejudices and extraordinary ignorance about the world—not to mention an unwillingness to temper either by learning from and about others. I do believe, however, that my assessments are well supported and reasonably objective—and that when the documentary record of Trump's tenure is finally released, my conclusions and the assessments of other critics will be upheld and may even prove to be too mild.

I relied heavily for my research on the outstanding journalism of the *New York Times*, *Washington Post*, *The Guardian*, CNN, and other media—the very sources Trump condemned as "fake news" and the reason for dedicating this book to a free press. Rarely did their reporting of Trump and his administration's activities prove faulty, a sign that investigative journalism is alive and well. I also cited those writers whose interviews of the principals in the administration, or whose service in it, proved reliable and insightful.

I am grateful to a number of friends who helped bring this work to fruition: Walter Clemens, Glen Jackson, Larry Kirsch, Milton Leitenberg, Michael Marien, and Fred Sierles. I owe special thanks to Mark Selden for appreciating the value of the book, offering helpful suggestions, and shepherding it to a favorable decision.

Mel Gurtov, Deadwood, Oregon, February 2020

Chapter One

We Were Warned

"AMERICA FIRST"

Approaching his third year in office, Donald Trump was reported to be isolated and angry, at war with his staff and critics, under multiple investigations, yet convinced he was doing everything right and supposedly puzzled over the lack of appreciation.[1] Several months later, those investigations had so gotten under his skin that he raged against his Democratic critics, insisted he was "the most transparent president" in history, and vowed not to do any legislative business with them until the investigations—by then numbering twenty-eight—ended.[2] His behavior was mercilessly derided in the mainstream media—pathological liar, narcissist, paranoid, irrational, man-child—as was his management of the White House: free-for-all, undisciplined, lacking guardrails. The Democrat-controlled House of Representatives, after the 2018 midterm elections, was all about impeachment, galvanized by a whistleblower's account of the president's attempt to gain Ukraine's help in Trump's reelection campaign. A constitutional crisis loomed as the White House refused to comply with subpoenas and demands for documents.

Meantime, the United States of America was adrift, its reputation tarnished and its international leadership in doubt—in short, a nation in retreat. Mainstream publications lumped the "authoritarian" US president with leaders in China, Russia, Egypt, and Saudi Arabia—people Trump admired and called friends. Trump escaped impeachment in a mock trial in the Senate that rejected calling witnesses or documents, but his claims of acquittal rang hollow. Not since the Watergate scandal had the country experienced a more troubled time, or a greater threat to democracy.

That the United States faced such a dire situation should not have come as a surprise. Donald Trump made no secret of his "America first" views during the 2016 presidential campaign. Liberals and many conservatives responded caustically, calling him unfit for office and questioning his foreign policy positions and credentials. No critique was more powerful, or prophetic, than an open letter signed by fifty former senior foreign policy officials in Republican administrations, from Richard M. Nixon's to George W. Bush's. Here is an excerpt:

> From a foreign policy perspective, Donald Trump is not qualified to be President and Commander-in-Chief. Indeed, we are convinced that he would be a dangerous President and would put at risk our country's national security and well-being.
>
> Most fundamentally, Mr. Trump lacks the character, values, and experience to be President. He weakens U.S. moral authority as the leader of the free world. He appears to lack basic knowledge about and belief in the U.S. Constitution, U.S. laws, and U.S. institutions, including religious tolerance, freedom of the press, and an independent judiciary.
>
> In addition, Mr. Trump has demonstrated repeatedly that he has little understanding of America's vital national interests, its complex diplomatic challenges, its indispensable alliances, and the democratic values on which U.S. foreign policy must be based. At the same time, he persistently compliments our adversaries and threatens our allies and friends.[3]

This extraordinary takedown of candidate Trump proved accurate in every detail, though my analysis draws the line at its advocacy of a return to traditional foreign policy interests and values that have condoned interventionism, systematic human rights violations, and ever-higher military spending. In any case, the Republicans' critique did not affect Trump's election or his foreign policy views. Foreign policy was not a major issue in the 2016 election, thanks in part to outgoing president Barack Obama's decision not to make public the discovery of Russian attacks on the electoral system in Trump's favor. Thus Trump had a virtual free pass not just on Russian interference and possible coordination with Trump's campaign, but also on some of his most cringeworthy ideas during the campaign, such as abolishing the North Atlantic Treaty Organization (NATO) and making more use of nuclear weapons. Health care, the climate crisis, and Trump's impeachment were at center stage as 2020 began, but the onset of the coronavirus changed everything, propelling the pandemic to the forefront and making responsibility for it a major issue in US-China relations and in the presidential election.

Trump's international priorities were major departures from the positions of previous Republican administrations, not to mention Democratic ones—which may explain why every living president distanced himself from Trump's declaration of "America First." Whereas George H. W. Bush proposed a "new world order," George W. Bush touted the "war on terror" and "axis of evil," and Barack Obama advocated engaging longtime adversaries,

Trump disparaged grand internationalist visions. He suggested in his inaugural address that the only thing that mattered was putting America first. "I'm the Lone Ranger," Trump proclaimed, and in most respects he was.[4]

During Trump's tenure it was common to find analysts suggesting that he had defined a new and lasting foreign policy consensus built around anti-immigration sentiment and trade protectionism.[5] Trump certainly identified with those issues as he took office, believing that they won him the election.[6] That led to the notion that Trump wanted to take America back to the future, that is, to the 1920s and isolationism or even to the 1930s and the rise of fascism. Rather, I think Trump capitalized on economic, political, and cultural disruptions that emerged in the 1990s and became full-blown crises of capitalism and democracy by the time Trump ran for office. Trump's behavior at times conjured up visions of earlier times, but he faced international problems that, while not entirely new, were far more profound and interdependent than anything political leaders had previously faced, such as China's rise, a global economy in disarray, a climate crisis, a pandemic, and uncertain alliances. As for isolationism, it is true that Trump had no personal interest in either a "globalist/internationalist" agenda—playing a lead role in multilateral organizations, espousing free trade, extending intervention in overseas conflicts, and strengthening alliances, for example—or in a progressive agenda, such as protection of the environment, democratic governance, and a strong commitment to human rights. But Trump could not avoid entanglement in old and new geopolitical challenges abroad, from Africa and the Middle East to Northeast Asia. His hope to displace internationalism also had to contend with the contrary views of many of his advisers, not to mention the foreign policy bureaucracy, a public still largely supportive of strong US involvement abroad, and the tumult of impeachment. But foremost among his challenges was his own largely incoherent philosophy and impulsiveness when called upon to act. In short, there was no Trump Doctrine.

This book is a critical examination of Donald Trump's foreign policy: the influences on it of his character, business philosophy, and leadership style; and his administration's policies toward key countries and regions. Trump conducted foreign policy with little attention to American ideals, institutions of government, national interests, diplomatic tradition, or—most extraordinarily—systematic policy formulation. Yet he did bring to the office ideas about the proper direction of foreign policy—ideas prompted by nationalism (as he claimed) and populism (as the media insisted). Neither label fit well: His nationalism was ethnic, based on white identity, and his populism was authoritarian—anything but antiestablishment.[7] No matter; Trump doggedly pursued those ideas in defiance of advisers and anyone else who questioned him. My job as a longtime student of US foreign policy is to try to explain and, from a human-interest perspective, assess the Trump phenomenon—

most importantly, his administration's impact on people and planet in an era of permanent war and climate crisis.[8]

THE "LONE RANGER" RIDES AGAIN

Donald Trump was not entirely new to foreign affairs. Observers agree that 1987, which happens to be the year Trump first visited Moscow in hopes of building a hotel there, marks Trump's debut as a commentator on international affairs. His main concern in those days was about the excessive cost of US alliances.[9] In full-page ads that year, Trump argued that wealthy nations could afford to pay for their own defense, which would help America's economy grow and show that the country had backbone.[10] "We are defending some of the world's wealthiest countries for nothing," he said in 1990.[11] Trump thereafter regularly talked down the virtues not only of defense alliances in Europe and Asia, but also trade arrangements with allies and just about everyone else. He called for "renegotiating" all such agreements.[12] China later became his favorite target for unfair trade practices, but Japan, which he accused of "openly screwing us," came first. He admired leaders in both countries for being "strong"—in China, for cracking down on dissent, and in Japan, for making "our leaders look totally second rate."[13] "America First" emerged as Trump's answer: a tough-minded president willing to end freeloading and promote a stronger home economy.[14]

Trump proved quite consistent on trade and alliances. As discussed later, he was so convinced of Chinese perfidy on trade, and equally convinced that they had tricked the United States into paying for their economic rise ("We have rebuilt China single-handedly"),[15] that he unleashed a trade war in 2018. By that time China had risen to become international enemy number one on Trump's list. His determination to reduce US overseas obligations resurfaced many times, such as his insistence that NATO allies pay a greater share of the common defense bill, and his administration's reduction of foreign aid to countries and United Nations programs judged unfriendly to the United States or unreliable in serving US interests. Everyone was ripping off America, he said: the Chinese, the Mexicans, the Japanese. Certainly, there were legitimate issues of fairness here, but Trump blew them out of proportion and allowed them to color his economic views, as when he said, "These countries are much richer than us. We're not a rich country. We're a debtor nation."[16] What he neglected to mention is that on his watch, the US budget deficit climbed more than $1 trillion and government debt, more than $2 trillion, all due in substantial part to his very un-Republican indifference to a balanced budget and increased government spending.

Trump's emphasis on America getting its money's worth earned him the title of transactional president. But that title was overused; virtually every action he took was explained as transactional. His presidency in fact was only partly defined by financial and other deal making. Trump was a man with a strong sense of entitlement, an instinct for revenge, a get-tough attitude, a contempt for others' views, and (as his comments on the United States "rebuilding" China and "debtor nation" showed) a strong tendency to exaggerate. But above all, he was obsessed with winning: "I can only say: my whole life has been about winning," and "when I do something, I win. . . . My natural inclination is to win," he told interviewers in 2016.[17] All these characteristics were honed in a long and not entirely illustrious business career.

The best clues to Trump's thinking and behavior as president may actually lie in his business philosophy and practice. As head of the Trump Organization, he concerned himself chiefly with cutting a good real estate deal without regard for who sat on the other side of the table. Numerous sources—not to mention Trump's own (ghostwritten) book, *The Art of the Deal*—point to an aggressive, take-no-prisoners model—a model in large part learned from the lawyer Roy Cohn, Senator Joseph McCarthy's front man who was later disbarred for unethical conduct; and from Trump's father, Fred Trump, from whom Trump inherited a great deal of money along with the fine art of cheating on taxes and notorious self-promotion.[18] His own business experience was a further endorsement of that model, for Trump had fought back from multiple bankruptcies in his career. He knew about losing—he was, after all, the self-declared "king of debt"—as well as about winning. The patterns in this model are the following:

- Rule by instinct, not by prearranged plan.
- Go for the jugular. Find points of leverage.
- Winning is everything.
- Demand absolute loyalty. Seek revenge on the disloyal.
- Trust no one. Test friendships.
- Fight rather than compromise.
- Lie whenever necessary; pay no attention to the truth.
- Defy rules and norms; do whatever you must to secure a deal.
- Never apologize, never admit defeat.
- Keep all power to yourself; trust nobody beyond the family.

These patterns of personal behavior translate directly into treating foreign affairs as though governments are run just like businesses—at least those Trump ran. To wit:

- Information is not as important as personal instinct.
- Maintain a tight circle of advisers.
- Be suspicious of experts and the "deep state."

- Play to win, not to negotiate differences.
- If attacked, counterattack with a vengeance.
- Communicate to the world in tough but equivocal language.

   Trump seemed to believe governing was *just another opportunity* to bring glory to the Trump brand. In earlier days, when Trump was first amassing the signs of wealth—boats, airlines, the Trump Tower—he allowed that they were all actually "props for the show," the show being Trump himself.[19] Hence, for Trump the line between brand and business—and as president, between brand and governing—did not exist. How could it? At the time he campaigned, his international business interests alone—real estate holdings, management, and branding agreements—comprised 131 companies in eighteen countries.[20] When elected, Trump refused to put his business empire in a blind trust or divest, instead putting it in the hands of his two eldest sons while retaining ownership. Filings for Trump trademarks worldwide continued unabated.[21] His intent was clear: He was counting on greater personal enrichment while in power. What he did not count on was governing under a microscope and amidst legal, constitutional, and bureaucratic constraints. Accusations of corruption and conflicts of interest put the Trump empire in federal and state courts, making the brand a liability. As matters turned out, the brand did not fare much better than the man.[22]

THE FITNESS ISSUE

Trump's egotism infused his personal and international instincts, which may explain why the US foreign policy establishment focused as much on his personality as on his policy views. The critique of Trump that opens this chapter is one example. There are plenty of others. Thomas Pickering, a former US ambassador to Russia with a long history in the diplomatic service, said the following in an interview on the eve of Trump's initial summit in 2018 with Russian president Vladimir Putin in Helsinki, Finland: "Trump's own kind of unbridled, egotistical narcissism seems to be the major definer of [summitry under the Trump presidency]. U.S. national interests take a second or third place. Reality TV as an instrument for promoting Trump, his ego, and his political success ranks in his mind and his actions way above promoting U.S. national interests."[23] James Clapper, director of national intelligence under Obama for seven years, wrote in a memoir: "I don't believe our democracy can function for long on lies. We have elected someone as president of the United States whose first instincts are to twist and distort truth to his advantage, to generate financial benefit to himself and his family, and, in doing so, to demean the values this country has traditionally stood for." When Trump fired back at Clapper, John Brennan, a former director of the CIA, defended him. Addressing Trump, Brennan said: "Your hypocrisy knows no bounds. Jim Clapper is a man of integrity, honesty, ethics, & morality. You are not."[24] Brennan called Trump's performance at the Helsinki summit "nothing short of treasonous," and said Trump was "drunk on power."

What those criticisms of Trump indirectly bring out are the large gaps in Trump's preparedness for the highest office: the absence of governing experience or military service, the deficiencies of character, and the great distance from the lives of ordinary people. Trump's business background certainly prepared him for making deals—by bullying, not by compromising—but for little else, especially shaping foreign and national security policy. As would soon become apparent, Trump had no conception of what it meant to be a commander in chief of the world's most powerful military, imagining that threats to use it, plus occasional flattery—as he learned from business and legal dealings—would suffice to defeat opponents. Nor did Trump convey any understanding of poverty, social welfare, climate change, or race relations. He pretended to be Everyman, despite all evidence to the contrary—as when he said about the federal workers who were going without pay during the 2018–2019 government shutdown, "I can relate" and "they'll make adjustments."[25] Yet he seemed to succeed with his so-called core of supporters, who rallied to Trump's brash anti-elite message and the simple solutions he offered to international problems: a bigger military, protective tariffs, a promise to win so often that "you may get bored with winning."

Trump prided himself on being a disrupter, a chaos *meister*, a rule bender—qualities admired by his strongest supporters but unsuited to managing a superpower. When he took the reins of government from Obama, Trump was woefully unprepared but, worse yet, apparently not convinced he needed to *be* prepared. By one account, Trump thought the whole idea of a transition team was ridiculous, apparently because winning the election had seemed far-fetched. When he did win, he summarily fired the team (led by his one-time friend, former New Jersey governor Chris Christie) and discarded Christie's detailed transition plan. Trump then installed a hodgepodge of loyalists who either had no prior experience dealing with the work of government agencies, or had ties with the very industries they would be regulating, or were friends of the Trumps.[26] Rather than learn the policy ropes, the main job of these people was to remove Obama-era appointees. This managerial failure was not accidental: It reflected Trump's unfamiliarity with government, his (and the far right's) distaste for Obama, and his stubborn belief that he had all the tools he needed to run things—early signs that arrogant self-regard and bureaucratic chaos would be hallmarks of the Trump years.[27]

If it is possible to bring together all these personality and behavioral traits in one sentence that conveys their meaning for Trump's presidency, I offer this: *Donald Trump viewed the presidency as an opportunity for him to do*

whatever he felt like doing, free from legal, moral, or bureaucratic con-
straints, but also free to convert personal prejudices and greed into public
policy—in short, carrying on just as he had in his business and personal life.
But those characteristics also provided the glue for his critics and the basis of
his impeachment.

So I begin with the two sides of Donald Trump that are equally problematic when it comes to leadership: his personality and his approach to carrying out foreign policy.

Chapter Two

President Trump, in Person

THE "STABLE GENIUS"

Political scientists are generally loath to draw personality profiles of political leaders, much less attempt to psychoanalyze them in search of explanations for their behavior. They prefer to analyze the policy issues and positions that political leaders espouse, the assumption being that regardless of personality, political leaders take stands based on "rational" considerations, such as their personal philosophy, the views of their trusted advisers, public opinion, and decision-making style—the latter including the advisory system, organization of the bureaucracy, and evidence of groupthink. I do delve into all those matters. But Donald Trump represents a wholly different figure, one with an outsize personality but without a strong political identity or interest in organizing a bureaucracy to improve information flow and leadership. He had changed his mind about party affiliation and political issues numerous times. He had ideas, of course, and he conveyed them with enormous self-confidence in his ability to manage any project with minimal help. ("I have a gut, and my gut tells me more sometimes than anybody else's brain can ever tell me," he told interviewers.)[1] His stubbornness and enormous ego account for the strength of his convictions. During his campaign he claimed to know more than anyone else about just about everything, evidently because of superior instincts. Unfortunately for him, these supposed attributes were also his worst enemy.

Trump described himself as a "very stable genius," indicative of his penchant for self-inflation. He exaggerated his successes and rationalized his failures, creating a myth of himself as a self-made man.[2] He constantly blamed others rather than accept responsibility for his actions. He walled off emotions and took actions that to most people would be heartless and lacking empathy—such as by showing callous indifference to human suffering.[3] Trump was forever on the attack, abusing his public office by railing against people he disliked and whom he could hurt for political advantage. Trump responded angrily, even vengefully, to each and every criticism or perceived slight. He seemed paranoid about people and groups that he believed were out to get him—the special counsel's office (SCO) under Robert S. Mueller III, the bureaucratic "deep state," the media, and the FBI, for example—or failed to serve him with absolute loyalty, such as Attorney General Jeff Sessions.[4] (Trump demanded nondisclosure agreements from his staff, a fruitless attempt to prevent them from ever saying critical things about the president, vice-president, and their families.)[5] He had difficulty learning from mistakes and accepting setbacks—witness his unceasing efforts to build a wall on the Mexico border despite the unpopularity of the wall and Mexico's adamant refusal to pay for it as Trump had pledged it would. He was unable to rise above petty politics when the occasion demanded it, such as his disrespectful reaction to the death of Senator John McCain, a Vietnam War hero who had butted heads with Trump several times over policy;[6] or his lashing out at "very dishonest and corrupt people" who sought his conviction at the Senate impeachment trial—in a speech at a national prayer breakfast traditionally devoted to bringing people together.[7]

In a word, this was a president who, just when you thought he had hit rock bottom with low-class behavior, went even lower the next day. Psychiatrists and psychologists, normally reluctant to analyze someone they have not personally examined, made an exception for Trump, whom they found to have significant personality disorders, chief among them narcissism and lack of empathy.[8] How else to diagnose a man who claimed to have won awards that either did not exist (such as for Michigan's man of the year) or were not given to him (such as for *Time* magazine's man of the year)—or who rarely had a word to say about human rights at home or abroad?

These observations, shared by many biographers and others with first-hand experience, lead me to another: that Donald Trump entered the race for president, and then occupied the White House, with an enormous chip on his shoulder. Some say he felt embarrassed and humiliated after being roasted by President Obama at the annual White House Correspondents' Association Dinner in 2011. (Obama's taunt was partly over the birther issue—the lie that Obama was not born in the United States—which Trump had by then already begun pushing.) And it certainly seems that Trump was motivated in part by a determination to erase Obama's legacy—on everything from health care and the environment to Iran policy. Perhaps; but the larger humiliation might be that for years he was not taken seriously as a presidential candidate by the political elite in New York or elsewhere. The Republican Party establishment vehemently opposed his candidacy, and Trump had to bear the sharp-edged criticisms of him by the likes of Jeb Bush, Ted Cruz, Marco Rubio, John

Kasich, Chris Christie, and Mitt Romney—all active or former officeholders at the time. We may never know how hurtful Trump considered these attacks to be, but judging from his retorts—the nasty nicknames for his opponents, his dismissive attitude toward them, and his undisguised hostility toward Obama, Hillary Clinton, and anyone associated with them that carried into and throughout Trump's time in office—Trump probably felt spiteful and determined to show all his detractors that he didn't need to build on anyone's legacy, or anyone else's money.[9]

What should be added to Trump's possible longtime defensiveness about his capacity is the questionable *legitimacy* of his presidency. Apart from the fact that he lost the popular vote in 2016 by about three million, it is entirely possible, perhaps even likely, that Trump could not have been elected without two unique interventions, one from Russian hacking and trolling in US social media, the other from Trump's criminal payoffs to suppress stories about his infidelities. Neither of these factors probably made a difference to his core—the millions of Trump defenders who admired his defiance of political conventions, his seeming toughness, and his campaign promises to help ordinary people. Trump's lies and provably false statements were of no consequence to them; he channeled their anger toward the system's unfairness.[10] Yet that core rarely accounted for more than 40 percent of the electorate, and his approval rating was consistently the lowest in US history. Those facts may explain the White House's constant efforts after the 2018 midterm election defeats and numerous investigations of Trump to turn the legitimacy issue around. It cast the Democrats as radical-left Trump haters out to (in Trump's words) "win an election in 2020 that they know they cannot legitimately win."[11]

"TRUMP AT WAR" IN AMERICA

As the White House circled the wagons in mid-2018 in an increasingly desperate attempt to turn public attention from the president's Russia problem, Trump was constantly on Twitter attacking his favorite enemies: the press, the Department of Justice, the FBI, Hillary Clinton, liberals in general, and anyone else who criticized or acted against him. Stephen K. Bannon, once one of Trump's chief strategists and still an influence on him, portrayed Trump as engaged in a monumental struggle: "This is Trump at war—war with the elites; war with the permanent political class; war with the opposition party media, tech oligarchs, the Antifa anarchists. This is the reason Trump is president—to take on the vested interests in this country for hard working [sic] Americans."[12] In fact, Trump's attacks had nothing to do with protecting "hard working Americans," much less warring with "the elites." While Trump convinced many workers that the system was rigged against them, and that only he could speak for "the people," as president he took steps to keep the system rigged in favor of the wealthiest Americans, starting with lower corporate and personal taxes and cabinet and agency appointments.

Trump's preferred method of communicating to the public, via rallies and Twitter, tells us much about how his version of populism became synonymous with demagoguery. Rallies substituted for public events and yelling a few words to reporters substituted for press conferences. The slogans and political targets were the same as those employed during his campaign, starting with "Lock her [Hillary Clinton] up!" Had Trump been a *popular* president, he would have assumed the role of unifier and harmonizer seeking to expand his base. Yet here was Trump still calling, repeatedly, for jailing his presidential opponent, denouncing the "witch hunt" to investigate Russia's election interference and his impeachment, and condemning as "fake news" anything critical of him. (The *New York Times* editorial board, in a November 30, 2019, editorial, "Who Will Tell the Truth about the Free Press?" noted more than 600 occasions when Trump used that expression.) Once the Mueller report came out, he renewed the call, saying that Clinton, some "dirty cops" at the FBI, and the Mueller investigators had conspired to carry out a "coup."[13]

The incessant tweets, sometimes numbering in the hundreds a day, were often intemperate, childlike, conspiratorial rants—rambling, illogical, nagging, threatening, and in poor English to boot. Often the subject was some pet grievance rather than public policy, raising questions about not just his competence but also his psychological balance. After all, what is one to make of a president who used the bully pulpit to lash out at people he disliked— leading figures in sports (e.g., Colin Kaepernick and LeBron James), journalism (e.g., CNN's Jim Acosta and Don Lemon), and Hollywood (e.g., Arnold Schwarzenegger); media owners and editors (e.g., Jeff Bezos, owner of the *Washington Post* and founder and CEO of Amazon); even *Saturday Night Live* comedians. Where possible, Trump would punish these critics—for example, by insisting that the Pentagon award a $10 billion computer contract to Microsoft rather than Amazon.[14]

Trump detested weakness and pounced on anyone he believed displayed it. Power is denoted by fear, he once proposed.[15] During his presidential campaigns his bullying techniques were on full display, as he seemingly tolerated physical assaults on hecklers and gave his rivals snide nicknames designed to humiliate as well as divert attention from the issues. This is the man who once demanded that Obama release his college transcripts, but threatened his own high school to ensure that his academic records were buried, probably out of fear that they would reveal a less-than-stellar student.[16] His tweets and comments in the White House were replete with disdainful comments about those he considered weak or in some way vulnerable.[17] He dubbed them "losers," like Attorney General Sessions for not undermining the Mueller investigation, George Conway ("a stone cold LOSER & husband from hell!" of Kellyanne Conway) for challenging Trump's mental balance,[18] and Justin Trudeau after the Canadian prime minister criticized Trump's trade policies. "Weak politicians" was how Trump characterized Republicans who opposed his tariff war. A "total joke," Trump said of the "globalist" Koch brothers' PAC, Americans for Prosperity, after Charles G. Koch criticized Trump's "divisive" rule and "destructive" protectionist trade and immigration policies.[19]

To apologize is to be weak, Trump believed. Even when caught in a flagrant lie, he rarely backed down and instead tried to weasel his way out of the lie. When he finally did apologize for promoting the myth of Obama's birth record, he offered a follow-up lie that Hillary Clinton had made the claim first.[20] More than once, Trump criticized Sweden's liberal immigration policy, citing a terrorist attack that had never happened. When Trump blamed "both sides" for the violence at Charlottesville, Virginia, in August 2017 during a neo-Nazi demonstration, he at first acceded to his staff's insistence that he issue a correction. But then he reversed himself, saying, "You never apologize. I didn't do anything wrong in the first place. Why look weak?"[21] In response to the public outcry that followed his decision to separate parents from children in the name of border security. Trump backed down. But far from apologizing for the policy or reappraising it, he and his team devised ways to keep hundreds of the children permanently separated. Trump summarized a summit meeting with North Korea's leader, Kim Jong-un, in 2018 by saying: "I think he's [Kim] going to do these things. I may be wrong. I mean, I may stand before you in six months and say, 'Hey, I was wrong.' I don't know that I'll ever admit that, but I'll find some kind of an excuse."[22] Indeed, he always did.

WHOSE SIDE ARE YOU ON?

Trump was not just "at war" with his detractors; he saw himself as in "a war every day" with his own appointees. All it took to become Trump's enemy was not agreeing with him, not to mention publicly disputing him. Disagreement amounted to disloyalty, which (as we will shortly see) is why the attrition rate among his cabinet and staff was exceptionally high. Any of them who too forcefully challenged his ideas, attempted to upstage him, or on leaving office spoke critically about his character and competence immediately came under fire. Take Trump's former assistant and *Apprentice* contestant, Omarosa Manigault Newman, who was fired as an adviser and retaliated by publishing a very unflattering memoir and revealing tape recordings of conversations in the White House. Trump turned on her, calling her a "low life" and a "dog," saying he kept her on only because she "only said GREAT things" about him. Michael Cohen was Trump's longtime lawyer and fixer until he opened up to Mueller about Trump's order to pay hush money to cover up affairs and other potentially impeachable offenses. Trump then spent many days tweeting that Cohen was "weak" and a consummate liar. On retiring, Paul Ryan, speaker of the House, was hailed by Trump as having "a legacy of achievement that nobody can question"—until, that is, Ryan said in interviews that Trump "didn't know *anything* about government" and was a deplorable leader. Trump responded with numerous tweets excoriating Ryan, including: "Couldn't get him out of Congress fast enough!"[23] And there's Anthony Scaramucci, briefly Trump's communications director, who not only turned on Trump but tried to forge a coalition dedicated to defeating him in 2020. "Nobody ever heard of this dope until he met me," said Trump in one of numerous attacks. Finally, and most impactful of all, were Trump's actions when John Bolton, the national security adviser, wrote a memoir after leaving office that upended Trump's contentions about the withholding of US aid to Ukraine. Trump not only attacked Bolton's credibility; he tried to quash the book on grounds of revealing highly classified information, and he cited executive privilege in attempting to prevent Bolton from testifying at the Senate's impeachment trial. Bottom line: If you weren't for Trump, you were against him.

He carried his angst, and vindictiveness, with critics to the point of creating what amounted to an enemies list, one that reminded many—for example, Admiral Mike Mullen, retired former chairman of the joint chiefs of staff[24]—of Richard Nixon's list that John Dean, then White House counsel, revealed in the Watergate hearings. The distinctive feature of Trump's list initially was that it included people who worked for Obama—fifty in the National Security Council (NSC) in 2017—but later extended to people (twenty-six in all) whom Trump branded "treasonous."[25] Among his enemies were several former top intelligence officials, such as James Clapper and John Brennan, who regularly criticized Trump in the media. When Rex Tillerson opened up about his time as secretary of state, criticizing Trump for his impetuousness, among other things, Trump—who once had praised Tillerson as a "world class [*sic*] player"—immediately turned on him, calling him "dumb as a rock" and "lazy as hell."[26] Once Defense Secretary James Mattis resigned with a stinging rebuke of Trump's foreign policy and drew favorable attention for playing the role of Trump's minder, the president moved up Mattis's end date by two months and did a complete about-face in his evaluation of Mattis, turning a great choice for the job into a questionable one.[27] Jerome H. Powell, Trump's pick to head the Federal Reserve, wasn't in the job very long before Trump called him his worst appointment after the stock market tanked at the end of 2018. Later, at a major financial conference, Trump said, "My only question is, who is our bigger enemy, Jay Powell or Chairman Xi?"

Then there's the FBI: As James Comey's memoir describes, Trump heaped praise on his leadership of the FBI, but once the president's constant pressure on Comey to demonstrate loyalty and quash the Russia investigation failed to pay off, Comey was history.[28] From then on, Trump heaped abuse on Comey. Christopher Wray, Trump's third FBI director, also came under attack when he supported an inspector general's report that exonerated the FBI of blame for investigating Russian election interference in 2016. (At a political rally, Trump called the FBI "scum.") Last are all the distinguished State Department and intelligence specialists on Ukraine who defied the White House and testified as to Trump's attempt to get Ukraine's president to investigate a political rival. One was Ambassador Marie Yovanovitch, whom Trump ordered recalled in May 2019 after telling Ukraine's president she was "bad news."[29] She and the other officials, all with many years of distinguished service, became "Never Trumpers" in the president's eyes.

On the other hand, loyalty to Trump paid off—loyalty that seemed to amount to servility. Appointments to key offices seem to have been made with the highest priority, not to competence or experience, but to willingness to do his bidding and not seek the limelight. He sought to pack the Federal Reserve with an economist and a former pizza executive who had both personal and professional strikes against them, but could be relied on to keep interest rates low. Former Fed governors derided Trump's disregard for its independence in installing yes-men.[30] He installed Justice Department leaders (Matthew Whitaker and William P. Barr) who ensured that before the Mueller report was given to congressional leaders, their boss was protected from accusations of collusion with Russia. Barr's handling of the report put him in line as Trump's next fixer, earning him lavish praise from the president, which Barr further earned by going abroad in search of help from other countries' intelligence services to discredit the Russia interference story, and, in a move without precedent, dropping the government's case against Michael Flynn, Trump's first national security adviser.[31] Trump appointed an internal revenue legal counsel who could guarantee that Trump's income tax returns would never see the light of day.

What all these appointments also had in common is that they undermined the integrity of what are supposed to be independent bodies not subject to presidential interference. And that was their purpose: to deinstitutionalize the US government and thereby expand presidential power. As two former government lawyers put it in the wake of the Michael Flynn case, "Mr. Trump, Mr. Barr and those echoing them have used the Flynn case to make condemnation of federal law enforcement official U.S. government policy." In a word, the villains were the FBI and the (former) Justice Department, not Flynn.[32]

A number of observers were struck by how Trump acted like the *capo* of a Mafia-like gang. His intolerance of dissent, his corruption, and his and his advisers' lawlessness all fit the Mafia image. During his days in New York real estate, Trump did business with mafiosi—Russian as well as American.[33] Trump even *sounded* at times like a gang leader, such as when he said "nobody disobeys my orders" when the Mueller report revealed the opposite, or when he called the report a "total 'hit job'" after initially saying it proved his "total exoneration."[34] Convinced that Ambassador Yovanovitch wasn't loyal to his cause, Trump told supporters at a private dinner, "Get rid of her! Get her out tomorrow. I don't care. Get her out tomorrow. Take her out. Okay? Do it."[35] And who can forget the cabinet meeting that saw each member take turns extolling Trump's virtues and the privilege of serving him—the sort of ego-satisfying exercise one might expect in a gang or a dictatorship. But nothing quite surpassed his response to an interviewer's question about whether Trump would call the FBI if offered anything of value by a foreign country in an election. That's a crime, of course, and the FBI director had earlier testified to that. But Trump said he never called the FBI in the past, so if a foreign power had "information—I think I'd take it."[36] Which turned out to mean, if Russia, Ukraine, or China could help in his election or reelection, Trump would have no compunctions about taking that help.

Michael Cohen underscored the gang metaphor, describing how Trump would speak to his underlings in code when wanting them to do something illegal or unethical.[37] Trump's pressure on the president of Ukraine to do him a "favor" by investigating a political rival amounted to a "Mafia-like shake-down," said one congressman. A gang engages in just such willful and re-peated violations of the law, and in Trump's case that resulted in four former Trump campaign officials going to prison and seven associates pleading guilty, including Cohen. James Comey discovered the gang while serving it: "Holy crap, they [Trump's team] are trying to make each of us an *"amica nostra"*—friend of ours [meaning their gang]. To draw us in."[38]

Trump was capable of flattery, which he used with people he thought he could outsmart—for example, Kim Jong-un. Following their summit meeting in 2018, Trump praised Kim to the skies ("a very talented" and "very smart guy" who "loves his country very much"), spoke admiringly of how one so young could take over "a tough country with tough people," and claimed he had developed "a very special bond" with Kim. A White House official put it this way: "He loved the summit with Kim Jong Un. He thinks he can sit down eye to eye with these guys, flatter them and make a deal."[39] Kim wrote personal letters to Trump that convinced the president that dismantling North Korea's nuclear weapons was going to happen. "We fell in love," Trump said at a political rally. But flattery works both ways; foreign leaders learned that it was the surest way to win Trump over. "Love" led Trump to dismiss concerns about North Korea's missile tests. Elaborate welcomes by Xi Jinping when Trump visited China and Crown Prince Mohammed bin Salman when Trump visited Saudi Arabia ensured US silence on their human rights abuses, as did Vladimir Putin's defense of Trump against critics. These men improbably became Trump's best friends, as though national policy differences no longer mattered.

But they did matter. "Great chemistry" with authoritarian leaders meant that the US president would *never say a critical word* about their policies or reject their "word" when contradicted by US intelligence (and common sense).[40] Trump was made to look totally out of touch when excusing their outrageous behavior, such as when he welcomed Egypt's President Abdel Fattah el-Sisi to Washington in 2019 by saying, "I think he's doing a great job." He later—supposedly, jokingly—referred to el-Sisi as "my favorite dictator."[41] This, for a leader who had jailed thousands of critics and human rights advocates and had arranged to be president for life. Despots like el-Sisi used Trump's praise as cover for pursuing policies adverse to US interests, such as using US-supplied weapons for repression. With Putin, Republicans as well as Democrats excoriated Trump for pandering to a leader who had authorized interference in the 2016 election. Trump consistently avoided saying anything critical of the Russian leader, even going so far as to acknowledge—and then dismiss—Putin's assassinations and poisonings of opponents.[42] "What, you think our country is so innocent?" Trump countered. With the Saudi crown prince, the tight personal relationship between him, Trump, and especially Jared Kushner, the president's son-in-law, meant overlooking the sordid human rights record of the House of Saud, which includes mass executions. It set the table for Trump's rejection of sanctions when (as described later) the CIA concluded that the prince was responsible for the murder of a prominent critic.

Then there is the case of Libya, a country mired in civil war and with a fragile central government supported by the UN. To the astonishment of many observers, Trump in April 2019 reversed US policy and told a Libyan general who had launched an attack on Tripoli that he had US support. Yet Secretary of State Mike Pompeo, speaking on behalf of "the administration at the highest levels," earlier had expressed opposition to the general's action and urged an "immediate halt" to it. A White House statement explained Trump's move in terms of "fighting terrorism and securing Libya's oil resources."[43] Once again Trump ignored the implications of embracing a disreputable strongman who just happened to profess hatred for "Islamic terrorism" and concern about the flow of oil.

IT'S ALL ABOUT TRUMP

Trump was most comfortable talking about Trump, sometimes in the third person. He practically awarded himself the Nobel Peace Prize for agreeing to meet with Kim Jong-un ("but I would never say it") and boasted of doing "the best," "the most beautiful," "the greatest" in everything. His poll numbers were better than Abraham Lincoln's, he said in Britain, and the gross domestic product (GDP) under his administration was double or triple what it had been—embarrassing remarks, but quickly overtaken by the next day's exaggeration. When the world seemed about to crash down around him with the indictments, convictions, and grants of immunity to some of his closest associates, Trump responded by predicting "the market would crash, I think everybody would be very poor" if he were impeached. He doubled down on that prediction as it came closer to reality, saying "civil war" was possible. He gave himself an "A+" for his performance in office,[44] issued a Thanksgiving Day (2018) message that mainly gave thanks for his own leadership, and even went so far (before the UN General Assembly no less) as to claim, "In less than two years, my administration has accomplished more than almost any administration in the history of our country."[45] That remark drew mocking laughter from some of the assembled diplomats.

Rarely did Trump credit anyone else with achievements. It was all his doing, as he prattled during a NATO meeting. "Trade wars are good, and easy to win" was a typical boast. "They [China] kill us [in trade]. I beat China all the time. All the time," he said in 2015. When he launched his trade war with China in 2018 and China's economy took a hit, Trump boasted that "it's only in trouble because of me." In his own mind, he was the only president who could make peace with the North Koreans: "If not for me, we would now be at War with North Korea," he tweeted in July 2018, and said (in response to criticism from John Bolton) that if not for him (Trump), the United States would be in "World War Six." Trump claimed greater expertise than his commanders on military matters, saying, for example, that he "knows more about" alliances that his defense secretary and former NATO commander, General James Mattis. Trump was the one president who could revitalize the US economy—and in fact had built the best economy "EVER." And he considered himself politically invulnerable: As he once said, he could kill someone in the middle of Fifth Avenue in Manhattan and get away with it because of his exceptional popularity. Everybody loved him, even when they didn't—as in Scotland and Ireland, where he was so unwelcome that his trips there had to be canceled.

The fact that the mainstream media found fault with issues that he believed deserved credit only added to his grievance list. Never mind that the media's constant attention to Trump's antics helped him win election. (As the presidential candidate Pete Buttigieg said, "It is the nature of grotesque things that you can't look away.") Or that he was actually successful at cowing enough of the media that freedom of the press in the country as a whole suffered.[46] So when media attention turned elsewhere, as happened in October 2018 when a pro-Trump man mailed pipe bombs to a dozen prominent Democrats, Trump's anger was aroused: Why aren't they covering my forceful reaction to the migrant caravan headed our way from Central America, or my policy on opioids? That incident, which Trump could have used to demonstrate compassionate leadership, instead became a launch point for yet another attack on the "bad and hateful" media.[47] Not once did he refer to or contact the potential victims of the bomb threat.

These characteristics lead me to conclude with what may by now seem obvious: Donald Trump is a deeply flawed human being. Yes, we're all flawed; but Trump is in a class by himself, lacking some of the basic ingredients of a fully developed person: empathy, a sense of humor, a sensitive and sympathetic ear, a taste for the arts, an enjoyment of people, a willingness to listen, an appreciation of his limitations.[48] Ego, power, and quest for celebrity are Trump's drivers; tolerance, modesty, and self-examination are missing from his makeup. He is not merely non-intellectual—he is said to have read and touted only books favorable to himself[49]—but also anti-intellectual, a man very reluctant to seek, much less accept, expert advice. His narrow business history may account for some of those features of his character; it certainly seems to have shaped his performance in office. But Trump evidently did not devote time to self-reflection; he was too busy flaunting his wealth and pursuing the limelight—and women. He never got enough of either of those.

Chapter Three

Taking Sides

DAMN THE EXPERTS

I know we're used to it by now, but it still amazes me how often the government has to tell you not to pay attention to the president.

—Trevor Noah

The foreign policy establishment's concerns about Donald Trump were borne out soon enough. A widely published picture of Trump's foreign policy team on March 31, 2016, showed twelve white males at the table, the meeting chaired by Jeff Sessions, then an Alabama senator, and with Trump present. Clearly, personal loyalty ranked first in importance. Trump's team did not include anyone who had come out in favor of another Republican candidate or, worse yet, had been critical of Trump. That also eliminated most of the Republicans who had once served under Ronald Reagan or the Bushes and, therefore, had international experience. When Trump's transition team made its way through the State Department, a number of political appointees and noncareer officers were axed immediately, as previously noted. At the NSC, now headed by the rabble-rousing Michael Flynn, briefing documents were rebuffed and "Obama holdovers" were sidelined.[1] In short, the Trump team wasn't visiting to learn. One senior official is quoted as saying the team showed a "deep distrust for professional public servants."[2] That situation foreshadowed a rocky relationship between the president and the foreign and national security policy bureaucracy—not just at the State Department and the NSC, but throughout the intelligence community (IC), notably the Central Intelligence Agency (CIA), Director of National Intelligence (DNI), and FBI. It also foreshadowed a foreign policy making–process that would be haphazard at best and dangerously indecisive at worst.

Once Trump took office, bureaucratic infighting was fierce, Trump's ad hoc tweeting proved unstoppable, and efforts to create a chain of command failed miserably.[3] Policy advice depended on catching Trump's ear, but that depended on gaining access to a leader who had no idea how government functions and seemingly little interest in finding out.[4] Advisers were there to be ignored or tolerated, many accounts agree, but Trump did not feel he needed them; he was his own best adviser, particularly when it came to foreign policy.[5] Beyond him, policy making was often a family affair: Daughter Ivanka Trump and son-in-law Jared Kushner, whom Trump named senior advisers and were impolitely called "Jivanka" behind Trump's back, were clearly members of his inner circle, with a few longtime pals as close advisers and enablers: people like Rudolph (Rudy) W. Giuliani, Trump's personal lawyer; Steve Schwarzman, chief executive of Blackstone investment group; Donald Trump Jr., the eldest son; and Michael Cohen. Everyone else was cast as "natural predators," according to Reince Priebus, Trump's first chief of staff.[6]

Ivanka and Jared were a constant presence in the White House but were widely regarded as unwelcome interlopers.[7] And with good reason: Neither had any experience that even remotely qualified them for their jobs.[8] Yet here was Kushner acting like a secretary of state, made point man on Middle East policy, the North American Free Trade Agreement (NAFTA), and various domestic programs. Thanks to Trump's intervention, which he and Ivanka lied about by denying, Ivanka and Jared obtained top-secret security clearances against the advice of the FBI, the CIA, and two White House officials.[9] Both were found to have conducted official business with foreign governments on personal electronic accounts, in violation of federal law and announced White House policy. The Trump campaign's attack on Hillary Clinton for having just such an account went ignored.

The White House staff itself was frequently in turmoil under Trump. In his first two years in office, Trump went through two chiefs of staff, Priebus and General John Kelly. They easily had the toughest job in town after the president's. Both had to deal with an irascible, unpredictable personality who might say or do anything, at any time, without warning. Each was reported to have tremendous difficulty restraining Trump's use of Twitter, controlling access to him, and watching over his communications with foreign leaders. Neither succeeded. Bob Woodward quotes Kelly as saying of Trump: "He's an idiot. It's pointless to try to convince him of anything. He's gone off the rails. We're in crazytown."[10] Nikki Haley, his first ambassador to the United Nations, wrote in her memoir, *With All Due Respect*, that Kelly and Tillerson tried to recruit her to find ways around Trump to "save the country." Little wonder that Trump could not readily find a replacement for Kelly, eventually settling on an "acting" appointment of Mick Mulvaney, his budget director—a man who, while running for reelection to Congress in 2016, said he could only reluctantly support Trump because "he's a terrible human being."[11] What also emerged is that Mulvaney had pumped himself for chief of staff months before the position became available on the basis that he would let Trump be Trump, which surely was music to Trump's ears.[12]

Trump's preparation habits reflected his distaste for expert advice and, as Tillerson said, being "lazy as hell." He disliked reading reports, preferred pictures to text, ignored briefing papers, and attended only about three briefings a week instead of daily. Often his statements on public issues revealed appalling ignorance or, at the least, intellectual vacancy.[13] Policy—the arguments for and against, the background, the implications—did not seem to interest him: At his first meeting with military leaders in mid-2017, what was supposed to be a thorough briefing on strategic issues devolved into intermittent Trump blasts at alliance costs and insistence on a military parade that would rival France's Bastille Day parade.[14] Leaks from White House staff revealed an uninterested and inattentive chief executive—one who spent far more time watching television, vacationing, and tweeting than attending meetings or reading reports.[15]

Trump's first meeting with Putin, in Hamburg in 2017, found Trump ill-prepared and at a disadvantage, according to Tillerson.[16] The Helsinki summit in 2018 underscored Trump's distaste for preparation: According to one news report based on extensive interviews with White House staff, Trump was given a lengthy briefing book for use in dealing with Putin. He ignored its advice on issues to bring up with Putin, instead launching into a widely panned recounting of his election success and criticism of his own intelligence community.[17] Likewise when it came to the Middle East: His advisers all seemed to share the view that Trump had no need of briefing papers or background information. He would somehow absorb whatever he needed to learn.[18] In fact, Trump never had any contact with the highly experienced envoy to the international coalition fighting the Islamic State (ISIS), yet attacked his integrity after the envoy resigned in protest of Trump's decision to withdraw US forces from Syria at the end of 2018.[19]

Trump's relations with the IC were tenuous from the start. Its heads were not regularly consulted and even less often relied upon, since their views tended to be directly opposite of Trump's on most major national security issues.[20] Whenever those views were made public, Trump went on the attack.[21] He already knew that Obama's top IC appointees were unanimous in believing that Russia, at Putin's direction, had hacked into the Democratic National Committee's e-mails and otherwise interfered with the election. That put those IC officials on Trump's radar, and as their very public criticisms multiplied, Trump decided on the unprecedented step of removing Brennan's security clearance. When he made his move on August 15, 2018, he also threatened to remove the clearances of several other former intelligence and national security officials critical of the president. It was a frightening display of political retribution.

The riposte from former senior intelligence officials was swift and impactful. Fourteen former officials who served in both Democratic and Republican administrations, including six former CIA directors, signed a joint letter taking Trump to task for his "deeply regrettable . . . attempt to stifle free speech."[22] Within days, more than 230 additional names joined the letter list. Some joined because of the free speech issue, while others added that national security itself would be jeopardized by isolating longtime intelligence experts from advising current colleagues. Few voices rose from the Republicans' ranks in support of the protest.

Not surprisingly, such a difficult work environment led to the resignation or firing of an unprecedented number of senior officials in Trump's first three years—by one count, fifty-nine.[23] Several of these departures were connected with Trump's anger over failure to implement a very harsh immigration policy. The State Department, whose influence had been withering away ever since the 9/11 terrorist attacks, suffered more than most agencies. Only 63 percent of senior positions had been filled as of April 2019.[24] Many key people left, among them the senior US official in China; the ambassadors to Panama, Mexico, and Russia; the assistant secretary for Latin America; and the above-mentioned US envoy on ISIS. Most expressed anguish over Trump's negligence in foreign affairs, the disarray in policy making, and his unethical behavior.[25] Three senior State Department and Pentagon officials known for their strong support of NATO also resigned. Glaring gaps in diplomatic representation emerged, notably in the Middle East as well as in international organizations, which ranked low in the administration's estimation.

As one longtime diplomat concluded, the Trump administration had determined on "unilateral diplomatic disarmament" precisely at the moment when diplomacy was most needed.[26] One measure of this disarmament is the number and financial contributions of political appointees to ambassadorships. The figures for Trump appointees are substantially higher than for previous presidents.[27] By far the most powerful blow against Trump's indifference to the diplomatic corps, however, was delivered by Ambassador Yovanovitch, the longtime foreign service officer whom Trump recalled in 2019. She was a victim of conspiracy theories and the president's determination to leverage US aid to Ukraine in order to investigate his chief political opponent at that time. Yovanovitch's testimony during the Trump impeachment inquiry was a masterful rendition of traditional patriotism, personal integrity, and truthfulness.[28] Contrary to her boss, Pompeo, who refused to defend her against the recall, Yovanovitch spoke to the damage being done to the State Department as an institution:

Today, we see the State Department attacked and hollowed out from within. State Department leadership, with Congress, needs to take action now to defend this great institution, and its thousands of loyal and effective employees. We need to rebuild diplomacy as the first resort to advance America's interests and the front line of America's defense. I fear that not doing so will harm our nation's interest, perhaps irreparably. [29]

TWO CAMPS

The other key ingredient in Trump's policy making besides the denigration of expertise was the philosophical division between the nationalists, with whom he identified, and the globalists (or internationalists). To Trump, the key difference between the two groups was defense of national sovereignty: To his mind "the future does not belong to globalists. [It] belongs to patriots." [30] The nationalists included Bannon; Bolton, Trump's third national security adviser, and Robert O'Brien, the fourth; Commerce Secretary Wilbur Ross; the second secretary of state, Mike Pompeo; the US trade representative, Robert Lighthizer; and two hard-line policy advisers, Stephen Miller on immigration and Peter Navarro on trade. Over the first two years of Trump's presidency, and for some time beyond that, the internationalist view was usually represented by Defense Secretary Mattis; Secretary of State Tillerson; the head of the National Economic Council, Gary D. Cohn, and his successor, Larry Kudlow; Treasury Secretary Steve Mnuchin; the second national security adviser, H. R. McMaster; Director of National Intelligence Dan Coats, and other intelligence community leaders; Jared Kushner; and the Joint Chiefs of Staff.

Whatever the issue—sanctioning Iran and North Korea, trade with South Korea and China, climate change, the Mexico wall, NAFTA, NATO, US forces in the Middle East—the consistent nationalist position was usually *withdrawal and sanctions* if the United States could not get what it demanded, whereas the internationalists just as consistently argued for *maintenance* of commitments and *negotiation* when possible. Withdrawal did not always close the door to further discussion; it often was used as a threat to gain leverage, whether with another country or with opponents in Congress. The tactic sometimes worked—for example, in the US–South Korea trade deal[31] or when Trump threatened Mexico with escalating tariffs if it didn't stop Central American migrants from reaching the US border. More often it didn't, as when the Chinese offered only modest trade concessions in response to Trump's pressure tactics,[32] or when his withdrawal from the nuclear deal with Iran failed to win support from allies, or when aid to the Palestinian Authority did not force it to negotiate with the Israelis on a US peace plan, or when a modified NAFTA initially failed to win congressional Democrats' approval. For the nationalists, *winning* was the name of the game—no deal was often better than any other kind of deal—even if it carried high risks.[33]

The internationalists may have had the numbers, but generally they proved no match for the nationalists. For one thing, the internationalists had to make their case for upholding international obligations while also restraining Trump from acting impulsively. For another, nearly all the internationalists either resigned or were fired before the start of Trump's third year in office or soon thereafter, with nationalists replacing them. That left the field to Trump loyalists, with important consequences, one of which was reorganization of the NSC. Under O'Brien, the NSC's professional staff was both significantly trimmed and refocused, "less on transnational issues like global economics and nonproliferation, and more on bilateral and geographic priorities."[34] Following Trump's agenda thus became more certain.

On the policy side, Iran is an example of the nationalists' overriding influence. Trump decided to withdraw from the Iran nuclear deal despite appeals from the internationalists to stay in it, and the nationalists overcame internal objections to push for regime change. Trump's refusal to sign the final document of the Group of Seven (G-7) meeting in Quebec in June 2018, which upheld the standard American idea of a "rules-based international order," is a third example. Often, the best the internationalist camp could do was water down Trump's demands, such as on total troop withdrawal from Syria and Afghanistan and closing the US-Mexico border to stop migration. Sometimes even that didn't work, as when Trump defied his secretary of state and reversed policy on Libya in support of an anti-Islamic general, or when he decided to impose tariffs on Mexico, reportedly against the advice of his trade representative and even Kushner.[35]

A division of the policy-making community into two camps is inevitably an oversimplification. Among the nationalists the use of force was a key point in dispute. Trump, while having no compunctions about threatening and sanctioning other countries, seemed attuned to the political risks and financial costs of going to war or widening US involvement in a war to which it was already committed. His ego also fed that tendency—the belief he could charm authoritarian leaders like Kim Jong-un and Xi Jinping into making policy concessions. Those views clearly were not shared by his chief advisers, notably John Bolton, who brought a well-known reputation for having a quick trigger finger—ready to attack enemies, tending to shape intelligence to suit his purposes, and with little regard for costs or values.[36] Bolton's excessive hawkishness on Iran, North Korea, Afghanistan, and Venezuela, and his disdain for Trump's chumminess with dictators, led to his removal in September 2019, whereas Pompeo, while sharing ideological common ground with Bolton, survived by knowing better than to challenge Trump outright.[37]

SHAKEDOWN: TRUMP'S SECRET AGENDA IN UKRAINE

The President engaged in this course of conduct for the benefit of his own presidential reelection, to harm the election prospects of a political rival, and to influence our nation's upcoming presidential election to his advantage. In doing so, the President placed his own personal and political interests above the national interests of the United States, sought to undermine the integrity of the U.S. presidential election process, and endangered U.S. national security.

—*The Trump-Ukraine Impeachment Inquiry Report*, December 2019[38]

The privatization of policy making, in which the professional analysts are deliberately sidelined and individuals who are not members of the policy-making community or confirmed by the Senate implement the president's wishes, has been a practice of presidents of both parties. The Iran-Contra affair during the Reagan years stands out as an example. Reagan agreed to a covert action, orchestrated by Lieutenant Colonel Oliver North at the NSC, to illegally fund the Nicaraguan Contras via arms sales to Iran, using Israel as a conduit. But whereas Reagan's operation was a coverup in pursuit of a policy, Trump's was a coverup in pursuit of personal advantage. Trump's personal lawyer, Rudy Giuliani, led the "domestic political errand" (as one former State Department expert put it) that sought to bribe a foreign leader in return for help in Trump's reelection. But Trump was blindsided by his worst enemy, the leaker; unlike Reagan, he refused to acknowledge the secret action when caught, instead characterizing his crime as a "perfect call."

It was a whistleblower in the IC who, in September 2019, plunged the Trump administration into the worst of its many crises. The whistleblower reported in an official complaint that the president, in a July 25 telephone call, had urged the new president of Ukraine, Volodymyr Zelensky, to find dirt on Trump's chief political opponent, former Vice President Joseph Biden, and Biden's son, who had been on the board of a Ukrainian energy company. The news jump-started impeachment proceedings in the House and a vote to impeach that threatened to end Trump's presidency. Trump responded with predictable abuse, going so far as to equate the whistleblower with spying that is punishable by execution. But the whistleblower followed the letter of the law, as the acting director of national intelligence, a Trump appointee, acknowledged.

Unlike previous presidents, Trump showed no interest in supporting either Ukraine's resistance to Russian military pressure or the anti-corruption efforts of reform-minded Ukrainians. He had a dark view of Ukraine, completely at odds with specialists throughout the intelligence community—that Kyiv, rather than Moscow, had interfered in the 2016 election (and to the advantage of Hillary Clinton); that Paul Manafort, once Trump's campaign manager, had been wrongly accused of corrupt practices in Ukraine; that the very journalists and politicians in Ukraine who were exposing government corruption were actually enemies of America; and that in fact it was the Bidens who had engaged in corruption.[39] This view not only echoed Putin's line; according to some inside sources, the line *originated* with Putin.[40] Giuliani had plenty of experience in Ukraine to seek dirt on the Bidens. In 2017, when Ukraine was led by a different president, Giuliani apparently tried to leverage Ukraine's desire to ingratiate itself with Trump by burying documents that covered Manafort's corrupt activities there. Giuliani succeeded then, helped by various associates who were later charged with illegal campaign contributions to pro-Trump groups.[41] By May 2019, when Giuliani sought a meeting with the newly elected Zelensky, he wrote to him in a letter that he had Trump's "knowledge and consent."[42] That was the moment, according to one of Giuliani's associates, Lev Parnas, when Trump and Giuliani began the arm twisting of Zelensky.[43] And it appears that Giuliani had help from a Ukrainian oligarch with close ties to Moscow and to Russian organized crime.[44] But Trump could not enlist the help of Bolton.[45]

Nothing Trump's aides could say dissuaded Trump from believing in what his top Russia expert on the NSC called a "fictional narrative" that played into Putin's hand, repeating Russian talking points on social media.[46] The reality was that Manafort was tried and convicted of illegal campaign financing, the reformers had the backing of the US ambassador to Ukraine, and no evidence ever emerged of the Bidens' corruption.[47] But Giuliani had Trump's ear—"See Rudy" was the order of the day—and he used Trump's authority to engineer the recall of Yovanovitch, making her the object of a right-wing smear campaign and subjecting her to surveillance and possible death threats.[48]

Trump's plan, engineered by Giuliani with help from two friendly US diplomats and Energy Secretary Rick Perry, was to deny Zelensky an official visit to Washington and about $400 million in additional military aid unless Zelensky publicly promised an investigation of Ukraine's supposed interference in 2016 and, even more importantly, of the Bidens. The transcript of the July 25 telephone call with Zelensky, along with the testimony of multiple expert witnesses and, during Trump's impeachment trial, Bolton's unpublished memoir, confirmed that Trump had indeed pressured Zelensky to "do us a favor though."[49] William B. Taylor, chargé d'affaires and acting US ambassador in Ukraine, testified that the call's purpose was clearly illegal, as White House staff evidently recognized by "locking down" the record.[50] Gordon Sondland, US ambassador to the European Union (EU) and a $1 million contributor to Trump's campaign, also testified, saying that all the US officials involved with Ukraine "understood that these pre-requisites for the White House call and White House meeting reflected President Trump's desires and requirements." He had no recourse, Sondland insisted, since "the president directed us" to work with Giuliani, and "we were playing the hand we were dealt."[51]

Trump ordered that Zelensky be put on the spot, asking him to contact Giuliani and Attorney General Barr and reminding the Ukraine president that the United States had been "very, very good" to his country but that relations had not been "reciprocal." Soon enough, Zelensky found out exactly what Trump meant: The military aid, mainly Javelin anti-tank missiles, depended on his "favor." Trump insisted his sole concern was corruption in Ukraine, but he had never held up any previous aid to Ukraine because of alleged corruption. Trump apparently confirmed the hold on the aid within hours of his July 25 call, with orders to his budget office to keep the story quiet.[52] "Clear direction from POTUS to continue to hold," the chief budget officer for the weapons systems wrote to concerned Pentagon officials.[53] Trump refused to heed concerns expressed at an Oval Office meeting in August by Bolton, Pompeo, and Defense Secretary Mark T. Esper that withholding aid was not in the US national interest. Those officials not only believed that national security interests demanded release of the money, they were also well aware that impounding the money violated a law that requires either releasing funds approved by Congress or providing an explanation for withholding them.[54]

In fact, Taylor said in his October 22 statement that he was told "everything" involving Ukraine was on hold until Trump got his way with Zelensky. Taylor was astonished when he learned that Giuliani and company were running an informal channel that bypassed him and other State Department officials working on Ukraine.[55] So was Michael McKinley, Pompeo's top assistant, who said that after "37 years in the Foreign Service, . . . I had never seen" such scandalous behavior. Taylor pushed back, saying it was "crazy to withhold security assistance [to Ukraine] for help with a political campaign."[56] McKinley resigned, angry as well at Pompeo's failure to speak out in defense of Yovanovitch.[57] These officials were not alone. At least four other intelligence officers were so alarmed by how Giuliani and Trump were politicizing relations with Ukraine, both before and after Trump's phone call, that—with encouragement from Bolton—they met with the NSC's legal adviser.[58] One of those officers was Lieutenant Colonel Alexander S. Vindman, the top Ukraine expert in the White House. His testimony was perhaps more devastating than Taylor's, since Vindman had personally listened in on the July 25 phone call. Vindman corroborated the whistleblower's and Taylor's accounts, raising particular concerns about the national security implications: Aid to Ukraine would be threatened if it lost bipartisan support. He and some colleagues also found it entirely "inappropriate" that Sondland would endorse investigating a Trump political opponent based on a "false narrative."[59]

Trump's attempt to get foreign help to smear an opponent, with US aid and an official visit as bribes, was a major abuse of power. He seemed oblivious to the legal implications of these acts, evidently confident that just as he had survived the Mueller report on his 2016 campaign's reliance on Russian help—starting with Trump's now-famous line, "Russia, if you're listening, I hope you're able to find the 30,000 e-mails that are missing"—he could also survive requests to Ukraine and China to interfere. Typical of his style, Trump weaponized his crime, making himself the victim, openly repeating (and justifying) his demand for action against the Bidens, and urging the "impeachment" of his House accusers for "treason." As the impeachment inquiry produced credible evidence from nonpartisan sources, Trump became increasingly desperate, demanding that the whistleblower's identity be revealed, suppressing potentially incriminating testimony from aides, and calling on Republicans to defend him by resurrecting the false 2016 election story.[60] But throughout the impeachment inquiry and Senate trial, Trump succeeded in blocking virtually all White House officials' testimony and documents related to Ukraine, reinforcing the accusation of abuse of power even as he saved his presidency.[61]

The national security implications of Trump's actions were not lost on his detractors—namely, Trump's refusal to provide Ukraine with the means of self-defense against Russia until Trump got his pound of flesh. The fact that Trump's gambit failed—the aid was released in September, two days after the July 25 transcript was revealed, probably to try to undercut accusations of a quid pro quo[62]—does not alter either his crime or his pursuit of policies favorable to Russia.[63] Indeed, soon after the impeachment of Trump, new information emerged that further solidified the connection between the Kremlin and Giuliani in pursuit of damaging information on Joe Biden.[64]

ALL IN FOR THE ISRAELI RIGHT

Policy making on the Middle East's most intractable conflict provides a second striking example of how, under Trump, experienced diplomats were sidelined in favor of personal ties to governments that were useful to Trump's political agenda. All Trump's initial advisers on the Middle East were devoted to Israel's cause: Jared Kushner; Jason D. Greenblatt, chief legal officer in the Trump Organization and, along with Kushner, a key figure in crafting a plan to resolve the Israeli-Palestinian dispute; David Friedman, a lawyer who would become US ambassador to Israel; and Richard Roberts, a physician and pro-Israel donor. All of them lacked diplomatic experience but were fervent supporters of Trump.

During his 2016 campaign, Trump pretended to be understanding of both sides. Once in office, however, Trump revealed his hand, which entirely favored the Israeli rightists led by Prime Minister Benjamin Netanyahu and, not coincidentally, the priorities of Trump's biggest campaign contributors, such as the casino magnate Sheldon Adelson. The president moved the US embassy from Tel Aviv to Jerusalem and recognized Jerusalem as the Israeli capital; looked the other way while the Israelis added more Jewish settlements in disputed land; terminated (against the State Department's advice) aid programs that provided refugee relief to Palestinians as well as funds for their education, housing, and security forces; closed the Palestine Liberation Organization's (PLO) Washington office; and rejected a right of return to Israel for Palestinian refugees. These steps made Trump's promised peace plan predictable—and dead on arrival when it was finally unveiled in January 2020.

To solidify his pro-Israel stance at home and abroad, Trump interceded in Israel's elections every time Netanyahu faced defeat. The Israeli leader was in the fight of his life to retain office while facing corruption charges. Trump called for US recognition of Israeli sovereignty over the Golan Heights, which Israel illegally seized from Syria, annexed (in 1981), and occupied—a move that previous presidents had refused to make, violated international law, and had no international recognition.[65] It prompted Netanyahu, who won a narrow victory in April, to proclaim Israel's right to annex Israeli-settled portions of the West Bank, essentially creating South Africa–style Bantustans.[66] Naturally, the Palestinians were outraged. They broke relations with Washington and all but rejected the Kushner-Greenblatt plan before it was even officially presented. The Palestinian Authority had no role in the plan's creation, yet were being asked to give up their dream of a viable separate state in exchange for what Kushner said would be "the opportunity to do commerce and . . . improve their lives." Kushner spoke like a colonial ruler, saying Palestinian self-rule would depend on their being "capable of governing," and suggesting that Israeli authority over all disputed territory would prevail indefinitely.[67] "Land for peace," long the bedrock condition of a peace plan, now was being trashed, and Palestinian claims in the West Bank and Gaza would be transformed into "autonomy." Even Pompeo privately admitted that for some people, "this is going to be a deal that only the Israelis could love."[68] He was right.

"Some people" meant Netanyahu, whose ambition was to make Israel exclusively a Jewish state. But he failed to put together a ruling coalition, and in September 2019 a second round of national elections took place. Trump again interceded, but it was all for naught.[69] Netanyahu lost out to Benny Gantz, a former general who had support from the Joint List of Arab Palestinian parties. But Gantz, too, was unable to form a government, putting national leadership in limbo and prompting another US intervention: a State Department announcement in November 2019 that the United States would no longer regard the illegal Israeli settlements as being in violation of international law.

In 2020, with Netanyahu facing a third national election and Trump's impeachment trial underway, their common political needs provided the backdrop for the unveiling of Trump's Middle East plan. Trump announced the plan with Netanyahu (but not Gantz) at his side; Palestinian leaders, who had no part in the plan's drafting, were left to denounce it from afar. The plan was a charade: It endorsed Israel's annexation of most of the Jordan Valley in the West Bank while giving the impression the Palestinians might one day have a separate state in the land that remained, and called for an undivided Jerusalem to belong to Israel. Palestinians outside Israel would have no right of return. The administration's reversal of decades of US policy was now complete, probably putting the final nail in the coffin of a two-state solution to the Palestinian-Israeli conflict despite the fact that polls showed Israelis and Palestinians alike preferred two states to any other option for resolving the conflict.[70] In spring 2020, Netanyahu and Gantz formed a coalition government with a rotating prime ministership, leaving few obstacles to Israel's annexation ambitions.

COMPROMISED

Not until after the 2016 election did we learn about the extent to which several of Donald Trump's associates had secretly made contact with foreign governments and their associates that may have given those governments leverage over the new administration's policies. The most consequential contacts involved the major Gulf states that aligned with its anti-Iran policy—Saudi Arabia and the United Arab Emirates (UAE)—and Russia. Secret meetings during Trump's campaign reportedly led to an agreement on a "social media manipulation effort" funded by Saudi, UAE, and private sources, including an Israeli company. Trump's son, Don Jr., is said to have hosted a meeting on the plan at Trump Tower in New York. It is also possible that the Russians were in on the plan, which would have violated US law on foreign involvement in elections.[71] Also under investigation were illegal donations to Trump's campaign and his inaugural committee by sources in Saudi Arabia, UAE, and Qatar. Using American intermediaries and the front of a political action committee, Rebuild America Now, Middle East sources may have donated large sums, initially to keep the campaign afloat and then to buy access to the new president.[72] Trump in turn counted the Saudis among his best customers for buying and renting properties, which included Trump Tower apartments. As noted below, the Qataris learned from the Saudis how much money talks and followed suit with their own rentals.

By comparison, the secret contacts between the Trump campaign and Russians connected to the Kremlin were far more extensive and consequential for US policy. Far from being carefully managed diplomacy, the contacts amounted to influence peddling by both sides—the Russians seeking out people close to the new president and Trump's associates who were looking for business opportunities, all done in the name of improving US-Russia relations. The Mueller report counted 140 contacts between Trump's campaign and associates and Russian nationals, including at least six contacts by Trump himself, starting from 2013 and extending through the campaign and into the transition period.[73] Besides Cohen, Sessions, and Flynn, the chief campaign officials who had contact with Russians were George Papadopoulos and Carter Page, foreign policy advisers; Roger J. Stone, a longtime Trump associate and convicted go-between who facilitated contact between WikiLeaks and Russian hackers of Democratic National Committee e-mails; Manafort, who advised the pro-Russia president of Ukraine and in 2017 turned over polling data to a Russian with ties to intelligence agencies; and Ivanka Trump and Jared Kushner. Kushner had secret discussions with a Russian banker and a Russian diplomat,[74] and was part of a group of Trump advisers, including Don Jr., who met with Russians offering "dirt" on Hillary Clinton in 2016.[75] Trump personally constructed the lie about the purpose of that meeting and all the others, strongly suggesting Moscow's hold on him.

Except for Trump's children and Kushner, all the others were either convicted or pleaded guilty to lying about their activities. Flynn, along with K. T. McFarland, his deputy at the NSC, also lied to Congress and the FBI about conversations with the Russian ambassador to Washington to remove US sanctions on Russia. Flynn conveyed to the ambassador that not retaliating for Obama's sanctions on Russia would go well with the new administration, as indeed it did.[76]

The first Russia contact apparently occurred as early as 2015 when, as the Mueller investigation found, a high-level Russian offered Michael Cohen "synergy on a government level."[77] But well before that, biographers uncovered "a 35-year relationship between Trump and Russian organized crime" that gave Trump access to cash that the Russian mafia would launder.[78] The numerous contacts that ensued with the Trump campaign suggested that the Russians saw in him a vehicle for ending US sanctions, and he saw in the Russians a chance to make lucrative real estate and other deals with Vladimir Putin's personal approval. The contacts did not result either in a Trump hotel deal in Moscow or in a Trump-Putin meeting, both of which Trump's associates sought "from the day I announced to the day I won," and thought they had in hand.[79] But they did pay off when the Russians threw their social media and hacking campaigns into support of Trump's candidacy.[80]

The Russia contacts so concerned the Obama administration that in the days between Trump's election and his inauguration, it systematically brought together its intelligence and analyses not only in order to ensure that they would be available to future investigators, but also out of suspicion that Trump officials had colluded with Russia during the election and might destroy or cover up the intelligence.[81] The FBI initiated a counterintelligence probe of Trump in May 2017, shortly after he fired Comey and bragged about it to senior Russian officials.[82] The accusation of the former Republican foreign policy officials, quoted in chapter 1, that Trump would be "a dangerous President and would put at risk our country's national security" was given new life.

What connects all these nefarious activities is that the Trump administration's dealings with Russia and Middle East countries may have *compromised* the participants. By operating secretly, Trump and his associates exposed themselves to manipulation by foreign governments. Kushner's financial contacts exposed him to manipulation by four governments: China, Mexico, Israel, and the UAE.[83] Saudi Arabia recognized early on that it could leverage Kushner's inexperience and emerging personal ties to the monarchy—ties that, as will be discussed later, may have led Kushner, with Trump's endorsement, to downplay the crown prince's role in the murder of a Saudi critic and other human-rights abuses, and work with the Saudis on a nuclear energy deal.[84] These were among the reasons for the initial denial of Kushner's top-secret security clearance.

As for the Trump-Russia connection, we know that Trump feared Mueller's appointment as special counsel spelled "the end of my Presidency."[85] The president had lied, repeatedly, about his and his representatives' personal interactions with Russian officials and businessmen—"I don't know Putin, have no business whatsoever with Russia, have nothing to do with Russia," he said on one occasion in 2016—and now the jig was up.[86] Perhaps oblivious to the crime he was committing, Trump made many attempts, through subordinates, to impede or curtail Mueller's investigation and hide evidence from him.[87] Publicly, Trump denigrated the Russia investigation and challenged Mueller's integrity on an almost daily basis, conveniently ignoring that the special counsel's work led to thirty-seven indictments, including a dozen Russian intelligence officers among twenty-six Russians in all, and convictions of several key Trump officials and campaign associates.[88] All those efforts clarify that the president was running scared, afraid—I would have to imagine—that his indebtedness to Moscow and Moscow's support of his campaign would be exposed, with untold damage to his legitimacy.

Mueller's investigation was unable to prove *corrupt intent* on the part of Trump or any of his campaign aides—neither sufficient evidence of a conspiracy with Russia as legally defined nor obstruction of justice that rose to the level of a crime. But his team's report accomplished four things that could have constituted grounds for impeachment or indictment. It added to the extensive public record of Trump's efforts to undermine the investigation, to lie and misrepresent the facts, and to engage with Russian officials. It reinforced and elaborated on all the previous press findings of Russian interference in 2016 for Trump's benefit. It showed that the Trump campaign was willing and able to partake of Russian interference—that is, collusion by any ordinary understanding.[89] Lastly, the report, far from clearing the president of obstruction, presented at least ten possible instances of it, though leaving to Congress how to pursue the finding.

Trump's claim of "total exoneration" was therefore far from the truth. Had Trump been anyone other than the president, and had Mueller not adopted a narrow view of collusion—defining it in terms of "conspiracy law" rather than coordination by "an agreement" between the parties—Trump would probably have been subject to indictment.[90] Several hundred former federal prosecutors agreed.[91] On the obstruction charge, the Mueller report made the telling conclusion that while the president had not "committed a crime, [the report] also does not exonerate him."[92] Even some of Trump's die-hard defenders pronounced him guilty, such as Judge Andrew Napolitano of Fox News, who wrote that "ordering obstruction to save himself from the consequences of his own behavior is unlawful, defenseless and condemnable." Needless to say, the judge went from being a Trump favorite to being called "very dumb."[93]

Chapter Four

Foreign Policy by Improvisation

Patriotism is the exact opposite of nationalism. Nationalism is a betrayal of patriotism by saying, "our interest first, who cares about the others?"
—Emmanuel Macron, president of France, November 11, 2018[1]

You know what a globalist is, right? . . . A globalist is a person that wants the globe to do well, frankly, not caring about our country so much. And you know what? We can't have that.
—Donald Trump, at a 2018 rally in Houston[2]

POLICY MAKING OFF THE CHARTS

As the new administration got underway, two of Trump's senior officials—H. R. McMaster and Gary D. Cohn—wrote that "America First doesn't mean America alone," presumably to reassure allies of Trump's priorities following his initial visit to the Middle East.[3] The op-ed offered the usual Washington rhetoric about commitments to friends, opposition to enemies, and preservation of national interests (particularly anti-terrorism), all encompassed within the notion of putting America first. Left unspecified was the *price* of US friendship and the meaning of the assurance that America would not act "alone." Since Trump was always concerned about price and often pushed for action alone, his endorsement of the op-ed is uncertain. All the more so as an important feature of "America First" turned out to be its improvisational character.

Scholars and practitioners alike struggled to make sense of the "unconventional" foreign policy the Trump administration pursued. Beyond an emphasis on sovereignty over globalism—"The U.S. will always choose independence and cooperation over global governance, control and domination," Trump said before the UN General Assembly on September 25, 2018—he expressed no coherent doctrine, philosophy, or strategic vision in his international thinking.[4] But Trump believed he was acting on superior instinct.[5] He was the man of action; he seemed to regard strategy as an academic exercise best left to his national security team or, sometimes, to his son-in-law. Improvisation carries a price, however: uncertainty and unreliability. Trump left it to others to justify, modify, or discount what Trump had done. Advisers and foreign governments alike had to figure out if Trump meant what he said. Moreover, Trump could blow hot and cold, sometimes changing overnight. Thus, he would act disdainfully toward European allies one day, for instance, on trade issues, then agree the next to avoid further tariff fights. He would call China's president a great friend one day, then attack China the next. Or he would *seem* to agree that the Russians meddled in the 2016 election, then qualify or even dismiss the charge the following day.

Trump's supporters will argue that improvisation proved successful, pointing for example to his diplomacy with North Korean leader Kim Jong-un and his dueling with NATO leaders over military spending. Trump broke previous patterns in dealing with both—with North Korea by threatening war but winding up becoming the first US president to hold a summit with Pyongyang's leader and with NATO by forcing its members to confront their longstanding commitments to spend more on defense. These moves certainly shook up the bureaucracy, but were they foreign-policy successes? The North Korea summits (see chapter 6) did not lead to agreement on denuclearization, and so far as the North Koreans were concerned, never were meant to. And the demand on NATO not only did not accelerate its plans on defense spending; it produced a near-crisis in relations over the US commitment to common defense. Both cases, moreover, revealed wide gaps between the president's views and those of his subordinates.

When it came to money matters, however, Trump was more predictable. It was pay-as-you-go: international commitments depended not on past promises but on what was in it for him and his administration. He had already dropped strong hints that NATO was an expensive investment ("We're paying too much," he said on the campaign trail),[6] and questioned Article 5 of the NATO treaty that calls for collective defense commitments by all the parties.[7] Trump fell in line with the false accusations of Saudi Arabia and the UAE that Qatar, home to the largest US base in the Middle East, was promoting terrorism. Trump's support came, suspiciously, following the secret meetings that reportedly took place in Trump Tower and right after Trump's first overseas visit, to Saudi Arabia. Not to be outdone, Qatar bought a $6.5 million apartment in a Trump complex in New York, put in multimillion-dollar orders for US weapons, and launched an all-out lobbying effort that netted support from the US Secretaries of State and Defense. These moves eroded Saudi claims and its blockade of Qatar; the Qataris got what they paid for.[8]

South Korea, another close US ally, also found out what it means when money talks in US policy. In the course of intense name-calling and saber-rattling between Trump and Kim Jong-un, Trump demanded changes in the US–South Korea trade agreement and further demanded that South Korea pay for the US missile defense system (known as THAAD) that they had agreed to deploy. The new South Korean president, Moon Jae-in, suspended deployment amidst great public anger in Korea over Trump's demands.[9] Trump caused further consternation in Seoul in 2019 when he sought to quadruple South Korea's annual payment for US troops stationed there, using a figure—$5 billion—that seemed to many to have been taken out of thin air. The matter remains unresolved as of the spring of 2020.

I suggest that America First was a populist image—political advertising, if you will—behind which lay efforts to weaken any countries and institutions that stood in the way of expanding Trump's own brand and the wealth and political authority of white America. As a nationalist and nativist approach, America First ran against the globalism of all presidents who preceded Trump in the post–World War II era. All of them believed in American exceptionalism—the uniqueness and universal attractiveness of the American experiment. Though Trump did not, his foreign policy was not isolationist: Instead of pulling in US horns and proclaiming Fortress America, Trump wanted to reorder an unfair system—"negative internationalism," Richard Falk called it. He wanted better deals at lower prices, whether with European allies, next-door neighbors, or adversaries such as China; and he searched for ways to reduce the US military burden abroad while at the same time being totally prepared to impose sanctions on governments that resisted US demands. Nor was Trump a populist in the usual sense of merely being anti-establishment. His populism was illiberal: He had no interest in promoting democracy or human rights, evidenced by his enthusiastic embrace of authoritarian leaders.

Because of Trump's deal-making style, many commentators labeled his international approach transactional. Friend or foe, no matter; Trump was prepared to defy diplomatic norms in order to get what he wanted, just as he conducted his business ventures. The most glaring example was his out-of-the-blue attempt to buy Greenland from Denmark, a move that, when rejected as "absurd" by the Danish prime minister, drew angry comments from Trump and cancellation of an official visit he was scheduled to make to Denmark. His approach to international trade and alliances provides many other examples. But there are also plenty of counterexamples, such as Trump's antagonism to international organizations; his apparent lack of interest in global poverty or climate change; his policies on North Korea, Africa, and Latin America (discussed in chapter 6); and his failed attempt to eliminate most US foreign aid.[10] The MAGA slogan fell into this latter category; it was an appeal to a narrow-minded nationalism, with promises of a return to a past America, one that provided jobs for hardworking men and greater profits for companies that invest or expand operations in the United States. Promise isn't performance, of course; MAGA actually took from the middle class and the poor and gave to Trump and his supporters in Congress and among donors.[11] That explains why those billionaires who at first worked against Trump, such as Charles G. Koch and his foundation, and some giant corporations hurt by Trump's tariff wars, ultimately fell in line behind him. Self-interest dictated politics as usual.

All previous presidents and their administrations could be captured within the realism-idealism framework. That is, their foreign policy was shaped by an uneasy balance between power politics and universal values: preparedness to use force and threat on behalf of a hard-eyed notion of national interest on the one hand, and professed support of freedom, the rule of law, and human rights on the other. Together, these elements constituted the "liberal international order" that evolved from World War II institution building: the UN, the Bretton Woods system of international financial organizations, and the security alliances starting with NATO.[12] Ever since 1950 and the NSC-68 strategy paper, US administrations have been concerned less with threats from particular entities—the Soviet Union and China during the Cold War, terrorism since then—than with protecting from serious disruption a world order favorable to US interests.[13]

Proponents of the liberal order understand that the stakes are very high when the order is challenged: the economic and strategic architecture crucial to America's rise to global predominance and the values and ideals that underlie it.[14] The challenge has usually come from the left, on the argument that US-created global institutions promote corporate capitalism, require military interventions abroad to protect it, and spread false doctrines of freedom while accepting (and sometimes concretely supporting) the trampling of human rights. The challenge from Trump was quite different. He seemed out to destroy strategic consistency and diplomatic tradition. His administration never attempted to define US national interests; openly disparaged notions of international community, international law, and global responsibility; and sought to reduce, if not eliminate, the US role in major international institutions such as the UN.[15] Rhetoric about "making America great again" had little to do either with upholding longstanding US strategic interests abroad or promoting US values, ideals, or institutions.

That kind of narrowly defined realism could, in theory, serve America well in that it would reduce the longstanding sense of obligation of US leaders to determine world order by use of force and pressure. But that view also minimized other US obligations, such as to environmental protection, poverty alleviation, and corporate responsibility. The world to Trump was only consequential insofar as the United States derived maximum benefit from it, *regardless* of what allies, rivals, human rights groups, and international organizations wanted. "I'm for America First & the American Worker—a puppet for no one," Trump wrote to a "globalist" conservative group.[16] In short, Trump and fellow nationalists believed the United States did not need allies, friends, or multilateral groups unless they conformed to US self-interest. As Stephen Bannon explained in a speech to a mainly Japanese audience in 2017,

> America first. It's not America as isolationist. It's not America alone. It's never been that. Donald Trump's never said that. It's America engaged in the world as never before, but is in partnership that is also on America's terms, not just as a part of these faceless international organizations, these globalist institutions run by people in Davos, and people in Brussels, and people in Geneva.[17]

The context for this comment is important: Bannon was describing a China threat in the most expansive terms and urging Japan and other US allies to unite against Beijing—a project he later undertook outside the administration.[18] Thus, "partnership" was only acceptable "on America's terms," diminishing the value of multilateral institutions and coalitions and making clear that the United States would only obey rules it wrote.

Traditional Republican foreign policy, represented by Reagan and the Bushes, professed commitments to anticommunism, high military spending within balanced budgets, a strong position on terrorism, free trade, global corporate expansion, and promotion of freedom and liberty abroad. Donald Trump overturned virtually all of these. He embraced dictators left and right, rarely espoused the virtues of freedom or democracy, dramatically increased the national debt, reveled in trade wars and managed trade, and sought to weaken or ignore multilateral institutions that stand for rules-based global order. Even terrorism lost top status as a threat to national security; officially at least, Russia and China replaced it. Only high military spending remained under Trump, who repeated the standard Republican mantra about the Democrats having weakened the military. The military budget under Trump skyrocketed, reaching nearly $1 trillion in fiscal year 2020—with full approval, I should add, from most Democrats.

THE POLITICS OF TRUMP'S FOREIGN POLICY

Trump's audience was politically defined: those who somehow felt threatened by globalization and changing demographics—by the rising immigrant population, government regulations, and multiculturalism, for instance. These supporters—mainly older, working-class, white males and females, Christian, resentful of others who received a helping hand from government, and without college degrees—were, surprisingly, not very different from those who voted for previous Republican presidential candidates. [19] Many wanted to go back to the way things were, when they considered themselves rightfully on top—even when their paycheck and status showed otherwise. By no means all racists, they nevertheless feared that they would soon be in the minority in America, ignored in favor of other ethnic groups.

Like any opportunistic authoritarian leader, Trump stoked popular resentments: "The mutual distrust among Americans has been Donald Trump's most important political resource," David Frum wrote. [20] Trump presented them not with reasoned arguments but with symbols of racial and cultural threat: the Mexico border wall, the immigrant criminal, the disloyal Muslim. He shrewdly ignored both the benefits of immigration and elements of globalization that hurt his base but were useful to him personally, such as the oil producers, trade wars, Russian hacking, and licenses to sell Trump brands in countries with cheap labor. The Republicans in Congress overwhelmingly refused to talk about the divisiveness, not to mention the racial connotations, of Trump's message. [21] Their silence, motivated partly by fear of offending the far right and hurting their reelection chances and partly by the financial rewards of Trumpian economics, gave Trump the opportunity to take over the party. "Moral corrosion," the columnist David Brooks called it. [22]

This corrosion extended to foreign policy. Stalwarts of the party's traditional views, such as Senators McCain and Jeff Flake, were sidelined. Trump was given free rein. As Thomas L. Friedman wrote after the Helsinki fiasco, Trump could say and do what he pleased:

> The fact that Trump's party and his network always look for ways to excuse him has been hugely liberating for Trump. He can actually deny he said things that were recorded—like his trashing of the British prime minister. He can take one side of any issue (like trashing key NATO allies to satisfy his base) and, when he gets blowback, take the other side (claim to love the Atlantic alliance). And he can declare that he really meant to ask why "wouldn't" Russia be the one hacking us instead of why "would" it, as he did say. [23]

Perhaps the most remarkable aspect of the Trump presidency was *how little a political price* he paid among the overwhelming number of Republicans (anywhere from 80 to 90 percent) and some independents who supported him no matter his personal failings or even his embrace of Russia. "It's just going to be in his DNA," said a senior Republican senator in dismissing Trump's racist attacks as merely defensive. [24] Therein lay the nub of the constitutional crisis Trump's behavior brought on: the refusal of nearly all Republicans to confront a leader whose unfitness for office was obvious to many. They alone were in a position to alter history, and far from acting decisively on Trump, they enabled him, putting loyalty and self-interest ahead of defense of democratic institutions. At the close of the Senate impeachment trial, only one Republican—Mitt Romney—voted to convict, even though several voiced "disappointment" at Trump's behavior and hoped he would change. Far from changing, he was emboldened.

THE MYTH OF THE DEEP STATE

Bureaucratic self-interest and autonomy is a reality of government decision-making. Every president has complained at some point about bureaucratic leaders acting against his wishes. They often do: Heads of government agencies have many tools at their disposal to defy or weaken presidential preferences and protect their turf, such as leaking, withholding, and manipulating information, and delaying execution of decisions. Bob Woodward's book *Fear* has several stories depicting resistance to Trump's actions and behavior, even including hiding signing papers from him to prevent his making a presumed serious policy error.[25] But these same bureaucratic leaders also provide the intelligence and analysis that a president normally relies on and is expected to utilize. They offer policy alternatives for presidents to accept or reject. They plan ways to implement presidential directives and respond to foreign leaders' overtures.

Under Trump, however, there was a serious disconnect between what a president expected of them and what the experts and agency leaders believed was their job.[26] The result was more than simple confusion over policy: The president and the bureaucratic leaders took off in opposite directions, often due to Trump's impulsiveness but just as often to his profound distrust of experts who might disagree with him and thus demonstrate disloyalty. As John Kelly put it after leaving his post as chief of staff, Trump's bureaucracy had no guardrails: "The system that should be in place, clearly—the system of advising, bringing in experts, having these discussions with the president so he can make an informed decision, that clearly is not in place."[27]

In Trump's imaginings, evidently not widely shared in his cabinet but pushed by some informal advisers given to conspiracies,[28] a permanent "deep state" held the political system captive and subject to the will of elites from both parties. The deep state was never clearly defined, but its geography seemed to encompass all government agencies having anything to do with national security and intelligence gathering—a police state in disguise. Politically, its most important characteristic was opposition to Trump's views, especially by officials who had served under Obama. This notion was absurd on its face, since it also embraced many of Trump's own appointees, people he initially praised to the skies, such as Rex Tillerson, John Mattis, John Kelly, and John Bolton—the last, once an outspoken enemy of the deep state until he turned against Trump in the Ukraine scandal, at which point the pro-Trump Internet crowd painted Bolton as a deep stater, and Mick Mulvaney said it was "100 percent true" that a deep state was seeking to undermine Trump's agenda.[29]

Trump's paranoia owed much to Steve Bannon, who preached that Obama appointees and other bureaucrats opposed to Trump's agenda, especially in national security policy, were out to undermine his authority. In Bannon's view, Putin's nationalism was a model for what the "Judeo-Christian West" ought to be doing in opposition to centralized governance in the United States and Europe.[30] But there was no deep state, only a "complacent state," as one career foreign service officer put it upon resigning—a bureaucracy that complies with an unjust president rather than protests over his disregard for protection of human rights and other ideals.[31]

Trump's remedy for the deep state was to find ways around it. One way was to keep the intelligence community out of the policy-making loop; another, to demand loyalty of the people who headed it; a third, to make interim appointments; and a fourth, to unilaterally expand presidential power. When Trump and his team met heads of the intelligence community for the first time, the team "had no questions about what the future Russian threat might be." It was only interested in eliciting from the IC confirmation that Russian interference "hadn't elected Trump."[32] Or consider why Trump, on five different occasions when he met with Putin, never revealed notes from the meetings or put them into the classified record. No president had ever been so secretive.[33] Nor had any previous president, perhaps with the exception of Nixon, ever demanded personal loyalty from the head of an independent agency. Yet here was Trump telling James Comey, "I need loyalty. I expect loyalty."[34]

Besides firing people, Trump undermined the bureaucracy by making interim appointments, thus avoiding a formal Senate confirmation process. Trump acknowledged that acting status made it easier to replace people, but what he did not admit is that it made it easier to get rid of disloyal people and shuffle in partisans.[35] "Acting" heads of department and senior White House posts became the norm; there were fourteen midway through 2019, including temporary Secretaries of Defense, Labor, and Homeland Security, White House chief of staff and head of communications, and directors of the Federal Emergency Management Agency, Immigration and Customs Enforcement, and the Food and Drug Administration. Worse yet, Trump left numerous posts below cabinet level vacant—for instance, nineteen senior Pentagon positions, including Secretaries of the Army and Air Force; and one third or more positions in the State, Treasury, and Homeland Security Departments.[36]

But the most destructive Trump remedy, applicable to opponents in Congress as well as to "deep-state" bureaucrats, was to expand presidential power. He did it in ways that defied not just tradition but often the law as well. With Ukraine, he used military aid approved by Congress as a hammer to get Ukraine's president to investigate a leading Democrat. He as much as invited three foreign governments to give him election help. He diverted military funds to build his pet project, the Mexico border wall. He ignored war powers legislation in a violent act that nearly started a war with Iran. His military aid to Saudi Arabia continued despite that country's criminal behavior in the war in Yemen. His executive orders on immigration stripped away basic humanitarian and international legal obligations. He bypassed normal channels to pardon far-right and high-profile criminals, using that absolute power to cater to his base and to the rich and powerful like himself.[37] Most damaging was Trump's refusal to allow a single White House official to testify or a single document to be turned over at either his impeachment inquiry or Senate trial, using executive privilege to obstruct investigations of his abuses of power. All these examples are discussed in later chapters, but one more now follows.

Policy on Turkey is a particularly revealing example of distrust of the deep state and its companion, presidential hubris—qualities that Trump happened to share with Turkey's president, Recep Tayyip Erdogan. In 2019 Trump announced that US forces would be quickly pulling out of Syria, contrary to the advice of most of his National Security Agency heads. They rightly feared exposing Kurdish forces, America's most effective ally against ISIS, to a Turkish attack. Trump relented, threatening to "devastate Turkey economically if they hit Kurds."[38] But then he overturned his own decision following a phone call with Erdogan, defying his advisers again by ordering US troops withdrawn from the Turkey-Syria border area. Republican leaders in Congress and other normally pro-Trump conservatives joined with Democrats and the foreign policy establishment in railing against Trump's betrayal of the Kurds.[39] Trump beat a retreat, warning Erdogan of the terrible consequences if his army attacked the Kurds. But it did, causing a huge new refugee flow, heavy losses of life and property, the restoration of Bashar al-Assad's rule in northern Syria, and a predominant role for Russia in the region's future. ISIS got a new lease on life with US withdrawal, though Trump—in somewhat of an about-face—ordered troops to defend Syria's oil fields from seizure by ISIS. Faced with a backlash at home, which included senior Republican senators' sharp criticism of Turkey's attack on the Kurds, Trump imposed ineffectual trade sanctions that did not include US military assistance to Turkey—and then removed them when Turkey declared a ten-day "pause" in the fighting. Trump was left looking impotent and wholly out of touch, an easy mark for Erdogan, and once again shown to be obliging to Moscow.[40]

Could Trump's critics inside the administration fight back? On September 5, 2018 the *New York Times* published an anonymous op-ed attributed to a "senior official" in the Trump administration.[41] The author claimed to represent a "resistance" force within the White House that was trying to "preserve our democratic institutions while thwarting Mr. Trump's more misguided impulses." The op-ed condemned Trump's "amoral" behavior, antidemocratic leadership, and some aspects of his foreign policy while also supporting Trump's domestic agenda. Trump's reaction was predictable: attack the author for disloyalty and "treason," and the "gutless" *New York Times* for publishing the piece.[42] The op-ed's author, conscious that the op-ed might be seen as ratifying the notion of a deep state, said it represented a "steady state," showing yet another way otherwise loyal bureaucratic leaders register disagreement with the boss's agenda: go public. The Ukraine scandal showed the power of going public as a number of senior policy professionals defied the White House and exposed the president's abuse of power, bringing on a new round of White House attacks on the State Department, the intelligence community, and the FBI. "Radical bureaucrats," White House aides railed.[43]

TWO TERRIBLE DISORDERS

In two respects Trump's mental state could not be hidden: his lifelong racism and his persistent lying. Donald Trump made little effort to hide his prejudices. Giving a few jobs to nonwhites and cloaking fear-mongering of Mexicans with talk of border security was not enough to cover for a long history of racist remarks.[44] These continued unabated into his presidency, to the point where he was *legitimizing* racism. "Hispanic, any Hispanic here? I think so. Any Asians? Asian? Asian? Any Asian?" That was Trump at a rally in September 2018 in Las Vegas.[45] He attacked a Muslim member of Congress for daring to say that some Americans exhibited dual loyalties to Israel and the United States, then turned around and told a Jewish audience that Netanyahu was "your prime minister."[46] He told four progressive minority congresswomen that they should "go back" to their home countries—three of them were born in the United States—where they might fix "totally broken and crime infested" situations.[47] This terrible slur, which Trump's rallies picked up with chants of "send her back," ignited a fierce reaction. But Trump, true to form, insisted, "I am the least racist person you have ever met," and said (reportedly under pressure from his family) he was "unhappy" with the crowd's chant and tried to stop it (which tapes disproved). He finally reversed himself by maintaining the chant was "patriotic," not racist.

The Trump administration was dominated by white faces. Not a single African American worked in the West Wing of the White House once Omarosa Manigault Newman was fired in December 2017. Trump rarely appealed for racial equality, and his economic and social policies reflected unfamiliarity with and lack of interest in the experiences of nonwhites, abroad as well as at home. Steve Bannon insisted that the winning strategy for Trump in 2016 was to appeal to the "common man," by which he meant white people, with three themes, the first of which was to limit immigration.[48] Trump followed suit, beginning his campaign by saying Mexico was sending "rapists" and criminals across the border—though he had no problem employing undocumented Mexican and other workers for low wages at his Mar-a-Lago country club. He said during the campaign that a Mexican-American judge was biased in a lawsuit against Trump University because of his heritage.[49] Despite a deluge of criticism, he refused to retract reference to white nationalists parading in Charlottesville, Virginia, as "very fine people on both sides."[50] He disparaged refugees from (among others) Haiti, El Salvador, and Nigeria, and was overheard asking congressional leaders why, in preference to Norwegians, "are we having all these people from shithole countries come here?"[51] As the 2018 midterm elections approached, Trump played the race card all-out, focusing entirely on fear of immigrants and endorsing a video that was so provocative it led even Fox News to join other media outlets in pulling it off the air. Central American refugees "haven't done a thing for us," Trump insisted as he authorized a cut in aid to three countries in 2019. His indisputable misogyny aside—he was accused by more than a dozen women of one or another form of sexual impropriety, and paid off two of them for their silence during the 2016 election campaign[52] — Trump made minority women—especially politicians, professional athletes, and journalists—a special target of his tweets, calling each of them some version of "dumb."[53]

One writer explained Trump's ability to get away with racism and sexism this way: These biases "are not bugs, they're features. They're the reason he is so popular amongst Americans who believe, as Laura Ingraham [the far-right commentator] recently put it, that demographic changes in the US constitute a 'national emergency.'"[54] She was right, according to various polls.[55] Trump's racism thus drew on his followers' worst fears and often silent bigotry. His "politically incorrect" comments were "one of the reasons the American people love him," said Sarah Huckabee Sanders, the White House press secretary.[56] For more than two years he refused to condemn white supremacist violence or equate it to terrorism—his Charlottesville comment and his response to the March 2019 assault by a white supremacist on two mosques in New Zealand were the signature events—and when he finally did, in response to the mass shooting in El Paso in August 2019, he avoided mention of guns and took no personal responsibility for his own incendiary language (his frequent mention of an immigrant "invasion") that evidently motivated the shooter. The best explanation of Trump's refusal to consistently condemn white nationalist violence is straightforward: He was one.

Lying is second nature to Trump. Prior to becoming a presidential candidate, Trump had built his reputation on pretense—about his net worth, his business practices, his genius in economics, his "university," his supposed opposition to the war in Iraq.[57] He posed as another person to give the press uplifting stories about himself and feigned his love of the Bible. As described by Michael Cohen, everyone who worked for Trump was expected to lie for him; "that became the norm."[58] Indeed, just about every Trump appointee was found guilty of lying or dissembling. Some of them went to jail; others, like Cohen, turned on Trump or his associates to avoid jail or obtain reduced jail time.

Trump's life is filled with examples of unethical behavior, far in excess of what we might reasonably consider normal.[59] His lying seems almost pathological. As president he lied, misrepresented, and exaggerated all the time. Somewhere along the way he embraced Josef Goebbels' idea of the big lie: Say it often enough and it will be believed, and even after it has been proven wrong, deny everything. The birth myth about Obama; the Muslims who supposedly cheered the fall of the World Trade Center towers on 9/11; the historic crowds that actually weren't at his inauguration; the insistence that Hillary Clinton won the 2016 popular vote only because three to five million people voted illegally; the repeated false claims about voter fraud (only in state elections he lost), aid to Puerto Rico, and the national debt; the charge that the FBI engaged in politically motivated spying on his campaign; the prediction of Britain's Brexit vote, made *after* the fact; his claims that "we have the best economy in history," the "cleanest air" and "cleanest water"; the assertion that he was uninvolved with security clearances granted to Jared Kushner and Ivanka Trump, which in fact he had ordered over the heads of the FBI and CIA;[60] the repeated denials that he knew certain people who committed crimes despite photographic evidence that he had met them many times, such as the two Giuliani associates who pressured Ukraine's president for damaging information on the Bidens; the pretense that he knew nothing about the Russians' hacking of WikiLeaks to help his campaign when he may actually have sought to cover it up[61]—the president was seemingly incapable of telling or facing the truth. Even the most trivial matters evidently were worth lying about, such as the birthplace of Trump's father (New York, not Germany!). The *Washington Post*, which kept a running record of Trump's "false and misleading" statements, counted more than 18,000 by mid-2020.

Like Don Quixote, Donald Trump believed that "facts are the enemy of truth." Lying was part of Trump's toolbox, used with full confidence that his supporters would unquestioningly believe his every word. As E. J. Dionne wrote, Trump "believes that reality itself can be denied and that big lies can sow enough confusion to keep the truth from taking hold."[62] To any in his base who might have doubts, Trump announced, "What you're seeing and what you're reading is not what's happening." "Stick with us," he told supporters. "Don't believe the crap you see from these people, the fake news."[63] Faced with bad news, Trump found that he could change the public agenda instantly by turning to another subject—a deliberate strategy to impact the news cycle.[64] Or he would take an extreme position favored by his base, then backtrack and blame others for having been forced to do so. He was adept at making threats and quickly abandoning them, such as closing the border with Mexico, ditching NAFTA, and penalizing companies that wanted to move jobs abroad. No matter: It was really all about playing the nationalist card.

Even when confronted with incontrovertible evidence of a lie, such as the London *Sun*'s taped interviews in which Trump was highly critical of Theresa May's stance on Brexit and called the Duchess of Sussex "nasty," he denied his words. When his lies were exposed about the June 2016 meeting in Trump Tower—first, that he knew nothing about it; second, that he did not dictate a false statement about the purpose of the meeting; third, that seeking information from a foreign source about "an opponent" (meaning Hillary Clinton) was perfectly legal—Trump tried to gloss over the significance of lying about collusion with a foreign government. Though taped by his former lawyer, Trump refused to acknowledge that he paid to prevent a story of hush money to a model with whom he (allegedly) had an affair. When a study of the death toll in Puerto Rico from Hurricane Maria showed that nearly 3,000 people had died and not sixty-four as originally thought, Trump persisted in citing the lower figure, presumably in order to justify his administration's poor response to the emergency. Trump surely knew it was a lie to tell evangelical leaders time and again that he had done away with a law that forbids churches and charities from participating in elections—a lie not only because the law remains on the books but also because a president cannot remove the law. Just as he knew he was lying when he warned those same evangelicals they would face violence if his people didn't win in the November 2018 elections.[65] And when television showed Trump on two occasions in 2019 saying he would meet with Iran's leader with "no preconditions," he lashed out at this "fake news."

Some of these lies, often based on false right-wing reporting, had foreign policy consequences. For example, Trump, in an ongoing effort to belittle German prime minister Angela Merkel's government, mocked her liberal immigration policy and insisted it had caused a steep rise in Germany's crime rate. In fact the crime rate had dropped rather substantially. Trump falsely accused a Pakistani-American who had been a congressional staffer for Democratic members ("the Democrat I.T. scandal" and "a Pakistani mystery man," he said of the case) of stealing computer secrets. An extensive investigation cleared the man.[66] Months after pulling the United States out of the Iran nuclear deal, Trump picked up false accusations that part of the deal was Obama's grant of citizenship to 2,500 Iranians tied to the regime. The accusations had been pushed by a hardline member of the Iranian parliament.[67]

Trump's subordinates, no doubt used to his problems with the truth, had to come up with creative explanations. He used "alternative facts," adviser Kellyanne Conway said. He did not "knowingly lie," said Sean Spicer,

Trump's onetime press spokesman. His former campaign manager, Corey Lewandowski, actually admitted lying to the media for Trump.[68] One of Trump's former stenographers, whose job was to stick with the president and ensure that all his comments were recorded, wrote about the president's aversion to being recorded. That aversion caught up with him in the *Sun* interview. She wrote, "Mr. Trump likes to call anyone who disagrees with him 'fake news.' But if he's really the victim of so much inaccurate reporting, why is he so averse to having the facts recorded and transcribed? . . . It's clear that White House stenographers do not serve his administration, but rather his adversary: the truth."[69] Little wonder that Robert Mueller was never able to get Trump to agree to a sit-down interview during the Russia probe. Mueller had to settle for Trump's answers in writing that, predictably, were filled with "I have no recollection."

FRIENDS AND ENEMIES

Trump's connections to the far right became crystal clear once in office, epitomized by his tight relationship with Fox News. Sean Hannity of Fox News, Trump's favorite station, was the equivalent of a top adviser.[70] His colleague Tucker Carlson, another informal adviser to Trump, is credited with influencing Trump's decision not to go to war with Iran. Carlson also was right on track with Trump concerning Russia, saying during the Ukraine investigation, "Why shouldn't I root for Russia?" Fox News chairman Rupert Murdoch was a Trump confidant and beneficiary of Trump's antitrust decisions, despite a rocky personal relationship.[71] And there were many other direct connections.[72] Fox's loyalty to Trump was evident on many occasions, such as when it killed the story of Trump's affair with Stormy Daniels precisely out of fear it would hurt Trump's election.[73] Fox became not just a sounding board for presidential policy and quite possibly the main source of Trump's ideas, but in a real sense the official propaganda agency—America's Pravda-equivalent, only one step removed from what MSNBC critics called Trump-TV.[74] His third press secretary, Stephanie Grisham, made a mockery of her title by failing to hold a single press conference during her nine months of service. Instead, whenever she had something to say, always in defense of Trump, she said it exclusively on Fox News. Most revealing of the Trump-Fox axis may be the moment Trump *attacked* Fox for not supporting him enough, saying, "We have to start looking for a new News Outlet. Fox isn't working for us anymore!"[75] But of course, it still was, just not in absolute lockstep.

Playing to the far right gained Trump support from conspiratorial opinion and gave him a convenient target: the legitimate media hostile to him. On the one hand, Trump disseminated easily disproven claims that he often got from

Fox News commentators.[76] Trump had high praise for Alex Jones, the conspiracy-minded, half-crazed radio commentator on *Infowars* whose tweets Trump sometimes retweeted. He allowed fringe groups like QAnon to gain legitimacy with a photo-op in the White House.[77] When Facebook banned several far-right commentators, including Jones, Trump embraced them by proclaiming defense of "freedom of speech," a justification his administration used again to avoid signing the "Christchurch Call" to combat online extremism.[78] On the other hand, Trump constantly sought to discredit the mainstream media, displaying a dangerous authoritarian streak. Harping on "fake news" whether at home or abroad, calling the press "the enemy of the people," denying access to journalists who asked tough questions, narrowing opportunities for give-and-take with the media, and urging followers not simply to disregard what the media had to say but arousing their anger and potentially violence against independent media—particularly CNN, the *New York Times*, and the *Washington Post*—are hallmarks of the dictator's way of focusing followers on *them*.[79] It could hardly have been accidental that CNN was among the recipients of pipe bombs mailed to several Democratic critics of Trump in October 2018. Only Fox News, *Breitbart*, *National Enquirer*, and other far-right media were exempt from Trump's attacks—except on the rare occasions when they criticized him.

To be sure, other presidents have gotten angry with the media just as they have with "the bureaucracy." But Trump's attacks were constant, and sometimes were accompanied by blaming the media for the "anger" *it* had aroused.[80] Those attacks reached dangerous heights in 2019 when the Justice Department brought charges against Julian Assange, the founder of WikiLeaks, for violating the 1917 Espionage Act. No journalist had ever been charged under that act; Assange's publication of classified government documents in 2010 brought to mind the Pentagon Papers case, which resulted in a victory for press freedom. Now the Trump administration was striking a direct blow at the First Amendment, and the press responded with predictable, fully warranted outrage. But Trump may have been playing an altogether different game with Assange in offering him a pardon if only he would exonerate the Russians.

There is another side to the story of Trump and the media, to be sure. Probably no president in memory was ever subject to so much mockery, unflattering imitation, personal attacks, and unsparing insults. For all the uncritical, fawning attention Trump got from his base, he was vilified just as much by the liberal (and other) media, commentators, and late-night comedians. When we think about his view of the world, we might factor in the decidedly negative treatment he received from the mainstream media while recognizing that he used that treatment to justify calling the media the enemy.[81] Yet the fact remains that despite the attacks from the left, Trump gained far more than he lost from the media's attention. The media soaked up his angry tweets, insults, and muddled rages, and dutifully reported his most absurd statements, perhaps as much out of fear of retribution as out of Trump's entertainment value. The media thus was complicit in Trump's election and durability and his attractiveness to his core followers. Too late, it recognized that it had helped create a monster. And for that unintended cooperation, Trump rewarded the critical media by looking for ways to undermine it and limit its access to him and his team.

TRUMP'S DEMOCRACY DEFICIT

A significant victim of Trump's disrespect for the institutions of government was the Constitution. He simply did not "take care that the law be faithfully executed," as the Constitution requires. Trump's alternative mantra was that presidential power is unlimited; whatever he said, goes—a recipe for lawless government. "So often," Rex Tillerson recounted, "the president would say, 'Here's what I want to do, and here's how I want to do it,' and I would have to say to him, 'Mr. President, I understand what you want to do, but you can't do it that way. It violates the law.'"[82] Trump's personal lawyers and some advisers sometimes weighed in when Trump was considering some ill-considered action. The courts were his enemy: After a judge ruled that the administration could not deport families to Mexico, Trump complained, "We're bucking a court system that never rules for us."[83] Indeed, lower courts were often all that stood between Trump and authoritarian executive orders on the environment, immigration, and voting rights. He insisted that the Department of Justice protect him at a time when the Russia investigation was in high gear. What he cared most about was that the law *serve him*, which it most certainly did once he found an obedient attorney general: William Barr.

With Barr at his side, Trump was positioned to defy House of Representatives committee requests for testimony and documents and subpoenas. One conservative commentator referred to the president's "criminal administration" as it became apparent that Trump would not respect the oversight function of House committees.[84] Decrying the House's "partisanship," Trump followed his longtime pattern: suing to avoid a congressional subpoena of his financial records and announcing that no current or previous official in his administration would respond to a subpoena to testify. In Trump's mind, the House was a subordinate body so long as it was in the opposition party's hands. Rather than deal with the political reality, as other presidents did, Trump was willing to create a constitutional crisis. Feeding such fears, he at various times implied that he would not step down if defeated for reelection, suggesting—particularly after the impeachment process began—that he was the victim of a "coup" orchestrated by treasonous Democrats.

Academic experts and the liberal media took Trump's comments seriously, an unheard of and ominous point of debate in a democracy.[85]

The constant efforts to discredit the mainstream media, interfere with the judicial system's normal functioning, ignore congressional oversight, undermine the IC, and embrace dictators point to a larger issue with Trump: his autocratic tendencies. In some cases Trump simply didn't seem to care, or want to learn, about the institutions or foundations of democratic governance—such as his persistent and false assertions that large numbers of people illegally voted in 2016, and therefore that states were justified in finding ways to restrict voting rights; or his disregard for the Constitution's emoluments clause; or his declaration of a national emergency in February 2019 in order to plunder the budget for more money for his border wall; or his appointment of "acting" department heads so as to avoid the Senate's "advice and consent" power; or his belief in the "absolute right" to order US corporations to leave China. His attacks on judicial rulings that didn't fall his way, his intrusions into ongoing legal disputes, and his anti-Muslim immigration orders, for example, showed a fundamental disregard for the rule of law and democratic processes. As the noted constitutional lawyer Laurence Tribe said, when Trump sought a way around the Constitution on a census case, "The combination of the president's abject ignorance and manipulative flexibility on these matters is, at a minimum, quite telling. It suggests all matters—constitutional and legal—are subject to his whim."[86]

Trump directly interfered with the work of independent agencies—the Department of Justice, the FBI, and the Federal Reserve—as though they were his personal instruments and could be used to further his political agenda. Dissatisfied with the head of the Federal Reserve, Jay Powell, whom he appointed, Trump not only called him an "enemy" but later excoriated Powell ("No 'guts,' no sense, no vision!")[87] when the Fed did not lower interest rates to Trump's liking. Trump sought to have the Justice Department and the FBI prosecute two of his most prominent political enemies, Hillary Clinton and James Comey—an abuse of power and potentially an impeachable offense, his lawyer told him.[88] When it came to Trump's convicted advisers, on the other hand, he directly intervened to influence lighter sentences, even trying to intimidate the judge in the case of Roger Stone. (Barr went over the heads of his prosecutors on the sentencing, supporting the president even as he publicly professed unhappiness that Trump was interfering. The four prosecutors resigned.) Trump also tried to sway those agencies' actions in Mueller's Russia investigation, as previously noted. Once the Mueller report came out, Trump gave William Barr carte blanche to pursue the supposedly dark motives behind the Russia investigation, investing Barr with the politically volatile power to declassify intelligence.

Trump clearly obstructed justice by urging FBI director James Comey to "let go" when Michael Flynn lied about conversations on sanctions with the

Russian ambassador—and when Comey refused and was fired, his replacement, Andrew G. McCabe, launched an investigation into Trump's ties to Russia, considering him a "national security threat" and possibly a Russian "asset."[89] Trump's prodding of the Justice Department to go after the anonymous op-ed writer, urging the department *not* to go after two Republican members of Congress who were caught in corrupt practices, and repeatedly calling his acting attorney general to express displeasure with his refusal to appoint Trump's choice of an attorney to handle the Michael Cohen case in the department's New York office, all crossed the line between presidential power and judicial independence.[90]

Thanks to lower courts, the rule of law was preserved in a number of instances of administration overreach. DACA (Deferred Action for Childhood Arrivals, the legislation that protects the children of undocumented immigrants) continued, press credentials were restored to a journalist critic of the president's, and dozens of attempted rollbacks of a number of Obama-era environmental protections were reversed. The administration's attempts to overturn federal law on the Keystone XL pipeline, drilling on some public lands, and transgender service in the military were also rebuffed by courts, though that did not stop Trump from finding ways around the rulings.

At bottom, Donald Trump—but not only Trump, for he was aided and abetted by unprincipled leaders of the Republican Party, starting with Senator Mitch McConnell[91]—never took to heart that the United States is a *constitutional* democracy, meaning his and all other officials' first loyalty is to the Constitution, not to the White House. He and they routinely violated democratic norms, most specifically *accountability*, tearing at the fabric of the American political system, not to mention undermining the very legitimacy that so obsessed Trump. But while many conservatives outside the administration took issue with Trump's failure to respect the rule of law and the Constitution, conservative officeholders were generally content with Trump's positions, such as on judicial appointments and immigration, or were too fearful of jeopardizing their own careers if they opposed him.[92] Former Secretary of State Colin Powell said as much, urging the Republican Party to "get a grip on itself . . . because they're terrified of what will happen to any one of them if they speak out. When they see things that are not right, they need to say something about it, because our foreign policy is in shambles right now."[93]

I'm reminded of an old classic: Richard Hofstadter's *The Paranoid Style in American Politics*. Rereading it helps give Trump's lies, his authoritarian style, and his true believers a historical context. In a word, we've been here before, though of course in a different form. Those whom Hofstadter called the "pseudo-conservatives" came to power under Trump, but this time they were not particularly interested in the threat from communism or from Russia. They were the aggrieved, the frustrated, the angry and sometimes violent.

Most of all they were conspiratorial, which Hofstadter called the central feature of the paranoid style. In Trump they had their deliverer from evil. In a worrisome ending to one of his essays, Hofstadter (writing in the early 1960s) considered it "at least conceivable that a highly organized, vocal, active, and well-financed minority could create a political climate in which the rational pursuit of our well-being and safety would become impossible."[94]

CORRUPTION BEYOND MEASURE

And then there's the extraordinary corruption of this president and his inner circle.[95] "Full-spectrum corruption," one longtime Republican official called it.[96] Trump brought to Washington a long history of fraudulent behavior—not just cheating on tax returns and insurance policies, as already mentioned, but also lying about properties offered for sale or investment,[97] stiffing contractors, making illegal use of his foundation, running a university that failed to meet its promises to students and was penalized for it, paying hush money to women he seduced, and failing to make promised charitable contributions. In office, Trump, in violation of the Emoluments Clause of the Constitution, profited immensely from his hotels and golf courses, making sure that foreign visitors (along with everyone else) were directed to use Trump facilities—and in effect letting foreigners, officially connected and otherwise, know that it would be politically wise to use those facilities.[98] Most egregious were Trump's effort to build a hotel in Moscow while running for president, and lying about it, and his decision—which he was forced under bipartisan pressure to reverse—to host the 2020 G7 meeting at his Doral, Florida, hotel.

To the Trump family, however, capitalizing on the presidency was an entitlement. Trump has never divulged (and clearly never intended to divulge) his tax returns, which would probably have revealed a history of illegal dealings, faked charitable contributions, and financial obligations to Russian and other foreign backers. As David Frum puts it, the Trumps brought to Washington "no vision. They came to loot."[99]

Every aspect of Trump's finances became the subject of an investigation. The New York State attorney general found that the Donald J. Trump Foundation had operated not as a charity but as a mechanism for supporting Trump's presidential campaign and paying personal expenses. The foundation was forced to close and ordered to pay a $2 million fine. Trump's entire family came under scrutiny inasmuch as they all hold titles in the foundation. Meantime, as Michael Cohen testified, the Trump Organization payments of hush money at Trump's direction were clear violations of campaign finance laws, yet neither he nor his two oldest sons were charged with a crime.[100]

Trump's inauguration committee, which raised an astounding $107 million, was investigated by federal prosecutors for the Southern District of New York for, among other charges, illegally raising money from foreign sources and money laundering.[101] Trump's unusual relationship with Deutsche Bank, which loaned Trump more than $2 billion for real estate transactions despite the bank's awareness that he was a bad risk, also came under investigation.[102]

The central issue here is that Trump and his family were unwilling to draw a line between the public and the private interest. Not only that, their repeated acts of corruption were in-your-face; they made no effort to hide them and were unfazed by law or ethics in carrying them out. Thus, the family's travels, sometimes for business purposes and always at great public expense; the use of Trump properties for official business, melding advertising with profits; and the refusal to end ownership and not merely management of Trump properties on taking office—all these were out in the open, a kind of dare to challenge obvious ethics violations. Several groups, notably CREW (Citizens for Responsibility and Ethics in Washington), did take the dare, at least trying to shame Trump. But with the exception of Trump University, the cases went in Trump's favor or carried on indefinitely, allowing Trump to avoid criminal and civil penalties—and continue to reap profits.

Trump famously promised to "drain the swamp" in Washington, but in fact he repopulated the swamp with people favorable to corporate interests. Blatant corruption and conflicts of interest were hallmarks of many of Trump's cabinet and others in his orbit, including his daughter and son-in-law. Jared Kushner was in good company with his father-in-law, making millions from real estate dealings with the Chinese, Qataris, and others, and paying virtually no federal taxes for many years thanks to clever tax lawyers.[103] Ivanka Trump benefited from licensing agreements granted with unusual rapidity by the Chinese government. Michael Cohen shamelessly gathered corporate payments intended to enhance access to the president. (By most reckoning, such lobbying violates US laws.) Rudy Giuliani contracted with various foreign governments to perform security services while also serving as Trump's lawyer, which gave him the appearance of being a US official. By also defending wealthy Venezuelan, Ukrainian, and other foreign clients with connections to their governments, Giuliani deployed his inner-circle status for both personal profit and Trump's political interests—all while shrouding these activities in the name of "national security."[104]

In the cabinet, EPA head Scott Pruitt catered to the chemical industry and used public money to protect himself and gain special privileges, even for his wife. Forced out, Pruitt was succeeded by a coal industry lobbyist and climate-change denier, Andrew Wheeler. Interior Secretary Ryan Zinke's kowtowing to energy interests and assorted ethical violations led to a host of legal actions, forcing his resignation—only to be succeeded by his deputy, David Bernhardt, another energy and agriculture lobbyist with numerous conflicts of interest.[105] Another lobbyist, Mark Esper, became Defense Secretary despite refusing to say whether he would stay out of contract decisions involving his former employer, the Raytheon Company. The business involvements of Commerce Secretary Wilbur Ross, Labor Secretary Eugene Scalia, and Transportation Secretary Elaine Chao also involved numerous conflicts of interest.[106]

Then there was the favoritism shown the biggest corporations by the Consumer Financial Protection Bureau, which became devoted to undermining consumer protection, and the shift of support from public to private education in Betsy DeVos's Education Department. In Trump's administration, it was hard to find a top official who was free of corrupt practices or conflicts of interest.[107] Democracy was for sale as never before, infecting every aspect of the policy-making process. Yet, Republican control of the House and Senate for the first two years under Trump meant that these unseemly violations of ethical and legal barriers went uninvestigated, unpunished, and rarely even remarked upon by conservatives. As one writer observed, Trump succeeded at creating a "culture of impunity" that the Republican Party readily accepted and the Democrats could do little to stop.[108]

TRUTH AND CONSEQUENCES

Trump's leadership style deserves attention because it has foreign-policy consequences, even if those consequences aren't immediately apparent. A reputation for lying sows mistrust. Bigotry prompts resentment. Corruption invites bribery and other compromising situations. Relying for information and opinion on a news organization that is merely an echo chamber closes off a crucial role of the professional bureaucracy. Paying off people to insure their silence turns out to be a tactic that can be used against oneself. Inattention to details gives opponents opportunities to take advantage. Bullying is likely to be met with anger. Putting ego before interests, and insults before handshakes, will quickly lose friends. Using bluster and pressure tactics to get one's way may risk a costly miscalculation. Failing to show empathy undermines credibility on human rights and gives a free pass for rule by violence. It also means not being able to see the world through others' eyes, such as Palestinian, Mexican, European, and Chinese.

Ignoring expert opinion because you suspect the experts are all part of a conspiratorial "deep state" causes loss of confidence in you and inspires disloyalty. Attacking those experts and their institutions, such as the press, encourages violence—and may lead to dangerous imitation.[109] It also risks counterattacks—not just by the press but also by officials in the FBI, CIA,

Department of Justice, and other agencies Trump consistently maligned. That much became clear in the wake of Trump's revocation of security clearances of former intelligence officials, who ramped up their criticism of him.

The imitation factor also applies abroad: The Trump era brought the US reputation to a new low and in the process attracted all the wrong leaders—autocrats—to his side. Violating democratic norms such as the sacredness of the vote, respect for the rule of law, and freedom of the press gave license to other national leaders to do the same. Trump's cry of "fake news" echoed from Tel Aviv to Rio de Janeiro and from Manila to Yaoundé, where journalists came to be regarded as dangerous opponents.[110] Stereotyping immigrants as threats, casting the poor as beyond redemption, displaying religious and racial intolerance, and enriching the already rich likewise are welcomed and emulated by autocrats, for if America can do such things, so can "we." Using social media to spread lies and misleading information encourages emulation—for example, by the far-right Brazilian president Jair Bolsonaro, who said he wanted to "Make Brazil Great Again."[111]

Chapter Five

The Costs of Inexperience

Trump runs his foreign policy a bit like "The Apprentice" reality show. There are many twists but no plot.
—Thomas Wright, Brookings Institution [1]

HIS OWN WORST ENEMY

The oft-noted disconnect between the foreign-policy bureaucracy and the president sometimes compelled the State Department, the Pentagon, and the intelligence community to devise ways around Trump to avoid indelicate controversy. Trying to restrain him from acting impulsively proved to be a full-time, but ultimately futile, task. Presidents, after all, report to no one, and Trump's more than occasional lapses of judgment could not be prevented or punished. I have in mind his failure to safeguard national security secrets, such as by using an unsecured cell phone that Russians and Chinese were easily able to tap into; divulging top-secret information to the Russians while bragging about his firing of James Comey; mispronouncing and misidentifying the names of countries and leaders; and botching basic geography. He was more than sloppy, he was devious: placing phone calls to other world leaders without the knowledge of senior staff, meeting privately with heads of state and preventing access to notes of the meetings—or no notes at all; and allowing Kushner, Giuliani, and other confidants to act as his surrogates without the knowledge of cabinet members. Acts like these revealed a president who was neither the smartest nor the most reliable guy in the room. And that made him the worst enemy of a coherent foreign policy.

Incoherence extended in potentially dangerous ways to Trump's rocky relations with the military. Trump had a fascination with military power, strange for someone who avoided military service thanks to five deferments because of student status and supposed bone spurs. He regularly touted the US military's capabilities, fed its already enormous budget (which he once said was a *substitute* for his avoidance of military service), and staffed his initial cabinet and advisory system with four generals—McMaster, Flynn, Kelly, and Mattis. None survived Trump's first two years, however. Whereas US presidents probably as far back as George Washington occasionally tangled with their military leaders, Trump openly criticized and insulted them. He once referred to "failed generals" and, early in his administration, in a widely reported meeting at the Pentagon with his senior military and civilian advisers, excoriated them ("a bunch of dopes and babies") for failing to "win" in Afghanistan and overselling alliances that had not returned money on US contributions to them.[2] He missed some important military ceremonies,[3] and pardoned soldiers convicted of war crimes against the advice of Pentagon officials. Trump also used the military for his own political purposes—such as for border security and for a July 4 parade that featured himself. After three years in office, literally half the active military surveyed had a negative view of Trump. But that didn't stop him from using the military in 2020 to suppress protests and demonstrate his toughness.[4]

Just as he famously discounted John McCain's heroism, Trump lashed out at Admiral William H. McRaven, who had overseen the killing of Osama bin Laden, for being a "Hillary Clinton fan." (This was another lie. But McRaven had criticized Trump's attacks on the press and his divisive leadership in a number of op-eds.) Several retired senior military commanders responded fiercely to Trump, calling his outburst "disgusting" and uninformed.[5] When retired general Stanley McChrystal called Trump untruthful and immoral after Trump's decision to leave Syria, Trump also called *him* a "Hillary lover" with a "big, dumb mouth."[6] Trump's bumpy relationship with James Mattis covered a range of issues, from transgender troops in the military and the Iran nuclear deal to maintaining strong alliance ties with NATO and South Korea.[7] After resigning, Mattis implied that their differences went even deeper when he urged Defense Department employees to "keep the faith in our country and hold fast, alongside our allies, aligned against our foes."[8]

Trump's problematic relations with the military, like his difficult relations with the rest of the US foreign policy and national security bureaucracy, muddied the waters about US policy goals. Members of Congress and foreign officials alike were often baffled by the simple question, What is US policy? In this chapter and the next, I explore a subject not dear to Trump's heart: *policy*. On Russia, was US policy to befriend Putin or was it to sanction Russia for its hostile acts? On NATO, was US policy founded on the traditional commitment to common defense or on how much the Europeans were willing to pay for security? On China, did US policy aim at finding common ground, competing economically, or treating China as a national security threat? On North Korea, was US policy based on Trump's belief (as tweeted) that "there is no longer a nuclear threat" from the North, or was it based on his advisers' view that "we're still waiting for them to take real steps towards denuclearization"?[9] In these and other instances, Trump tended to act on instinct, with little concern about foreign-policy consistency, whereas the foreign-policy bureaucracy took into account prior commitments, national interests, US capabilities, and ideological affinities. The point is not that bureaucratic leaders and experts always came up with the right answers to complicated questions, but that Trump saw no need to consult with them, weigh their advice, and act with caution and a set of alternatives.

SHERIFF WITHOUT A POSSE IN EUROPE

When Donald Trump was preparing to travel to Brussels in July 2018 for a NATO meeting, Bolton and Mattis reportedly urged NATO leaders to sign a final statement before Trump arrived, fearing that their boss might upend NATO unity with some personal attack. They succeeded, avoiding a destructive confrontation with Trump over defense spending, Russia, and other issues.[10] They recognized that when it came to Europe, there was no predicting what Trump would promise, whom he would alienate, and what protocols he might violate when meeting its leaders.[11] For Trump, the Europeans were not friends: He considered the EU a "hostile" group[12] and privately told advisers "several times" that the United States should withdraw from NATO because it was so costly.[13] One European commentator provocatively proposed even before the NATO meeting that it would be better for the Europeans to move on from trying to preserve the alliance, which Trump had effectively undermined, saying, "The challenge now for the leaders of Europe is learn to live in a world where America has no allies."[14] So far had Trump's America fallen in the minds of EU leaders that by early 2020, when Pompeo joined the latest European security roundtable, he faced a new phenomenon: "Westlessness," signifying serious loss of faith in the United States and a security partnership on the brink of dissolution.

Beginning with his first month in office and continuing virtually nonstop, Trump constantly criticized the alliance and its most important members—Germany, Britain, and France. He reserved his most brutal comments for his second go-round on NATO in July 2018. It was there, in language extraordinary for a US president, that Trump made his "obsolete" comment. He said Germany's trade surplus with the US was unacceptable and its gas pipeline deal with Russia made it "captive to Russia"; that the alliance was full of deadbeats who weren't paying their fair share for defense (set long ago at 2 percent of GDP); and suggested that US withdrawal from Europe might be a good money saver.[15] Trump continued his barrage in Britain, where he accused Prime Minister May of having a Brexit plan, which British voters had narrowly approved, that threatened a US-UK trade deal, and even suggested that Boris Johnson, who had just quit her cabinet, would make a "great prime minister."[16] He again took aim at the EU, advising May to "sue" it rather than, as May preferred, negotiate with it.[17] Making matters worse, he repeated these interventions on his second, and first official, visit to England in June 2019, by which time May was on her way out and Johnson was a leading candidate to succeed her.

Facts mixed with fancy in Trump's remarks. He neglected to acknowledge that NATO members had agreed years ago to a 2024 deadline for the 2 percent contribution; that the US contribution was not "70 or 90 percent," as Trump claimed, but 22 percent; that other NATO members contributed to common defense in ways other than money; and that the gas pipeline deal hardly made Germany dependent on Russia, much less a puppet.[18] Most fundamentally, Trump pumped up the narrative that supporting NATO, and other alliances, was not first and foremost in the interest of the United States. Trump eventually did declare support for NATO, saying, "The United States commitment to NATO is very strong, remains very strong. I believe in NATO." But few bought that line, especially when he is said to have threatened that the United States would "go it alone" if NATO members did not reach the 2 percent target by January 2019.[19] When that didn't happen, he reportedly set a new target: cost-plus-50, meaning European and all other allies would have to pay the full cost of US bases and forces plus 50 percent, which if actually implemented would represent a huge increase.[20] Europeans could be excused for concluding that a fundamental rift with the United States had occurred, caused by Trump's "go it alone" foreign policy.[21]

As his critical comments showed, Trump had no compunctions about interfering in European politics, encouraging an identity politics that threatened EU solidarity, gave voice to both right and left anti-immigration groups, and undermined democratic rule and liberal social policies. His interventions offered Russia an opening to take advantage of Euroskepticism with financial support, election hacking, direct contact with right-wing parties, and outright subversion orchestrated by a previously unknown elite unit within Russia's intelligence service.[22] Trump surely approved of Steve Bannon's and right-wing financier Robert Mercer's involvement with Britain's Leave.EU campaign—that is, Brexit—which Russian money may have supported.[23] Bannon marketed white nationalism around Europe, awaiting the next great far-right leader who would hire him (as Ukraine did Paul Manafort). Bannon had millions of dollars to spend thanks to Mercer's offshore (Bermuda) investments that siphoned money into Bannon's disingenuously named foundation, the Government Accountability Institute.[24]

Marine Le Pen, leader of what is now called the National Gathering party in France, disavowed Bannon's support because he wasn't a European, but did throw support to an emerging alliance of far-right parties promoted by Italy's Matteo Salvini.[25] But others found much to like in Bannon, whose money and reputation were hard to resist. Ask Nigel Farage, Brexit's main voice, who toyed with the idea of teaming with Bannon to form The Movement, which would be an umbrella organization for right-wing populist leaders around the world committed to an anti-globalist agenda.[26] Trump openly endorsed Farage, as well as Boris Johnson, to replace Theresa May and complete Britain's divorce from the EU. By the end of 2019 they had succeeded.

Elsewhere in Europe, the Trump-Bannon team's theme song about the dangers of immigration found receptive audiences. In Germany, Trump said Chancellor Angela Merkel had made a terrible mistake by admitting so many refugees into Germany. Neo-Nazis, represented by (among other groups) Alternative für Deutschland (AfD), are gradually normalizing the far right.[27] AfD is now the second most popular party, has strong support from Russia, and *Lügenpresse* (lying press), the German equivalent of "fake news," has gained legitimacy. As Merkel prepared to leave office in 2020, she and mayors around Germany warned about the far right's "politics of hate" that endanger any official who supports immigration. The far right is also in the ascendancy in Hungary, Poland, and Italy under fiercely anti-immigrant governments, with judicial and press independence greatly eroded in the first two countries and Europe's nationalist movement increasingly centered in Italy.[28] Only in France did nationalists suffer a major defeat with the rejection of Marine Le Pen's campaign for the presidency, though on the bright side, the Green Party made significant gains in Germany and elsewhere in European elections in May 2019.

With Trump in power, some historians were reminded of the rise of fascism in Europe. Trump was not another Hitler, but his disdain for democratic processes, his efforts to undermine institutions of international cooperation, and his thinly veiled incitements of supporters to violence did recall the Nazi era.[29] Social scientists saw in Trump's rise similar causes of the nationalist upsurge in Europe: the decline of the social-welfare state, economic downturn since 2008, failure of liberal parties to deliver on jobs and economic growth, scapegoating of immigrants, the role of social media in broadcasting both real and imaginary reasons for loss of faith, and the subordination of women.[30] Far-right European groups also benefited from millions of dollars in contributions from well-heeled Christian anti-LGBT organizations with ties to the Trump administration.[31]

SANDBAGGED: THE RUSSIA CONNECTION

Russia's attack on the 2016 US elections was "sweeping and systematic," said the Mueller report. The attack, most observers agree, had three motivations: disrupt democratic processes and the Euro-American alliance so as to undermine US moral and political authority in world affairs; weaken Hillary Clinton's campaign in response to her criticisms of Russian politics and foreign policy; and support Trump's campaign in the belief a Trump victory would restore balance in Russia-US relations.[32] The interference, said Mueller, took place in more than twenty-five countries in addition to the United States, starting with Ukraine. Even before Mueller's report, Russian hacking was abundantly documented by the US intelligence community and later by a more comprehensive Senate Intelligence Committee report.[33] The administration's top foreign-policy officials in 2017 agreed with the IC's findings, but Trump usually belittled them, probably seeing the findings as challenging the legitimacy of his presidency.[34]

Donald Trump campaigned on developing a friendly relationship with Russia. His very first public comment on Russia came at a press conference in which he questioned the wisdom of sanctions, a theme he repeated throughout the campaign. Once president, he abetted suspicions about his Russia connection by invariably accepting Putin's assurances over the findings of the intelligence community. In a May 2017 meeting in the Oval Office with the Russian ambassador and foreign minister, Trump said he wasn't concerned about Russian interference in the US election because the United States also interfered in other countries' politics—a statement that left his aides aghast.[35] After his first meeting with Putin in July 2017, at the G-20 summit in Hamburg, Trump took the unusual step of contacting a *New York Times* reporter from Air Force One to say how impressed he was with Putin's argument that Russia was about noninterference, which to Trump was more convincing than the argument of "political hacks," meaning Comey, Clapper, and Brennan.[36] Then, in Helsinki, as mentioned earlier, he said he took Putin's word over those who "think it's Russia" that interfered. That summit was a major stain on Trump's record and one more visible than most others. Far from holding Russia at least somewhat responsible for the poor state of US-Russia relations, he blamed the United States. Putin acknowledged that he preferred Trump to Clinton in 2016—hardly surprising in light of the clashes of view between Putin and Clinton when she was secretary of state.[37]

By the time Trump and Putin met again, at a G-20 summit in Osaka, Japan, in June 2019, Trump playfully told Putin not to "meddle in the election," prompting laughter from both. Yet just one month earlier, Trump's Defense Department had issued a white paper on Russian strategy that emphasized the Kremlin's "zero-sum" worldview, including the "belief that it must contain and constrain US influence and activities in Europe and elsewhere across the globe."[38] At Osaka, Putin actually confirmed part of that assessment, telling British interviewers that Western liberalism had "become obsolete."[39]

Russia policy stood out as the best example of the frequent gap in the Trump administration between the president's instincts and the views of his policy advisers. "The disconnect [between Trump and his advisers] is so profound," the *New York Times* concluded, "that it often seems Mr. Trump is pursuing one Russia policy, set on ushering in a gauzy new era of cooperation with Mr. Putin, while the rest of his administration is pursuing another."[40] Whereas Trump's most loyal advisers secretly worked to reduce sanctions, his defense secretary, the State Department professionals, and the CIA leader aligned with Congress to block removal of sanctions and impose new ones.[41] Trump constantly played to Moscow's interests, clamping down on any criticism that might offend Russia, downplaying the importance of NATO and other alliances, rejecting making defense commitments to Ukraine and Montenegro,[42] never commenting on Russia's deplorable human rights record or its subversive activities in Europe, pulling most US forces out of Syria, retreating in May 2019 from an initial warning to Russia over its military presence in Venezuela (see chapter 6), and withholding military aid to Ukraine.

In essence, Trump endorsed a Russian disinformation campaign and demeaned the conclusions of his own Russia experts. He simply was oblivious to evidence of Russian misconduct; reportedly, his staff was told not to raise the election interference because of the connection in Trump's mind with his legitimacy.[43] This, despite ample warnings from his FBI director, the IC, and a bipartisan Senate intelligence committee report that Russia would continue seeking to disrupt US elections. (As Robert Mueller said in July 2019 testimony before Congress, "They're doing it while we sit here, and they expect to do it in the next campaign.")[44] Unfazed, Trump, once cleared by the Senate, seemed intent on creating a new narrative about Russian interference to divert attention from the warning his intelligence agencies were issuing about further interference in the 2020 elections.[45] Nancy Pelosi, Democratic leader in the House of Representatives, put it succinctly: "All roads lead to Putin."[46]

Nevertheless, Congress, even when both houses were dominated by Republicans, was occasionally able to push through tough responses to Russian provocations.[47] Sanctions on Russia in fact were a rare show of bipartisanship. (Only five Congress members in both houses combined voted against sanctions on Russia in 2018.) The White House did all it could to erode their scope and effectiveness, even on one occasion removing sanctions on three Russian companies affiliated with an oligarch close to Putin. Nevertheless, from January 2017 to August 2018, 213 Russian entities and individuals were sanctioned. Sixty Russian consular officials were expelled in retaliation for election meddling, and export controls were applied in 2018 to goods that might have military uses. Ukraine's army eventually received US military aid. The March 2018 poisoning with the nerve agent Novichok in Britain of a former Russian spy and his daughter led to additional sanctions required by a law governing chemical weapons. (Two Russians with the state intelligence agency were responsible.) But all those actions, though getting Moscow's attention, fell well short of serious punishment, and their impact was weakened by Trump's silence on the Kremlin's behavior and the administration's inexplicable delay in implementing the sanctions.[48]

Trump had the option of going with his advisers or even upping the ante for the Russians. He chose neither, reportedly unwilling to listen to any talk from his staff about strengthening the nation's election machinery in advance of 2020 and rejecting authorizing retaliatory measures to weaken Putin's rule.[49] For example, the United States and its NATO allies might have reinvigorated a propaganda campaign aimed at Putin's oligarchy and human rights record. The US might also have enacted stiff regulations to control the routes Russia's so-called kleptocracy takes to bring money into the United States and buy favors for doing so.[50] Still more boldly, Washington might have revitalized "a policy of containment to protect the sovereignty, security, and democracy of all NATO members, because Moscow seeks to undermine all three," as advocated in a Council on Foreign Relations study published in January 2018.[51]

Alternatively, Trump might have tried an entirely different tack with Russia: engagement. He could have proposed, with support from a bipartisan group in Congress, that sanctions on Russia be reduced in proportion to Russian withdrawal from the Donbass region of Ukraine and confirmed non-interference in US and European elections. The administration might also have pledged not to expand NATO to include Ukraine provided it received guarantees of Russian respect for Ukraine's sovereignty. Clearly, however, neither Trump nor, for that matter, many in Congress or the State Department, were interested in such policy alternatives. And Putin made the case for engagement all the more difficult by refusing to acknowledge interfering in US elections, acting aggressively on Russia's periphery, and talking about invulnerable hypersonic weapons and full-out modernization of Russia's nuclear triad.

After Trump's awful performance at Helsinki, a number of prominent Americans began to use the *t* words—traitor and treason.[52] Commentators and Democratic politicians began openly asking what the Russians had on Trump. Why had Trump sought Putin's favor ever since the Miss Universe contest in Moscow in 2013? What could explain Trump's extraordinary deference to Putin?[53] Why, at every meeting with Putin, did the president either not include his own interpreter or confiscate the interpreter's notes, thus not sharing information on the meeting with anyone? The ranting of the liberal media—joined by a few prominent conservative commentators—about Trump's obsequiousness and the Republicans' spinelessness did not equate to a tipping point on his fitness for office. Politics ruled, so that when it came to taking firmer action, such as voting to protect Mueller's investigation or backing a joint resolution warning Putin about Russian interference, the otherwise pained voices of Republicans went silent. It was a pitiful display of captivity.[54]

What *did* Russia have on Trump? Two theses are prominent among critical observers. The first looks like a conspiracy to commit bribery: benefits to Trump's financial position in exchange for ending sanctions. Money framed Trump's pro-Russia policy—millions of dollars in Russian loans to Trump laundered through Deutsche Bank and banks in Cyprus;[55] Deutsche Bank's introduction of Russian investors to Trump's overseas projects; Trump real estate bought by Russian oligarchs at inflated prices to help Trump repay debts; and Trump's longstanding interest in Moscow real estate, mainly building a Trump Tower there.[56] "We have all the funding we need out of Russia," Eric Trump is said to have once remarked, and that's about as bold a confession as one can get on a compromising contact with a foreign adversary.[57]

The second thesis puts Moscow's election support of Trump ahead of financial interests. Trump may have welcomed Russian election interference for the simple reason that Russia could help deliver votes toward his reelection. That would explain his consistent refusal to denounce the interference or make preventing it a top priority. Every time he was with Putin or spoke with Putin by phone, Trump could have point-blank warned the Russian leader. But Trump said nothing, perhaps because Putin was all-in on helping his "friend," with the assurance Trump would continue trusting Putin's word and, where possible, supporting Russian policies.

It is hard to find fault with Trump's desire for "constructive dialogue" with Russia. As he said when side by side with Putin in Helsinki, "The disagreements between our two countries are well known. . . . But if we're going to solve many of the problems facing our world, then we are going to have to find ways to cooperate in pursuit of shared interests."[58] Shared national interests were not nearly as strong as other shared things, however: the status Trump provided Putin, a nationalist agenda that accorded with Putin's, a lack of interest in promoting human rights and democracy, and real estate transactions. Like Xi Jinping, Putin may have become less infatuated with Trump over time than when Trump was elected because Trump failed to deliver on ending sanctions and, flattery aside, wasn't as predictable as first thought. Trump's reaction, for example, to a Russian attack on Ukrainian ships in November 2018—"I don't like that aggression"—must have taken the Kremlin by surprise, though it did not include a condemnation of Russia that the State Department professionals had urged.[59] But Trump was still Putin's best bet for promoting Russian interests with the United States.

THE CHINA CONUNDRUM[60]

Ever since China's economic reforms began in 1978, the goal of US foreign policy has been to "manage" China's rise so that it might become a worthy member of the community of nations dominated by the United States and its allies. Republican and Democratic administrations alike have sent Beijing essentially the same message: The United States supports a "peaceful, stable, and prosperous" China that will play by international rules while internally carrying out liberal political reforms. For a time, especially in the early decades of reform under Deng Xiaoping, China did seem to conform to Western expectations. It made no attempt to challenge US predominance in the Pacific (or anywhere else), its military modernization was modest, and its singular focus was on rapid economic development. Granted, the crackdown at Tiananmen in 1989 showed that political liberalization was not in the cards for China for quite some time. But overall, China's behavior gave US leaders cause for optimism, particularly as economic reforms opened China to international trade and, later, foreign investment, and as China began joining various regional and international organizations. Beijing's embrace of globalization, it was widely assumed in Washington, put it on the road to liberalization.

What American leaders failed to perceive was that China's leaders never intended its economic rise to include political liberalization. The political changes that did occur were mainly to promote greater economic efficiency. China's ambition was to become a major economic player while sustaining the party-state system and preventing a Jasmine Spring, the equivalent of the Arab Spring. China's growing wealth, founded on a distinctive "market socialism," would also present a new model of development for Third World countries to follow, a no-strings alternative to the Washington Consensus, the term used to define the international financial institutions that typically impose conditions, such as "structural adjustment," on loans to developing countries. The notion during the George W. Bush years that China would become a "responsible stakeholder" in international affairs, meaning a supporter of US policy priorities, never gained traction in Beijing. Instead, as Xi Jinping told Barack Obama, China's goal was (and remains) having a "new type of great-power relationship" with the United States. The message? The stronger China becomes economically, the stronger the drive for influence, power, and an equal seat at the table.

That is China's world that Donald Trump stumbled into. He was far from ready to manage, much less forestall, China's emergence. In fact he had no idea about China, his only experience having been as landlord of a Chinese bank with an office in Trump Tower. Inexperience and an emerging "America First" mentality led Trump to cast China as a villain as far back as 2011, when he told CNN that China was an "enemy" and needed to be punished for its unfair trade practices.[61] Years later he also held China responsible for a climate change "hoax," lost US jobs, and currency manipulation. Shift to his presidency and we find that Trump's approach to China hardly changed at all: China remained the villain and continued to be scapegoated. Now China was accused of preventing North Korea's denuclearization, stealing US intellectual property, seeking military parity, and still refusing to level the playing field on trade. While Trump's national security and intelligence community focused on Russia, Trump was riveted on China, notwithstanding his supposed friendship with Xi.[62]

Trump cast the competition with China as a zero-sum game. Referring to trade, he said, "I raised 50, and they [the Chinese] matched us. I said, 'You don't match us. You can't match us because otherwise we're always going to be behind the 8-ball.'"[63] Matching, no; but each time Trump raised tariffs on Chinese goods, China answered with tariffs of its own. This happened several times during 2018–2019. A former head of the American Chamber of Commerce in Beijing wondered when the war might end, noting that Trump was "publicly demanding an unconditional surrender from Beijing."[64] He did not know Trump, who countered with the usual bluster: "They do not want me or us to win because I am the first president ever to challenge China on trade," Trump said before the UN Security Council in September 2018. "We are winning on trade. We are winning at every level. We don't want them to meddle or interfere in our upcoming election."[65] In mid-2019, with no sign the trade war would end anytime soon, Trump had returned to a theme he used years earlier: Who needs China?[66]

But he wasn't winning: The US trade deficit with China rose again in 2018, to about $419 billion, and was lower in 2019 only because overall trade went down. Trump's strategy seemed to be to keep escalating tariffs on Chinese imports until Beijing capitulated and made structural changes in its economy—most importantly, on subsidies for key industries. But pinning Xi to the wall was not a tactic that would go over well with a leader every bit as nationalistic as Trump.[67] Trump and company evidently did not take seriously the many Chinese press accounts of how Xi and the party leadership viewed the US assault: the references to a "new Long March," overcoming difficulties, and defending China's economic development path, which it now called a "core interest."[68] China retaliated, not only with its own tariff increases but also with a currency devaluation and tougher regulations for US companies doing business there. Chinese investments in the United States dried up. US consumers, taxpayers, farmers, and auto manufacturers were badly hurt.[69] And China did not suffer nearly as much as US sources had predicted—the onset of the coronavirus (COVID-19) in 2020 caused far more economic pain—mainly because Beijing shifted to markets in Southeast Asia and Europe and moved ahead with its alternative to the Trans-Pacific Partnership, the Regional Comprehensive Trade Partnership that includes twenty-five Asia-Pacific countries. [70] Thus, when a new "Phase One" trade agreement was announced in December 2019, it was more a win for China's trade hawks than for the Trump administration, which by then needed an agreement largely for political reasons. [71]

"Winning" against China counted for a great deal with Trump, but his own NSC did not entirely agree: Its 2017 strategy paper cast both China and Russia as the leading threats to the United States. [72] Yet China's own 2019 defense white paper, while critical of US global policies, did not characterize the United States as a national security threat and instead said domestic "separatism" (meaning Taiwan, Hong Kong, Tibet, and Xinjiang) was the main threat. Treating Beijing and Moscow as the chief threats to the United States gave them every incentive to tighten their relationship. Militarily, Russian sales to China of sophisticated arms such as surface-to-air missiles increased, and large-scale joint exercises took place. Economically, their trade greatly expanded. [73] US-China tensions apparently reduced Chinese and Russian incentives to curb illicit oil transfers to North Korea in violation of UN sanctions. [74] In the view of some observers, the level of cooperation between Beijing and Moscow was just short of a formal alliance. [75] Trump now simultaneously faced two main enemies.

Trump also provided China with another gift: new diplomatic successes. China's relationship with Japan suddenly warmed, just as Japan–South Korea ties were fraying over the longstanding reparations issue and without any US effort to mend the breach. [76] Japan's Prime Minister Shinzo Abe visited Beijing in October 2018, after he and Xi issued a joint statement in defense of the World Trade Organization and globalization, both objects of Trump's scorn. Among other things, Abe and Xi agreed to jointly support infrastructure projects within the scope of China's ambitious, multitrillion-dollar Belt and Road Initiative (BRI) that stretches across Asia to Africa and Europe. China's economic ties with Germany and South Korea also improved in the wake of US-China differences. [77] With another US ally, the Philippines, China took advantage of deteriorating relations between the Rodrigo Duterte government and Washington despite Beijing's aggressive pursuit of its territorial claims in the South China Sea. [78] US economic warfare against Iran after withdrawal from the nuclear deal gave China a propaganda victory as it excoriated Washington for "unilateral bullying [that] has become a worsening 'tumor' and is creating more problems and greater crises on a global scale." [79] As noted later (chapter 6), US pressure on Iran led Tehran to look to Beijing for arms and stronger political ties. [80] Likewise, as noted later, Iraq turned to China rather than be bullied by Trump to fork over half its oil revenues.

The task of promoting human rights in China became more difficult under Trump. Rarely did Washington raise its voice to defend human rights, and when it did, Beijing ignored it. One example is the US threat of sanctions in response to China's incarceration and "reeducation" of an estimated one to one and a half million Uyghurs and other Chinese Muslims in Xinjiang Province. The threat did not materialize until the trade war with China escalated in 2019, when it was applied to a number of Chinese firms that dominate the domestic Chinese and international market in surveillance technology.[81] But Trump said only a word or two on behalf of the Uyghurs, though Pompeo did more, calling China's repression "the crime of the century." The Europeans criticized China, but without letting that criticism stand in the way of their trade relations.[82] A more egregious example is the lack of a strong US response to the many weeks of large-scale popular protests in Hong Kong beginning in the summer of 2019. The immediate cause of the protests was a Beijing-backed decision by the Hong Kong authorities to impose an extradition bill that would have allowed dissenters to be shipped off to China for handling. But the protests evolved into calls for greater autonomy and democracy. Despite the sometimes brutal treatment of the protesters by police and Beijing-hired thugs, the Trump administration adopted a hands-off policy, reportedly looking at Hong Kong as a bargaining chip in the trade talks and later as an inducement to "investigate" the Bidens.[83]

Where Chinese leaders and analysts at one time had viewed Trump's presidency positively because of his business career, they now seem puzzled and frustrated by his behavior and its impact on American politics. "Some US watchers in China, myself included," wrote Wang Jisi, "find the country we have studied for years increasingly unrecognizable and unpredictable." He cited various negative features of US politics as well as the longstanding US insistence on a "rules-based liberal international order" that Washington neither defined nor lived up to. Wang is among those influential analysts in China who still believe in a cooperative relationship with the United States. But he warned that compared with crises in relations in previous times, "the current deterioration in relations may prove more permanent."[84]

The Trump administration's purpose, however, was clearly not to find common ground, much less resolve, outstanding issues. It was to elevate the "China threat" and, for him, deflate the Russia threat.[85] As usual, he offered no explanation. Nor did Vice President Pence in a major speech on China policy the same month.[86] Pence actually went far beyond Trump in accusing China of an extraordinary array of threats: to academic freedom, to fair trade relations, to strategic balance, to human rights. Some of Pence's criticisms were well founded and of long standing. But the thrust of it, from the distorted history of US-China relations to the magnification of the strategic threat posed by China, was right out of the Cold War. The speech left little room for reasoned dialogue, giving credence to the idea that the United States and China might fall into "Thucydides's trap," in which a rising power threatens to displace the predominant power.[87]

China's role in world politics is changing dramatically. It no longer seeks to "hide its profile and bide its time," as Deng Xiaoping advised. On the contrary, many Chinese foreign policy specialists speak of a post-American world, one that is not merely multipolar but also one in which China is the equal of the United States. Some Chinese specialists, such as Zhang Tuo-sheng, maintain that China will soon eclipse the United States in the Asia-Pacific balance of power.[88] In this new Asian order, China has the ability to defend its territorial claims in nearby waters, and possibly even deter the United States from protecting Taiwan. China can step in when US relations with longtime alliances fray (e.g., its alliances with South Korea and Turkey), challenge US policies on high-profile issues (e.g., on Iran and North Korea), be the leading voice on globalization, buy economic dominance and strategic access in developing countries, and be a global leader in energy conservation. Not all of China's initiatives have been universally applauded—BRI, which entails large Chinese loans to developing countries, has been welcomed by some of them but has also run up against charges, by scholars as well as US officials, of creating a "debt trap" and being environmentally destructive—but the sense in China that the United States is in retreat and uncompetitive is pervasive.[89]

The predominant Chinese view is not that China will *displace* the United States as the leading great power in Asia, but rather that it can outcompete the United States.[90] But in China's upper echelons there is a widespread view that the American experiment is failing; Donald Trump is presiding over an increasingly dysfunctional America, and his extraordinarily inept handling of the coronavirus pandemic proves it to Beijing. China's leadership, according to this view, has kept social problems from exploding and has avoided disruptive reforms of the one-party state—though events in Hong Kong and Xinjiang, and the coronavirus epidemic that caught the leadership flatfooted and desperate to maintain damage control revealed cracks in the armor, a leadership with plenty of reason to feel insecure. Yet under Xi Jinping, China has clearly elevated its international standing relative to the United States, in part by becoming a supplier of last resort of medical supplies.[91]

We have thus entered a new "bipolar order," according to one Chinese analyst. It will be marked not by war but by intense economic and technological competition, including cyber hacking, and a decline of multilateralism in favor of spheres of influence.[92] Trump bears considerable responsibility for that transformation, as many other China specialists argue, having abandoned strategic engagement with China in favor of strategic competition.[93] That shift became abundantly clear during COVID-19 as both leaderships traded blame and accusations over the origins of the virus. One consequence will probably be a significant degree of commercial, technological, and interchange decoupling—all areas that both Republican and Democratic administrations once regarded as crucial to building positive relations with China.[94]

Finding common ground and avoiding needless confrontations is therefore more urgent than ever, particularly since another wave of anti-China sentiment, with liberals joining in, has emerged in the United States.[95] China should be treated as a political and economic competitor, not a paramount military threat: *competitive coexistence*, in short. That means strengthening US alliances in Asia and commercial relations worldwide while also pursuing mutually advantageous engagement with China, such as on climate change, pandemics, and conflict management in the South China Sea and Taiwan Strait. Engagement does not exclude standing up for human rights (by either side, it should be added), negotiating better trade and investment terms, or confronting aggressive behavior in or beyond East Asia. But it does exclude treatment of the other as an enemy—meaning, for example, recognizing that China's achievements in artificial intelligence, 5G networks, and other high-tech areas have not been mainly due to theft of US intellectual property, and regarding the tens of thousands of Chinese scholars and students in the United States as assets rather than potential spies.[96]

Inevitably, China's military power will grow both qualitatively and quantitatively to match its widening economic reach, which now extends across Asia and the Mediterranean to Latin America. China is not a true military equal of the United States in spending or any other category of military power, but it is closing the gap.[97] The United States will have to adjust to that new reality; pursuing containment of China and trade wars are high-risk strategies with global consequences. The adjustment, as Kurt Campbell and Ely Ratner have written, starts with "a new degree of humility about the United States' ability to change China."[98] That means refocusing on revitalizing US strengths greatly diminished under Trump: its influence in multinational commercial and environmental forums; its alliances, investments in resource and energy conservation, the attractiveness of its ideals and innovative culture; and its political unity to solve urgent social problems. If US-China cooperation continues to go south, influenced by liberal as well as conservative voices, China's nationalists will gain influence and Wang Jisi's prediction of a permanent rupture will come true.

Chapter Six

The (Lost) Art of the Deal

The notion that the Trump administration's nationalist bent equates with isolationist or merely transactional impulses is easily debunked when we turn to its actions in specific international disputes. America First principles could sometimes be discerned in US policy, but for the most part policy making lacked strategic consistency and reflected an aversion to diplomacy. Sometimes Trump seemed to act on the belief that personal relationships would win out over conflicting national interests. At other times he was swayed by his ideologically inclined advisers to widen US intervention. In this chapter I explore US policy on several fronts: the failed attempt to denuclearize North Korea, the threat to Iran of regime change, the neglect of Africa, the erratic approach to the Middle East, and ideological warfare in Latin America.

"MAXIMUM PRESSURE": NORTH KOREA

When President Trump accepted the invitation of Kim Jong-un for a summit meeting at the end of 2017, the United States and most other governments responded to North Korea's development of sophisticated weapons of mass destruction and the means of delivering them with support for increasingly intense sanctions. The US president also threatened war, including use of nuclear weapons. Neither sanctions nor threats achieved the desired results, however: the North Korean regime remained defiant and committed to maintaining and developing nuclear weapons and long-range missiles. The summit on June 12, 2018, in Singapore, as well as a second summit in Hanoi in February 2019, took place while sanctions continued. Both were intended to lay a path to resolving the issue of North Korea's nuclear weapons. They didn't, for two principal reasons: different notions of what denuclearization means and the absence of a US diplomatic strategy for engaging North Korea.

Kim Jong-un was bound to be a challenge for the Trump administration. He surprised experts with the speed and scope of North Korea's nuclear and missile programs: six nuclear weapon tests and frequent tests of intermediate- and intercontinental-range missiles—thirteen in 2017 alone, including its first ICBM tests. Most analysts did not expect Kim to trade taunts and threats with the US president.[1] But Kim seems to have learned from the experiences of Iraq's Saddam Hussein and Libya's Muammar al-Qaddafi that "nuclear weapons [are] the major guarantee of their [North Korea's] security. There is no form of pressure that can convince them to budge on this, no promise that will seduce them into compliance; they believe that without nuclear weapons they are as good as dead."[2] Put another way, nuclear weapons are central to the survival of the Kim dynasty as well as to the survival of the Democratic People's Republic of Korea (DPRK)—its indispensable deterrent and principal bargaining chip.[3] For Kim, if denuclearization means the complete dismantlement and disposal of nuclear weapons, without rock-solid security guarantees, no deal with the United States is possible.

Nevertheless, Trump's team was convinced that "maximum pressure" would compel Kim Jong-un to succumb and commit to CVID: "complete, verifiable, irreversible denuclearization," the same objective George W. Bush and Barack Obama had failed to achieve.[4] As Trump apparently told advisers, who worried about the exchanges of threats between Trump and Kim, he wanted to keep Kim off balance by one-upping the threats. Trump showed a callous disregard for professional opinion. At one point Trump "rattled" his joint chiefs chairman, General Joseph Dunford, by asking for a plan to preemptively strike North Korea.[5] At another, Trump wanted to tweet an order to withdraw all US dependents from South Korea. Such an order, he was told, would convince the North Koreans war was imminent.[6] Trump believed he was in a "contest of wills" with Kim that, of course, Trump felt confident he would win.[7]

Kim Jong-un evidently thought his nuclear and missile program had advanced sufficiently that he could safely enter into talks with Washington. He also had a strategy for enticing Trump: starting dialogue with South Korea's liberal new president, Moon Jae-in, on improving inter-Korean relations while also professing interest in denuclearization. Trump jumped at Kim's invitation to a summit and the chance to make history. After all, no sitting US president had ever held a personal meeting with a North Korean leader. But the pitfall was the mistaken US assumption that CVID was a common aim, and that the North Koreans were mainly motivated by the prospect of US aid replacing sanctions. Andrei Lankov, however, pointed out that while Kim Jong-un had given highest priority to improving the North Korean economy, "regime survival is far more important to him than any economic growth, so no amount of promised economic benefits will lure him into surrendering his nukes."[8]

Had Trump applied his "art of the deal" to North Korea, he would have considered genuine engagement, meaning a strategic approach to peacemaking that centers on a carefully calibrated use of incentives and multiple levels and formats for dialogue—a process of trust building that requires considerable patience and forbearance over many months and perhaps years.[9] Such a process also means putting off the intractable issue of denuclearization to the end, allowing cooperative steps to take hold first. Based on two engagement success stories—the Obama administration's nuclear deal with Iran and its normalization of relations with Cuba—engaging North Korea also requires two other elements: empathy, meaning the ability to see the world through North Korean eyes, and mutual respect, meaning a willingness to accept North Korean representatives as legitimate negotiating partners. Liberal South Korean leaders, from Kim Dae-jung (1998–2003) to Moon Jae-in, understood North Korea's highest priorities—regime survival, security from threats, and international acceptance that would lead to normalization of relations with the United States—and fashioned a "Sunshine" policy in response.[10] Trump, on the other hand, accorded North Korea respect by agreeing to summit meetings but never displayed empathy.

A sticks-first, carrots-last approach did not mean the use of force, but it did mean reliance on sanctions on North Korean trade, banking, and export of labor. The UN Security Council passed several sanctions resolutions, each one expanding on the preceding ones. Clearly, the sanctions were painful, since they encompassed an estimated 90 percent of North Korean exports as well as North Korean laborers abroad. But Pyongyang found ways around the sanctions, even for its weapons exports, despite obstacles to its overall trade and banking systems. It had help from Russian and Chinese businessmen, lax border guards, cyberattacks, and oil smugglers offloading at sea.[11] The North Koreans also used the Internet very effectively to move money. But the primary reason for North Korean resistance has always been a militant nationalism: the North Korean leadership will preach doing more with less as a patriotic sacrifice made necessary by "imperialist forces."

China's role in the US-DPRK standoff offered little hope of bailing the administration out. The longstanding American notion, shared in the Trump administration, is that China holds the key to forcing changes in Pyongyang's behavior. As was demonstrated when Kim Jong-un met Xi Jinping three times in 2018 and twice in 2019, China wants to be actively involved in Kim's summit diplomacy with the ROK and the United States. That involvement may cut two ways, however: influencing a lowering of nuclear tensions on the Korean Peninsula, but also supporting North Korea in the event diplomacy fails and it again comes under US threat. The state of US-China relations will influence that direction. When, for example, Trump imposed new tariffs on Chinese exports in July 2018, Beijing seemed to have responded by trying to stiffen Kim Jong-un's insistence on a phased approach to denuclearization. Or so Trump believed.[12]

The alternative of diplomacy has worked in US and ROK relations with the DPRK. The 1994 Agreed Framework, under which North Korea froze its nuclear-weapons program in exchange for promised energy assistance, remains the best example. That trade-off restrained North Korea from producing fissile material for bomb making for roughly a decade. But we also have the 1991–1992 North-South Korea accords on exchanges and nuclear weapons, the agreements on economic cooperation reached under the Sunshine policy of Kim Dae-jung, and the September 2005 Six Parties agreement on the basis of "commitment for commitment, action for action."[13] Within the Trump administration, however, only Tillerson mentioned negotiating without preconditions. Early in 2017 he, along with Mattis, reassured Pyongyang that US policy did not seek regime change or Korean reunification.[14] But until the Winter Olympics in 2018, the White House had beaten down every suggestion of talks without North Korea's prior agreement to destruction or "dismantling" of its nuclear weapons.[15] Even then, the US administration was only willing to hold "preliminary" conversations with North Korea, not negotiations.

What US policy under Trump consistently avoided in its dealings with North Korea was *incentives* to create the conditions for a meaningful discussion of nuclear weapons. Kim Jong-un said as much when he met with ROK representatives following the Winter Games.[16] The trust-building element is key. As Kim reportedly told South Korean representatives, "If we meet often and build trust with the US, and if an end to the [Korean] war and nonaggression are promised, why would we live in difficulty with nuclear weapons?"[17] In a word, *engagement had to be seen in Pyongyang as strengthening regime and state survival.* North Korea therefore most likely also wanted international guarantees of North Korea's security, framed in a peace treaty to formally end the Korean War; an easing and eventual end to US and UN sanctions; and a way forward to normalization of US-DPRK relations. North Korea would also look to receiving long-term development assistance, increased trade and investment, and short-term food and fuel aid, thus also reducing dependence on China. But Trump was content to rely on sanctions even when they were obviously failing to alter Kim's negotiating position or missile testing.

Neither North Korean nor US goals were met at Singapore. "Peace and prosperity," "lasting and stable peace," "peace regime," "denuclearization," "new US-DPRK relations"—the joint statement was long on hope, short on substance.[18] It had nothing to say about actual denuclearization, a Korean Peninsula at peace, normalization of US–North Korea relations, economic or military incentives, verification of promises, and schedules for implementation. North Korea insisted that denuclearization would have to occur "step by step," whereas Trump insisted that sanctions would continue until denuclearization, or at least a timetable and weapon accounting, had been accomplished. To be sure, the North Koreans promised to work toward denuclearization and suspend nuclear and missile testing, which continued into 2019 when missile testing resumed. But they got much in return: an unexpected Trump decision to suspend US military exercises in South Korea, recognition as an equal at the negotiating table, implicit recognition as a nuclear-weapon state, and a declaration from Trump that North Korea was no longer a nuclear threat. The best that can be said of the summit is that it headed off the war of words and the possibility of a catastrophic miscalculation by either government. But their "very special relationship," as Trump put it with his usual exaggeration, was no substitute for the hard preparatory work needed for Kim to give up the nuclear option.

Trump was correct to describe denuclearization as a lengthy "process" that one summit meeting could not achieve.[19] However, the second summit, in Hanoi at the end of February 2019, again showed that personal diplomacy divorced from an engagement strategy increased the risk of failure. The Hanoi summit ended early without agreement, as Trump was unwilling to end sanctions in return for the closing of North Korea's main (but not only) nuclear enrichment plant at Yongbyon. Trump came with a weak hand, besieged by investigations at home.[20] But that did not prevent him from presenting Kim with demands on the last day of their meeting—demands that were in line with the "Libya option" advocated by John Bolton, a longtime advocate of using preemptive force against North Korea.[21] The US demand was that North Korea turn over its nuclear weapons and fuel to the United States and dismantle all nuclear, missile, chemical, and biological warfare facilities, among other steps.[22]

Still, agreement might have been possible if (as one North Korean official said) some US sanctions had been eased in return for the closing of Yongbyon. A modest success at Hanoi might then have paved the way for further steps, such as time points for establishing diplomatic relations and freezing or reducing North Korea's nuclear weapons in a verifiable way.[23] The North Koreans believed that after Singapore, they had taken the first steps in confidence building, enough to justify an end to sanctions. Some US analysts agreed.[24] Kim Jong-un said in April 2019 that there would be no third summit unless Washington came around on reducing sanctions.[25] But behind the scenes, Kim ordered the execution or purge of several officials whom he evidently held responsible for the failure of the Hanoi summit.[26]

Not only did the administration discard a chance to use sanctions as a bargaining chip; it also lost two other opportunities to advance the peace process. One was on the economic side. Kim Jong-un evidently had decided that once he deflected the US threat, he could turn all his attention to the economy. In April 2018, ahead of the Singapore summit, he declared an end to the previous *byongjin* policy of parallel military and economic development. His 2019 New Year's message reaffirmed the new direction. Kim's meetings with the Chinese apparently resulted in reassurances concerning trade as well as security. The Trump administration probably never considered how it might wean Kim away from total reliance on China.

A second opportunity came with the signing by Kim and Moon Jae-in of a September Declaration (September 18, 2018) to advance inter-Korean cooperation.[27] Though the declaration did not go beyond a pledge to pursue "complete denuclearization," it produced substantive tension-reducing steps, both military (such as no-fly zones and cessation of military exercises in the demilitarized zone area) and nonmilitary (such as resumption of joint commercial projects and opening of new rail connections). Rather than lend support to inter-Korean diplomacy, however, Trump sought to limit it. Much to the chagrin of the South Koreans, Trump, on learning of their plan to ease sanctions on the North, declared, "They won't do it without our approval. They do nothing without our approval." The South Koreans backed down from their plan, but continued to pursue economic ties with the North and some way to ameliorate horrific human rights conditions there.[28]

Notwithstanding the decision to hold a second summit with Kim Jong-un, Trump seemed to have Iran more than the DPRK in his sights.[29] At the same time that he and his advisers were warning Tehran (see below), Trump continued to praise Kim and displayed newfound flexibility about the time frame for North Korean denuclearization: "If it takes two years, three years, five months, doesn't matter," he said in September;[30] tweeted "we are in no hurry" in December; and just before the second summit said he was "not in a rush . . . I just don't want [nuclear or missile] testing."[31] Trump refused to budge from his solitary opinion that North Korea was not a threat, going so far as to disparage intelligence reports indicating that North Korea had as many as twenty secret ballistic missile bases and other hidden weapons.[32] Why so blasé? Perhaps Trump believed he had contained the North Korean threat inasmuch as Kim had pledged not to restart long-range missile and nuclear weapons tests. That singular achievement allowed his administration to focus on the Israelis and the Saudis, united against a common enemy: Iran.

But Trump neglected what the North Koreans surely had fixed in their minds: the lesson from Iran, that the United States could not be trusted to adhere to a nuclear agreement and therefore that they should give up nothing until they got something vital in return. And so it was: In 2019, the North Koreans began restoring a missile test site they had once indicated a willingness to scrap. Then Kim gave a speech indicating his displeasure with the US failure to reduce sanctions and said he would wait a year to see if Washington would reverse course.[33] The speech was quickly followed by a series of tests of shorter-range missiles, which Pyongyang said were in response to the resumption of US–South Korea joint military exercises. Some of the tests were of new and more advanced ballistic missiles, which violated the UN Security Council's ban and put US bases in South Korea and Japan within range. Trump, however, was not "disturbed" either by these tests or by the erosion of US-ROK relations. He tweeted (on August 2, 2019) that Kim Jong-un "will do the right thing because he is far too smart not to, and he does not want to disappoint his friend, President Trump!"[34] But the North Koreans, far from banking on friendship, were warning that their previous military commitments would be nullified.[35] Trading of personal insults resumed, and Pyongyang said denuclearization was off the table.[36] Trump's North Korea policy was in tatters, and only he refused to acknowledge the fact.

PURSUING REGIME CHANGE IN IRAN

Donald Trump brought to the White House a short but clear history of hostility toward Iran.[37] That was welcome news to US allies in the Middle East, especially Israel. Starting well before Trump's election and continuing thereafter, Israelis targeted Trump as their ticket to combating Iran. Obama's bitter relationship with Netanyahu, his criticisms of Saudi Arabia, and his determination to conclude a nuclear deal with Tehran were reason enough for the Israelis to hope for better treatment from the new president. Personal ties between Israeli officials and Trump's team, and money from the UAE and Qatar that apparently was funneled into Trump's campaign, facilitated their infiltrating and influencing a very inexperienced new administration. By the time Trump took office, policies favorable to Israel and its Arab neighbors were top priorities.[38] That meant undermining the US-EU-Russia-China nuclear deal—officially, the Joint Comprehensive Plan of Action (JCPOA)—that had taken thirteen years to negotiate.[39] Whether by insisting on major changes in its content, which none of the other parties supported, or by US withdrawal and renewal of sanctions on Iran, Trump was determined to get rid of what he called "the worst deal ever negotiated" by the United States. No one was happier than Benjamin Netanyahu, whose hostility to Iran finally found a partner in Washington.

Trump returned Netanyahu's glowing tributes to his leadership in ways already mentioned, such as moving the US embassy in Israel to Jerusalem. But abandoning the nuclear deal on May 8, 2018, was his most significant gift to Israel.[40] Both leaders' flawed efforts to justify abandoning the agreement—in Trump's case, by totally ignoring the positive response to the agreement of military leaders and nuclear scientists[41]—were meant to provide cover for their real aim: support of Israel's and Saudi Arabia's goal to destabilize Iran and ultimately bring about regime change.

It did not take long for Trump's new far-right national security team to put the hard line on Iran center stage. Pompeo took the lead in announcing "a new Iran strategy," which in fact amounted to "maximum pressure." Speaking before the right-wing Heritage Foundation on May 21, 2018, the secretary of state declared, "The Iranian regime should know that this is just the beginning. . . . After our sanctions come into full force, it will be battling to keep its economy alive. Iran will be forced to make a choice: either fight to keep its economy off life support at home or keep squandering precious wealth on fights abroad. It will not have the resources to do both." The US objective of regime change was barely hidden, as Pompeo urged Iranians to consider that their leaders were "most responsible for your economic struggles" and for "wasting Iranian lives through the Middle East."[42]

In the same speech, Pompeo listed twelve demands of Iran and gave every indication that the list was nonnegotiable.[43] He followed with an article that called Iran an "outlaw regime" whose "entrenched habits" of regional interference and corrupt leadership had to change.[44] He nevertheless said the administration hoped for negotiations with Iran, even though the administration surely knew there was no chance Iran would comply when threatened with what Pompeo called the heaviest sanctions in history. Bolton made that conclusion abundantly clear. Well-known before joining the administration for his advocacy of using force and sanctions against Iran, Bolton issued further warnings.[45] On August 22, 2018, during a visit to Israel, he said, "Regime change in Iran is not American policy, but what we want is massive change in the regime's behavior." "[Trump] has made it very clear—his words—he wants maximum pressure on Iran, maximum pressure, and that is what is going on." Bolton said the United States was prepared to push Iran's oil exports to zero, a threat the administration implemented.[46] Shortly after, when Iran-backed militants lobbed a few shells that fell harmlessly near the US embassy in Baghdad, the White House requested attack options on Iran.[47] In the spring of 2019 the administration deployed more US troops to the Middle East, and went around Congress to provide Saudi Arabia and the UAE with precision-guided weapons—all while US intelligence heads found that Iran continued to comply with the nuclear deal.[48] The administration never provided evidence of a new threat from Iran to US or other forces in the region that would have justified shows of force.[49]

Iran and the other parties to the nuclear deal were forced to respond to US policy. In November 2018, when Trump fully imposed sanctions on Iranian oil, banks, and airlines, Iran's leaders were defiant even while acknowledging the pain sanctions would cause.[50] Those Iranian banks engaged in international transactions, such as imports of food and medicine, were particularly hard hit. Iran's aid to Middle East allies, such as Hezbollah in Lebanon and militias in Syria and Iraq, had to be reduced, though that change seems not to have diminished their loyalty or commitment to Iran's cause.[51] As for the

Europeans, Britain, France, and Germany led the way (six other countries joined later) in 2019 in establishing a special purpose vehicle (SPV) called Instex to get around the US sanctions.[52] The Trump administration responded by ending waivers on sanctions for China and India, Iran's biggest oil customers, as well as for Japan, South Korea, and Turkey. "We will no longer grant exemptions," Pompeo said.[53] China, as the world's leading oil importer, was already paying Iran in yuan rather than dollars to get around US sanctions.[54] Embroiled in a trade war with the United States, China continued to import Iranian oil, out of defiance as much as need; and it significantly upgraded political and military ties to Tehran.[55] It remained to be seen how the other countries would respond.

Pompeo said threats and sanctions were part of a "strategy to create stability throughout the Middle East,"[56] but who could believe him when the strategy seemed focused on moving up the escalation ladder, baiting Tehran into a "provocation" to which US forces could respond. But Trump was not completely on board: When oil tankers were attacked in the Gulf of Oman in June 2019 and Pompeo immediately accused Iran, Trump backed away, telling his acting defense secretary that he did not want a war with Iran and describing the attacks as "very minor."[57] And when Iran's Revolutionary Guard shot down a US drone shortly afterward at a disputed location, Trump, saying he came within minutes of ordering air strikes, backed away again, supposedly out of concern about potential casualties but more likely with his reelection campaign in mind.[58] More confrontations followed: Britain seized an Iranian oil tanker, and Iran seized a British tanker. The United States downed an Iranian drone, and in September 2019 a drone and missile attack, apparently orchestrated by Houthi rebels in Yemen but possibly carried out from bases in Iran, severely damaged Saudi Arabia's oil-production facilities. Trump again declared that US forces were "locked and loaded" to retaliate against Iran, and Pompeo said the attacks were "an act of war." But Trump again stopped short, adding troops in Saudi Arabia and more sanctions on Iran rather than giving the go-ahead for war. The US goal remained regime change, however, as Pompeo as much as admitted.[59]

Threats of military action merely stoked Iranian nationalism and ratcheted up tensions, creating what amounted to a proxy war in the Middle East. The prime beneficiary was Iran's hard-liners in the Revolutionary Guard.[60] This much became apparent late in December 2019 when the United States conducted air strikes against Iranian-backed militia bases near the Iraqi-Syrian border. The strikes were justified as a retaliation for the death of an American contractor in a rocket attack. But pro-militia groups in Baghdad protested violently, endangering the US embassy, and the Iraqi government said the air strikes violated the country's sovereignty. The protests abated, but Trump was evidently persuaded, without consultation with members of Congress or US allies, that he needed a strong "deterrent" to any further Iranian move. He authorized an air strike to assassinate Iran's second most powerful figure, General Qassim Soleimani, an action both George W. Bush and Barack Obama had rejected because of the high risks of Iranian counterattacks. Iran's leaders threatened revenge. A decision supposedly based on deterrence suddenly and dramatically increased the chance of war—and, according to Iraq's prime minister, killed off an attempt at generating Iran–Saudi Arabia peace talks.[61] Trump insisted he wanted to stop, not start, a war, and Pompeo said all the United States wanted was to "get the Islamic Republic of Iran to simply behave like a normal nation." Tellingly, as in 2019, neither Trump nor any of his top aides could produce evidence that Iran posed an "imminent" new threat as claimed.[62] Nor was it clear why Trump, in an election year, would risk war after failing to retaliate over earlier confrontations with Iran. But in the end, Trump opted for avoiding war rather than "wag the dog."[63]

Leaders of both countries signaled that they wanted to contain the crisis. Iran did carry out an air strike in January 2020 against two Iraqi bases that housed US soldiers. Trump claimed no Americans were "harmed" and there were no US casualties, when, in fact, the Pentagon acknowledged that thirty-four soldiers had to be evacuated due to severe brain injuries. (Trump minimized their injuries, saying they were "not very serious," even after the total was raised to fifty.) War was avoided, but the US impasse with Iran remained, with no active diplomatic channel either to avoid another round of tit for tat or to restore the key elements of the nuclear deal. Meantime, thanks to Trump, Iran had accomplished what the ayatollah on his own could not: common ground between Iran and Iraq, Iraq's invitation to the US military to leave the country (discussed further below), huge anti-American gatherings in Iran that displaced popular protests against the regime's economic policies, and further division in Washington over Trump's Middle East policy, including renewed attempts to restrain his war powers.[64]

The option of negotiating with Iran was always out there, but the administration never showed serious interest in it.[65] Trump and his advisers on several occasions said he would talk to Iran's leaders with "no preconditions," but Iran's leaders said they weren't interested in direct talks anyway, declaring they would only negotiate with the United States if Trump returned to the multilateral nuclear talks. Even after both sides showed restraint following the exchange of attacks in January, Trump imposed new sanctions on Iran, and boasted of US military power rather than proposed negotiations sweetened with incentives. Tehran, which had already breached the nuclear deal by announcing it had exceeded the limit on uranium enrichment, now contemplated abandoning all limits under the JCPOA and building a bomb. Trump threatened European allies with new tariffs on auto imports if they did not initiate proceedings against Iran for violating the nuclear deal.[66]

The quandary Trump and his Iranian adversary found themselves in is that their respective strategies risked war by miscalculation with little prospect of achieving desired gains. Iran's military actions had no chance of reducing sanctions and relieving economic woes so long as Trump was president. Nor could US pressure tactics rein in Iran's nuclear program or cause the regime to collapse. In between lay diplomacy, which Trump and his top foreign policy officials were unwilling to seriously pursue. They were way off course if they truly expected Ayatollah Ali Khamenei to talk under threat and (as with North Korea) without US inducements. Trump thus squandered the opportunity Obama created with the nuclear deal with Iran to find common ground on other Middle East concerns, including Syria, Afghanistan, Yemen, and Iraq. As Obama discovered, threatening Iran only produced more resistance, whereas finding agreement proved possible with mutual respect, empathy, and an appreciation of the other side's history and interests.[67]

INDECISION AND INDIFFERENCE IN THE MIDDLE EAST, AFRICA, AND LATIN AMERICA

In the Middle East, Donald Trump's America First framework distorted effective and ethical foreign policy. Trump made much during his campaign about reducing US military involvement in the Middle East, a noble enough objective. But the follow-through came at great cost both domestically and internationally. Many expected Trump to start pulling out soldiers in Afghanistan once at the helm. As he said in an interview with the *Washington Post*, "Now, are we going to stay in that part of the world? One reason to is Israel. Oil is becoming less and less of a reason because we're producing more oil now than we've ever produced. So, you know, all of a sudden it gets to a point where you don't have to stay there."[68] Trump repeatedly demanded to know why the United States was still in Afghanistan, citing the costs in blood and treasure, the military setbacks, Pakistan's uncooperativeness (which led to a cut in US military aid), and the lack of an exit strategy.[69] He had to play the same numbers game as Obama: How many more soldiers should be sent to Afghanistan as each wave of bad news came in? A good question, especially as there was no sign either that the war was nearing a successful conclusion or that the military brass could be brought around to accepting that the war was unwinnable.

In Afghanistan, Trump not only inherited a war with human, economic, and environmental costs that defy imagination.[70] He also inherited a country mired in political intrigue, corruption, CIA-directed secret US warfare,[71] interference by Pakistan, and a Taliban force that controlled anywhere between one-third and one-half of the country. A stalemate with the Taliban seemed the most achievable outcome, and Trump's first instinct was to leave. In late 2018 he announced a roughly 50 percent cut in US forces in Afghanistan, to around 7,000.[72] But then US negotiations with the Taliban, which had begun in July, produced a possible peace deal that would cut US losses—and expenses. Trump was interested. The deal was to have two components: first, the Taliban's assurance, in return for US withdrawal in five years, that Afghanistan would not be used as a base for terrorist attacks on the United States; following that, a Taliban settlement with the Afghan government.[73] But when Trump pressed for a showy meeting of those parties at Camp David to finalize the plan—motivated, perhaps, by hopes for a Nobel Peace Prize and a pre-election victory—the Taliban backed down and Trump backed out, eliminating what might have been the last best hope for ending America's longest war in one of the world's poorest and most violent countries.[74]

Trump's Syria policy had been full of contradictions from the beginning, much like Obama's. The Obama administration struggled with the issue of intervention, including whether or not to provide military aid to the rebels, seek the removal of Assad, and punish his use of chemical weapons.[75] Trump vowed to be more decisive, but he produced no better results or end game. He cut off military aid to Assad's opponents and withdrew a demand for Assad's ouster. He also ordered a futile missile strike on a Syrian airfield following a chemical attack almost certainly carried out by Assad's forces, but did not follow up as Assad's use of chemical weapons continued. Meantime, deployed at a network of bases and airfields, the US military presence in support of Kurdish and Turkish forces in northern Syria actually increased several-fold on Trump's watch.[76]

All that came to an end in 2018 when Trump announced a US troop withdrawal of about 2,000. He justified it by saying the US mission to defeat ISIS had been accomplished even though ISIS was still fielding anywhere from 20,000 to 30,000 fighters. In typical Trump fashion, the decision seems to have been made on the fly, without consulting anyone, with no timetable for withdrawal, no thought about using withdrawal to leverage negotiations, and no consultation with the Kurds and other resistance forces fighting the Assad regime.

The spur-of-the-moment withdrawal decision exposed Kurdish forces and civilians to a Turkish onslaught, as described earlier. Coming right after Trump's telephone conversation with Erdogan, the decision caught the Pentagon and many Middle East governments by surprise. Trump's top national security advisers, the general leading the US mission in Syria, and key Republicans in Congress were left in the lurch.[77] Defense secretary Mattis refused Trump's request to endorse the Syria withdrawal and resigned. Trump was forced to backtrack, deciding to leave 200 US soldiers in place, assigned the mission of "protecting" Syria's oil fields. But not protecting civilians: When the Syrians and their Russian partners prepared for a major assault on Idlib Province in the fall of 2018, Trump officials issued a mild warning but nothing else.[78] Idlib became a humanitarian disaster: By 2020 nearly one million people were in desperate circumstances as the Syrian army and Russian air strikes pounded their encampments, causing a massive refugee flight toward the Turkish border. Trump also pleased Moscow by rejecting sanctions on Russian companies believed to be supplying chemical agents to Syria.[79] No wonder Putin expressed pleasure at Trump's idea to pull out of Syria.

Russia, and even more so China, further benefited from Trump's incoherent posture in Iraq. The Iraqi request for a pullout of US forces may have had more to do with oil politics than with the assassination of Soleimani.[80] According to Adil Abdul-Mahdi, Iraq's interim prime minister at the time, in fall 2019 Trump had demanded 50 percent of Iraq's oil revenues in return for completing certain infrastructure and energy projects. Trump threatened to incite mass protests if Abdul-Mahdi refused. The protests occurred, but Abdul-Mahdi did not back down. Instead, he turned to China, visiting Beijing at the head of a large delegation. The visit led to a major oil-for-development aid package within the BRI framework that Iraq now joined. The deal was a sharp riposte to Trump, made all the worse for him after the assassination of Soleimani, when US Arab allies in the region, in fear of igniting a regional war and starting with Saudi Arabia, distanced themselves from Trump's warlike threats to Iran. The US forces remaining in Iraq despite the request to leave are likely to find themselves in harm's way, less and less welcome for helping fight ISIS.[81]

Did the United States have anything resembling a Middle East policy? Early in 2019 Pompeo flew out to the region to try to quell confusion about US policy. Speaking in Cairo, Pompeo reassured "old friends" in the Arab world—every one of them a consistent human-rights violator—that "the age of self-inflicted American shame is over."[82] Such "shame" presumably meant turning a page from Obama and no longer talking about human rights, striving for a more balanced position on Israeli-Palestinian relations, or reaffirming an understanding on nuclear weapons with Iran. But in light of later developments, this appeal backfired. Threatening Iran, blocking Palestinian aspirations, wiping out Trump's Syria timeline, fumbling an Afghanistan peace, and occupying Iraq only reinforced a strong sense in the Middle East that US policy was at best inconsistent and out of touch with the chief concerns of all the governments there except Israel's.

In Africa, the Trump administration announced a "new strategy" in December 2018. But as outlined by Bolton, the strategy was less new than poorly purposed.[83] It was motivated by just two aims: countering terrorism and countering China. A principal motive of Bolton's speech was to proclaim reversal of US neglect of Africa in Trump's first term. "Nearly halfway through his term," one observer commented, "Trump has made no speeches on Africa, has not visited the continent, and was slow to appoint an assistant secretary of state for African affairs. . . . All this suggests that after 50 years of modest involvement in African security, the United States may be writing the continent off."[84] Sending Melania Trump to visit four countries in October 2018 was not exactly a statement of concern, and Trump's gaffes in attempting to show interest in Africa only made things worse.[85]

Fact is, US involvement in Africa was overwhelmingly military, dominated by US special forces counterterrorism operations under the Africa Command (AFRICOM). These originated from bases all over the Africa map. At its height, one investigation identified thirty-six operations in thirteen countries, often in partnership with autocratic governments.[86] The typical operation consisted of drone attacks followed by small on-the-ground missions in conjunction with African soldiers. All the partnerships were secret so as not to embarrass the host country. But they could also embarrass Washington, as when four special forces soldiers were killed in an ambush in Niger in October 2017. Trump seemed surprised that the military had such an operation. In 2020 Trump ordered a substantial reduction of the US force presence in Africa, about 5,000 soldiers, diminishing the counterterrorism mission. However, drone attacks, begun under Obama, significantly increased, incurring civilian casualties that went unreported.[87]

The China element in the US Africa strategy turned out to be all talk. Even though Bolton had warned that China had "the ultimate goal of advancing global dominance," putting the "balance of power" in Africa at risk of tilting to Beijing, US investment, aid, and trade with Africa was measly in comparison with China's. According to one report, "by 2016, China had become Africa's largest trading partner, foreign job creator, and source of foreign direct investment."[88] Critics warn that China's lending spree is a "debt trap," but money talks, Chinese banks have lots of it, and Africa's financial needs are huge. In 2018 Beijing hosted another China-Africa Cooperation forum with representatives of fifty-three African countries present. There, Xi Jinping again pledged (as at the previous forum three years earlier) $60 billion in development funds, mainly for infrastructure: ports, railroads, highways, and power transmission lines. These are on full display in Djibouti, where China opened its first military and intelligence-gathering base not far from a US drone base.[89] That led to speculation that China will follow with other security-related agreements in Africa, such as increased training and small-arms sales. Meantime, US investors, media, and educational institutions remained on the sidelines, with little encouragement from the Trump administration to regard Africa as something other than a backwater.

In Latin America, if polls are any guide, democracy and human rights are in trouble. Democratically elected and undemocratic governments alike— from Brazil and Guatemala on the right to Venezuela, Nicaragua, and Cuba on the left—have failed to deliver on corruption, crime, and inequality.[90] The Trump administration's chief concerns were not shaped by those issues, but rather by immigration and ideology. Trump, far from showing sympathy for the thousands of refugees fleeing violence in Central America, authorized cuts in US program aid, such as for education, that was actually designed to keep migration down in three source countries: Guatemala, Honduras, and El Salvador.[91] When it came to ideology, Trump took his cue from Bolton and Pompeo, who aimed to undermine the three socialist governments just because they were leftist.

The administration's attack on the left started with Venezuela. For several months in 2017 the administration held discussions with dissident members of the Venezuelan military and security forces about supporting a coup or even an invasion against the government of Nicolás Maduro.[92] In this instance US diplomats *were* consulted, and they apparently urged the military *not* to act against Maduro. The Venezuelan coup plotters hoped to get communications equipment. They were eventually rebuffed—not, apparently, because of the military's known human rights abuses or involvement in drug trafficking, but simply because the plotters seemed unlikely to succeed.[93] Once policy making shifted to Bolton and Pompeo, Cold War ideology and reversion to the era of US interventions in Latin America became the dominant motif, with Venezuela, Nicaragua, and Cuba the principal targets. "A sordid cradle of communism," Bolton called them. Very much in the spirit of George W. Bush's "Axis of Evil," Bolton said,

> We are also confronted once again with the destructive forces of oppression, socialism and totalitarianism. Under this administration, we will no longer appease dictators and despots near our shores in this hemisphere. We will not reward firing squads, torturers, and murderers. . . . The Troika of Tyranny in this hemisphere—Cuba, Venezuela and Nicaragua—has finally met its match.[94]

In fall 2018 the State Department announced that it would "use the full weight of American economic and diplomatic power to help create the conditions for the restoration of democracy for the Venezuelan people."[95] Apparently around that time, Trump rejected a meeting requested by Maduro.[96] Instead, as anti-Maduro protests took place, US interference intensified, evidently orchestrated with the Venezuelan opposition. This was no organic response to oppression; it came after some months of discussions among Trump's right-leaning advisers, and reportedly against the advice of State Department Latin America specialists. Pence publicly called Maduro "illegitimate," then secretly offered support to the leader of the national assembly, Juan Guaidó, if he declared himself the interim president of Venezuela.[97] Trump followed by recognizing Guaidó as the legitimate president and saying "all options are on the table." Guaidó was given access to Venezuelan assets in the United States, additional financial sanctions on the Maduro government followed, and Washington appealed to the Venezuelan military to switch loyalties to Guaidó. In a sign of desperation, American mercenaries tried to infiltrate the country in 2020, but they were either killed or captured. Regime change thus became official US policy, without any thought as to what direct interference in another country's politics would mean for America's reputation, international law, the safety of US diplomats and citizens in Venezuela, US criticisms of Russian intervention in Ukraine, and the possibility of fomenting civil war in Venezuela.

US policy was really just another version of the "maximum pressure" doctrine—or, from a Latin American perspective, gunboat diplomacy. To be sure, Maduro had become a dictator and Venezuela was imploding. Few Latin American governments recognized his staged election at the end of 2018. But the main problem there was a human security crisis marked by a dramatic decline in health and health care, runaway inflation, and a historic exodus of the population. Referring to US reliance on sanctions, a Congressional Research Service report in November 2018 said they might well exacerbate the human crisis, which is why "many Venezuelan civil society groups oppose sanctions that could worsen humanitarian conditions."[98] In fact, at that time Venezuela was finally reaching out for international assistance in response to the sanctions.[99] The call for regime change was an outright unlawful intervention in Venezuela's affairs, made without regard to the central problem there of alleviating human rights conditions and probably with no sense of how (or how well) Juan Guaidó might deal with them.

As it turned out, US policy makers made three serious overestimates about their strategy. Politically, they erred in thinking that Venezuelan soldiers would defect in huge numbers. They also were mistaken in thinking the opposition would unite behind Guaidó—"devilishly difficult," as Pompeo privately confessed.[100] Economically, sanctions did not drive Maduro from power, though that did not stop Trump from trying. Instead, he gave the private sector freer rein, "dollarizing" the economy—which meant that those who had US dollars could survive and prosper quite nicely.[101] But for poor Venezuelans, lacking dollars meant continuing to be poor and marginalized, thus continuing the country's humanitarian plight.[102]

There were alternatives to outside intervention that would aim at conflict prevention, minimization of human suffering, and avoidance of the use of force. One was diplomacy: urge Maduro to accept an amnesty offer from Guaidó and leave the country, or (as the EU demanded) get him to agree to hold new elections under international supervision. The Venezuelan military would probably have been relieved not to have to defend him; it was already divided over loyalty to Maduro. A second alternative was the UN's Responsibility to Protect Resolution (R2P), passed by the General Assembly in 2005. That instrument, which requires Security Council approval to invoke, is intended to apply to states in which large numbers of people are under threat and their government is unwilling and unable to provide for its citizens—in other words, failed states that threaten large numbers of their people. If Maduro insisted on staying on, the UN—not the US alone—could either have attempted to broker a deal between him and Guaidó or put the squeeze on the regime economically and politically under provisions of R2P, though a Russian or Chinese veto would probably have blocked sanctions.

As for Cuba, until Trump came along, Obama's policy of engagement was succeeding. Besides restoring diplomatic relations, engagement promoted tourism, small business, and increased contact in and with Cuba. Raúl Castro, Fidel's successor, allowed new opportunities for the private sector and for public dialogue on social issues.[103] Its superior health care system is a model for other countries, including the United States. But Trump saw in Cuba an opportunity to unravel Obama's legacy—and destroy the link between Havana and Caracas as well—such as by reinstating restrictions on travel, remittances by Cuban Americans, and investment so as to weaken Cuba's economy and undermine Castro's regime. "Cuba will be next" after Venezuela, Bolton declared.[104]

In Nicaragua, sanctions again were the chief US response to Daniel Ortega's autocratic government. He cracked down on dissent in 2018, with hundreds killed and arrested, and stood accused of crimes against humanity following an investigation by an independent group at the behest of the Organization of American States.[105] Instead of diplomatic engagement, Trump predicted "the days of socialism" were numbered in Nicaragua as in the other two countries. But financial sanctions were not going to deter Ortega. Instead, his government released some prisoners and opened talks with the opposition and other stakeholders.[106]

By contrast, the Trump administration found much to like in Brazil and Guatemala. Jair Bolsonaro, Brazil's far-right president who identifies with the darkest years of politics under military rule, became Washington's fair-haired boy in Latin America. Bolsonaro, said Bolton, is one of the "positive signs for the future of the region, and demonstrates a growing regional commitment to free-market principles, and open, transparent, and accountable governance."[107] In reality, Bolsonaro's increasingly unpopular regime is widely regarded as corrupt, dictatorial, and responsible for decimating the Amazon region. No wonder: Bolsonaro is the perfect counterpart to Trump.[108]

In Guatemala, the corruption-ridden government of Jimmy Morales drew tacit US support when it kicked a UN fact-finding commission (the International Commission against Impunity in Guatemala) out of the country, citing its threat to sovereignty. The commission, widely supported by Guatemalans and the country's constitutional court, and created by the United States as well as the UN, had honed in on Morales and his cronies and was set to put them on trial.[109]

In contrast with the narrowly focused US role in Latin America—Trump made only one visit to the region in his first two years[110] and, otherwise, US policy rested on sanctions and trade protectionism—China and Russia increased their involvement. China became a major player in Latin America's economy, accounting for roughly 9 percent of the region's exports and above that in specific sectors such as extractive industries (26 percent) and agriculture (14 percent).[111] China is also a major lender, crucial for heavily indebted countries such as Argentina, where China imports virtually all of Argentina's soybeans, the number-one export, and is busy constructing two hydroelectric dams.[112] Among the benefits for China of this economic activity is diplomatic recognition: the Dominican Republic, Panama, Ecuador, and El Salvador all shifted from Taiwan to the People's Republic in recent years. Venezuela, financially desperate, traded the sale of sovereign debt to China, in return for oil, and also turned to Russia, which provided several billion dollars in return for a major ownership interest in the state-run oil company, including its US affiliate Citgo.

Russia also became Venezuela's main weapons supplier and regime defender. In 2018 Russian advisers began serving in the Maduro government, and Russian strategic bombers showed up in Venezuela as part of joint exercises. Moscow upped the ante in March 2019, dispatching about 100 soldiers to Venezuela, allegedly to help protect Maduro, and an oil tanker to enable oil exports as an answer to US sanctions. These developments were clearly pokes in the US eye, as some observers said, but as international pressure on Maduro intensified, Russia's ties to him created a new challenge to the Trump-Putin relationship. For those around Trump who were itching for intervention, Russian and Cuban involvement on Maduro's side could have provided a pretext. But Trump backed away.[113] Following a phone call with Putin in early May 2019, Trump directly contradicted his secretary of state, who had said Maduro and other senior Venezuelan leaders were prepared to fly out of the country but that "Russians indicated he should stay." Trump said Putin "is not looking at all to get involved in Venezuela, other than to see something positive happen for Venezuela. And I feel the same way, we want to get some humanitarian aid" into the country.[114] True to form, Trump demurred on deeper involvement *and* took Putin's word over that of his own adviser.

Chapter Seven

Dealing Away International Responsibility

Protecting and promoting human rights, reducing and controlling nuclear weapons, and dealing with authoritarian regimes are among the most vexing policy issues for any US administration. Their common thread is their relevance to international responsibility and humane governance. President Trump showed little interest in human rights or nuclear arms control. As for authoritarian regimes that, like Saudi Arabia, also happened to be longtime supporters of US policy, he followed the script of previous presidents in turning a blind eye to their repression. But as the Saudi case study here shows, Trump took the "blind eye" further, protecting a regime that planned and carried out the murder of a US-based journalist.

ABANDONING HUMAN RIGHTS

In 1941, with the prospect looming of US involvement in another European war, President Franklin Roosevelt spoke of America's purpose in the world: to protect and promote "four freedoms." FDR drew a clear link between US security and the fulfillment of human rights at home. "Just as our national policy in internal affairs has been based upon a decent respect for the rights and the dignity of all of our fellow men within our gates, so our national policy in foreign affairs has been based on a decent respect for the rights and the dignity of all nations, large and small."[1]

Unfortunately, that way of thinking has had no place in the Trump administration, which has carried on a war on human rights at home, with virtually complete disregard for human rights abroad.

On the home front, two survey sources show how the US has declined as a repository of human rights—in particular, adherence to political rights and civil liberties. These sources are the World Justice Project's Rule of Law Index,[2] whose ranking is based on forty-four indicators of lawfulness, and Freedom House, which makes annual assessments based on implementation (not claims) of rights enumerated in the 1948 UN Universal Declaration of Human Rights.[3] The World Justice Project in 2018 ranked the United States nineteenth of 113 countries surveyed, 1 being highest. Among the weakest dimensions for the United States are labor rights, an effective correctional system, discrimination, respect for due process, and accessibility and affordability of the legal system. For comparison sake, note that Germany (6), Canada (9), and Britain (11) all ranked higher than the United States. Freedom House in 2019 ranked the United States eighty-sixth of 100 countries, 100 being highest; Canada (99), Germany (94), and Britain (94) again ranked higher. Trump's corruption, evasion of legal and institutional norms, and low regard for certain human rights—those of immigrants in particular—helped account for the US decline in the Freedom House ranking. It had been 90 in 2016.

In 2018 Philip Alston, the UN special rapporteur for extreme poverty and human rights, delivered a report on poverty in America. Before Trump, the rich-poor gap was already wide and the number of people, especially children, living in poverty was pitifully large. The UN report detailed how, under Trump, those people are even more vulnerable *because they are being deliberately targeted for political advantage.* Of course Trump, who had already withdrawn the United States from the UN Human Rights Council in June 2018 and from UNESCO in December 2018, rejected the Alston report, with US ambassador to the UN Nikki Haley deriding it as "patently ridiculous." The State Department thereafter rejected investigation of the Alston report's findings and took the unprecedented step of refusing to allow *any* visits by UN special rapporteurs.[4]

Parallel with the suppression of rights at home was the Trump administration extension of the sordid US practice of supporting authoritarian regimes, making the US party to repression of human rights abroad and, on occasion, a collaborator in crimes against humanity and war crimes. The usual pretext for such support is to maintain "stability" or counter terrorism. "Support" often takes the form of selling arms, as in the cases of Turkey despite widespread repression, Saudi Arabia in its bombing campaign in Yemen, and Abdel Fattah el-Sisi in his crackdown on dissent in Egypt. Israel should be added to this list, since the far-right Netanyahu government receives about $1.5 billion annually in arms that give it license to violently suppress Palestinian protests. Not surprisingly, the equally far-right US ambassador to Israel said Israel should be exempt from US law that requires a State Department report on whether or not US-supplied weapons are being used to repress human rights. Ambassador David Friedman made the astounding statement that "Israel is a democracy whose army does not engage in gross violations of human rights."[5]

In several other cases of egregious human rights violations, Trump either avoided commenting or offered excuses. He dismissed Kenya's homophobic attacks on gays, commended Duterte's drug war in the Philippines that has killed thousands, disputed with China on trade but said nothing about the mass incarceration of Uyghurs in Xinjiang Province, failed to support UN charges of genocide by the Myanmar military against the Rohingya people, and—as described at length below—dissembled when commenting on the murder in October 2018 of Jamal Khashoggi, a *Washington Post* writer, Virginia resident, and outspoken critic of Crown Prince Mohammed bin Salman. Even while exchanging nuclear threats with Kim Jong-un in 2017, Trump had nothing to say about the North Korean gulag. Yet UN reports found that there had been no improvement in human rights in the DPRK despite the reduction in tensions with the United States. Trump's hostility to a free press was welcomed in the many countries where journalists have been jailed and even murdered, without comment from Washington.[6] As Khashoggi wrote before he was murdered by Saudi hit men, "The Arab world is facing its own version of an Iron Curtain" on freedom of expression.[7]

Trump maintained he brought up human rights issues when he met with Kim Jong-un, and insisted that US missile attacks in response to Assad's use of chemical weapons were motivated by concern for Syrian children. But those claims cannot be taken seriously. After all, Trump publicly excused Kim, Xi Jinping, Putin, and other authoritarian leaders for their human rights record, saying they were great friends and there are "bad guys" in all political systems. He reserved his professed concern about human rights, and sanctions, for antagonistic rivals, notably Cuba and Iran—the very countries, probably not coincidentally, that Obama successfully engaged. What he and his administration failed to consider is that imposing sanctions and promoting regime change played into the hands of hard-line elements in those countries, resulting in increased repression of those wanting political change.

Discussion of sensitive human-rights cases often gets relegated to the annual State Department report on conditions around the world, a report required by Congress. Under Trump the report got short shrift. When the report for 2016 was prepared, Secretary of State Rex Tillerson rejected the usual practice of presenting it to the press, evidently to discount its importance.[8] The 2017 report, which came out in April 2018, "sugarcoated" several controversial issues, as one human rights NGO leader put it. These deceptions included Israel's conduct in the Occupied Territories (no longer labeled as such), high civilian casualties from Saudi Arabia's indiscriminate bombing in Yemen (referred to as "disproportionate collateral damage"), and women's reproductive rights (no longer mentioned).[9] For 2018, the department avoided any mention of the Saudi crown prince's direct role in Khashoggi's murder, had little to say about women's rights anywhere, and generally portrayed human rights as a secondary issue in foreign relations. [10]

It was therefore no surprise to hear Mike Pompeo announce that he had formed a special panel on human rights outside the State Department's own human rights office to *redefine* rights. "What does it mean," he asked, "to say or claim that something is, in fact, a human right? How do we know or how do we determine whether that claim that this or that is a human right, is it true, and therefore, ought it to be honored?" [11] Surely Pompeo knew that the answers to these questions have been on file with the State Department since 1945, and are supplemented by numerous UN conventions on specific rights. Raising the question was an ominous sign that "human rights" for immigrants, gay and transgender people, and other minorities would be narrowed out of existence.

AMPLIFYING THE NUCLEAR DANGER

In mid-2019 two experts on nuclear arms control wrote,

> The United States and Russia are now in a state of strategic instability; an accident or mishap could set off a cataclysm. Not since the 1962 Cuban missile crisis has the risk of a U.S.-Russian confrontation involving the use of nuclear weapons been as high as it is today. Yet unlike during the Cold War, both sides seem willfully blind to the peril. [12]

Neither Donald Trump nor Vladimir Putin seemed to be listening. Trump was especially taken with nuclear weapons, which was unfortunate in two respects. First, as his campaign comments revealed, he didn't have the slightest idea about the "nuclear triad," either their destructive capability or the history of efforts to constrain their use. [13] Second, Trump was reliably reported to have asked, "if we had them why can't we use them?" [14] Indeed, his go-ahead for production of a more "usable" (low-yield, tactical) nuclear weapon, with all the risks of increasing the possibility of its use, suggested the answer. [15] But that was not all: With little fanfare, Trump also accepted two other steps that increase the danger of nuclear-weapon use as well as the risk of theft by terrorists: a nuclear weapon in response to a cyber attack, and a new strategic role in NATO for forward-deployed nuclear weapons. [16]

When we also consider the decreased time now available for making a decision on actual employment of a nuclear weapon—the so-called fog of war, cyberwar capabilities, and Donald Trump's impulsiveness—it's understandable why some members of Congress publicly and some in the White House privately worried about what the nuclear codes in Trump's possession might mean in an international crisis. His threat to North Korea of "fire and fury" coupled with pursuit of options for using them heightened those concerns. What controls existed to constrain Trump's ability to launch a nuclear attack? Would senior military officials carry out his order to use nuclear weapons? Would the president consult them or civilian advisers, and if so, would a president—especially *this* president—listen to their advice?[17] Although a bill to prevent a president from ordering a nuclear first strike was before the US Senate, it lost traction with an easing of US-DPRK tensions. Nuclear "normalcy" was back: presidential launch authority remained ambiguous, and improvements in the nuclear arsenal—in Russia and China as well as in the United States—went on, justified as before by citing the need for improved, "credible" deterrence.[18]

Barack Obama began his presidency with an appeal for a nuclear weapon–free world and ended it by approving a roughly $1.2 trillion program for modernizing and maintaining nuclear weapons. Donald Trump had no interest in idealistic appeals. He not only sought even more money for nuclear weapons; he also wanted Congress to approve hundreds of millions of dollars to replace or improve the land- and sea-based nuclear delivery systems, which constitute about three quarters of all deploying US nuclear weapons.[19] In January 2019 the United States suspended participation in the Intermediate-Range Nuclear Forces (INF) Treaty with Russia signed by President Reagan and Russian president Mikhail Gorbachev in 1987. The Trump administration charged that Russia had consistently violated the agreement by deploying missiles near its western borders. Russia countered with its own charge—that US antiballistic missile defenses in Europe violated the treaty. Though the Obama administration had also been frustrated by Russia's apparent cheating on the treaty, it had refrained from pulling out, probably thinking it best to push for compliance in negotiations rather than leave the strategic weapons field to Putin. After all, what purpose would be served by a crash program to match Russian intermediate-range missiles, especially given European anxieties?

Trump, however, was evidently guided by Bolton's dogmatic opposition to *any* arms control agreement that called for US restraint. By the end of 2019, the administration had twice tested missiles that would have been proscribed under the INF Treaty, arguing that Russian tests had already broken the treaty. Trump did not respond to Russia's proposal of a joint moratorium on deployment of intermediate-range missiles. Resistance to that idea was consistent with the administration's opposition to two other international arms agreements: the UN Treaty on the Prohibition of Nuclear Weapons (TPNW), which was introduced in the UN General Assembly in March 2017, and the Arms Trade Treaty signed by Obama but not ratified by the Senate. The TPNW represents the first attempt to declare nuclear weapons illegal rather than merely seek to reduce their numbers, narrow delivery systems, or prevent testing—all measures that accept their continued possession and potential use. Among other limitations, the TPNW bans acquisition, testing, production, stockpiling, transfer, or threats to use nuclear weapons. The United States, along with all the other nuclear-weapon states, has rejected the treaty, and the Trump administration boycotted the negotiations on it.[20] The treaty on arms trading, originally negotiated in the George W. Bush administration, seeks to limit the transfer of all manner of arms to countries in conflict. Trump's decision to revoke US participation seemed to be in response to criticism from the National Rifle Association that the right to bear arms would be limited by international rules on gun sales. Around 130 countries had signed and/or ratified the treaty as of early 2019, but the United States joined North Korea, Russia, and Syria in refusing to sign.[21]

Trump's nuclear policy amounted to a return to the Reagan era, when the main subject of national security debate was how many and what kinds of nuclear weapons were sufficient for deterrence of the Soviet Union. Reagan's early answer was that you cannot have too many, and he budgeted accordingly. Trump seemed to agree, raising the ante for both Moscow and Beijing. But Reagan later surprised the world by coming close to agreement with Mikhail Gorbachev at Reykjavik, Iceland, in October 1986, on major reductions in strategic weapons—talks that eventuated in the INF Treaty. Now, at a time of "dangerously dysfunctional relations" between Moscow and Washington, which together have a stockpile of several thousand nuclear weapons, high-level nuclear diplomacy is again urgently needed to reestablish "a broad framework for strategic stability."[22] Their next chance will come in 2021, when the 2010 New START (Strategic Arms Reduction Treaty), the only remaining nuclear arms limitation agreement, is up for renewal.[23] But all the once available US-Russia dialogue mechanisms have become moribund, and Trump and Putin seem in no hurry to reactivate them.

REALISM WITHOUT APOLOGY: TRUMP AND SAUDI ARABIA

It's a classic narrative: the leader of a US ally visits Washington, the Pentagon and State Department are intent on selling him a large weapons package, a munitions maker seeks to capitalize on the visit, some senators resist and point to how US weapons are being used by that ally to kill civilians in a war, and the administration answers that the United States is not "a party" to the hostilities and must show good faith to the ally or risk losing its favor.[24] That was the Saudi Arabia story when its new leader, Crown Prince Mohammed bin Salman (widely referred to as MBS), visited Washington in April 2018. Contrary to the wishes of policy advisers such as Tillerson and Mattis, Jared Kushner had orchestrated Trump's first official trip abroad to Saudi Arabia in 2017.[25] Kushner sold the media and some in the administration on the king's reformist and modernizing intentions, starting with a few concessions to women's rights and a supposed distancing from the radical Islamist clergy. His narrative ignored MBS's repression of dissent, which extended to critics abroad, and indifference to women's inequality. Kushner also tried to hide his backing of the Saudis in a dispute with Qatar, a position he took after failing to get a business loan from Qatar. The dispute almost led to a war.[26]

MBS expected and received a warm welcome in Washington, where Saudi Arabia's strategic value to the United States, based on Saudi rivalry with Iran's Shiite regime and its role as a major oil producer and customer for US arms, was highly regarded. This assessment reversed Obama's belated conclusion that constant support of the Saudis was a mistake and should no longer be allowed to get in the way of other US interests, one of which was pursuing a nuclear agreement with Iran.[27] The Trump administration, with Iran as a common enemy and Israel as a common partner, offered MBS the chance to purchase another $1 billion in weapons, including Raytheon Corporation's precision-guided munitions. It also provided Saudi Arabia with weapons, logistical support, and intelligence in its bloody war in Yemen, where an estimated 10,000 civilians had died and epidemics of cholera and malnutrition had broken out.[28] And there were probably more personal considerations behind US policy: The Saudi elite was a reliable renter of hotel and apartment space belonging to Donald Trump and Jared Kushner.[29]

By some accounts, Kushner had become so close to MBS that he had not merely alienated other more experienced advisers to Trump; he had compromised US policy and lost any leverage Trump might have had with the crown prince.[30] The result was that US support of Saudi policies was not consistently returned. "It does seem like the Saudis are less concerned about U.S. views than ever before, both because they assume Trump won't care and because they think they don't need U.S. approval," said Gerald M. Feierstein, a former ambassador to Yemen who was the State Department's second-ranking diplomat for Middle East policy from 2013 to 2016.[31] MBS failed to endorse Kushner's pro-Israel peace plan, doubtless due to Trump's embrace of Netanyahu and US recognition of Jerusalem as Israel's capital. The Saudis rejected a UN-sponsored ceasefire arrangement in Yemen (which forced US ambassador Nikki Haley to withdraw her support of the plan), interfered in Lebanese politics (including the brief kidnapping of its prime minister), and were unwilling to resolve the dispute with Qatar. Kushner's closeness to MBS couldn't prevent those developments, and no US ambassador was available to pick up the slack. When one was finally nominated early in 2019, Saudi Arabia's horrendous human-rights record was on full display, moving Senator Marco Rubio to say of MBS, "He's gone full gangster, and it's difficult to work with a guy like that."[32]

But Trump found a way. His administration used every excuse imaginable for avoiding sanctions against its dear friend. Cutting off arms sales? "I think that would be hurting us," Trump said. "We have jobs we have a lot of things happening in this country." Ah, yes, jobs and "a lot of things."[33] Fact is, just as Rex Tillerson had said while secretary of state, the Saudis could not be trusted to follow through on any transaction. The numbers Trump put up were fantasies: The Saudis had actually bought only $14.5 billion of the $110 billion in US weapons Trump said they had agreed to buy, and their investments in the United States were nowhere near the $450 billion he claimed.[34] As for jobs, that depended on Saudi spending, and Trump could never get his figures straight. Each time he made reference to them, the number rose dramatically—from 400,000 to 500,000 and 600,000 and then to "millions." The actual number was probably in the low thousands.

Donald Trump was desperate to get MBS off the hook, even though he must have known of US training of the very people who killed Khashoggi.[35] He spoke about how painful it was to read of Khashoggi's disappearance and how he would mete out "severe punishment" if the Saudi regime was at fault.[36] (Trump was reportedly pained about civilian casualties in Yemen too.) But of course there was an "on the other hand." Khashoggi wasn't a US citizen, said Trump—the same absurd rationalization he made when asked about Putin-ordered assassinations. Trump dispatched Mike Pompeo to hear the Saudi leader's version of events, but that was merely a photo-op, all smiles and courtesies and assurances by MBS that he had no idea who might have taken the journalist away. (To sweeten the denial, the Saudi government on the very day of Pompeo's arrival was reported to have pledged $100 million to a US fund for Syria's "stabilization.")[37] However, a *New York Times* investigation found official connections between several of the hit men and the royal court.[38] When numerous angry voices rose from within Congress and the international community, and with the midterm US elections coming up, Trump changed his tune again, referring to "lies" and "deception" in the Saudi account, and still later calling it "the worst cover-up ever."[39] All this dancing around came to a head when the CIA concluded that the crown prince had almost certainly ordered Khashoggi's elimination.[40] Yet Trump refused to say the obvious, instead claiming uncertainty: "We may never know all of the facts surrounding the murder of Mr. Jamal Khashoggi"; "the CIA did not say affirmatively he did it";[41] and falling back on the real reasons for supporting the Saudi leaders: "They've been a great ally. Without them, Israel would be in a lot more trouble. We need to have a counterbalance to Iran."[42]

That explanation exonerated MBS—both Trump and Bolton refused to listen to tape recordings supplied by Turkey that a UN investigation reported clearly implicated the crown prince[43]—and underscored US economic interests (low-priced oil, arms sales, and a potential nuclear energy deal) in the relationship with Saudi Arabia.[44] Trump thus showed he would do the minimum, and so would the prince, when it came to gross violations of human rights. Jared Kushner did his part, having apparently advised MBS on how to "weather the storm."[45] Trump vetoed a War Powers resolution passed by both houses of Congress in 2019 to block military aid to Saudi Arabia in support of the Yemen war. Thumbing his nose at Congress, he used an emergency authorization to sell Saudi Arabia, along with the UAE, $8 billion in weapons; the agreement included Raytheon's sharing of smart-bomb technology with the Saudis.[46] (Raytheon's head subsequently was appointed acting defense secretary.) Congressional efforts to restrict nuclear technology transfers to Saudi Arabia were ignored—at least two permits for the transfer of nuclear expertise were approved *after* Khashoggi's murder[47]—and US intelligence and military cooperation with the regime was only temporarily suspended. MBS shrugged off responsibility for killing Khashoggi, and the Saudi repressive machinery remained intact.[48]

Someday, perhaps, a US administration will break the pattern of weaponizing friendships with authoritarian regimes in the false hope of maintaining influence. Such partnerships are tainted from the start as the United States becomes a partner in repression and the commission of war crimes.[49]

Chapter Eight

Business First

Consistent with economic nationalism, Trump aimed to improve the tax and regulatory climate for US businesses, discourage multinational corporations (MNCs) from continuing to expand operations abroad, reduce foreign investment in the United States, and take protectionist steps to limit competition. "Globalist" institutions were a prime target. Trump was determined, despite opposition from traditionally pro-trade Republicans, to replace US participation in multilateral organizations with bilateral negotiations and weaken the rule-making power of the World Trade Organization (WTO). As with other elements of his foreign policy, Trump acted with a reflexive determination to win, minimization of diplomacy, and nearsightedness as to human costs and consequences.

"TARIFF MAN"

Trump was very much in his element when it came to international trade. His game plan mirrored his approach to diplomacy in general: play chicken and see who blinks first. As he tweeted in July 2018, "'Tariffs are the greatest!' Either a country which has treated the United States unfairly on Trade negotiates a fair deal, or it gets hit with Tariffs. It's as simple as that—and everybody's talking!" "I am a Tariff man," Trump said by way of warning after a trade summit with Xi Jinping. The essence of his approach was to bait exporting countries—initially, the Europeans and the Chinese, later the Mexicans, Indians, Turks, French, Brazilians, and Argentines—with one tariff rise after another, challenging them each time to match him or come to the table hat in hand. Once the Trump administration had North America, Europe, and its Pacific partners locked into new trading arrangements, the strategy went, China would have to accede to US pressure in their trade war and even on military issues such as in the South China Sea.[1] The strategy didn't work.

In contrast with previous administrations that sought to outcompete China using arrangements such as the TPP, Trump aimed to contain and directly pressure China by aligning countries against it. Gordon Sondland, US ambassador to the EU, outlined that strategy in a speech that called on Europeans to join in compelling China to "act like a good global citizen in the business world and otherwise." But a united front with Europe posed problems, chiefly Trump's antagonism toward the EU and his pullout from both the Paris accord on climate change and the Iran nuclear deal. Nor would Europe be willing to sacrifice its trade and investment ties with China. Quite the opposite, as we have seen.

Relying on tariffs proved problematic. Early in 2018, when Trump was thinking about imposing high tariffs on steel and aluminum imports, he was warned by his more internationalist advisers, such as Gary Cohn, of the costs: major job losses in industries that rely on steel, and loss of support of key unions. The nationalists, led by Peter Navarro, disputed these views and eventually won out.[2] But Cohn was right and, if anything, underestimated the costs—for example, to American farmers and consumers. Industry groups complained about the high cost to them of Trump's tariffs.[3] Their counterparts abroad were similarly hurt—steel, aluminum, and auto exporters, for example. Chambers of commerce abroad, long cast by Trump as an enemy of economic nationalism, decried his protectionism, even when he announced the "Phase One" agreement with China at the end of 2019.[4] Key Republicans moaned about Trump's misunderstanding of the costs of tariff wars. Foreign corporations decided to virtually stop investing in the United States despite favorable tax and other conditions that normally should have increased the attractiveness of the US market. One writer called this trend the start of the "post-American world economy."[5] That writer could not have foreseen the destructive impact on the US economy of COVID-19, which greatly strengthened the prediction.

Trump proclaimed he was protecting US businesses and workers, citing (in 2020) "12,000 new factories under my administration, with thousands upon thousands of plants and factories being planned or built. We have created over half a million new manufacturing jobs." Even allowing for the statement's accuracy, in fact only some US manufacturing plants added plants and workers, mainly in high tech.[6] Most other manufacturers lost out, probably forever, to foreign competition, a workforce with special skills, and automation—all without reducing the US trade deficit, which remained high with China. In the long run, moreover, Trump may have created conditions for further economic decline. General Motors was a notable example: In November 2018 the company announced it was slashing 10 percent of its workforce in North America and closing five plants in response to a changing auto market and rising production costs. The decision, which would shift some production outside the United States, was made despite Trump's 2017 tax bill, which reduced the effective tax rate on corporations from 35 to 21 percent, and revisions to NAFTA on local labor content. Trump immediately came down hard on GM's decision, vowing to "cut all GM subsidies." Those same tax breaks were also supposed to result in a huge repatriation of capital by MNCs—as much as $4 trillion, Trump predicted—that would result in more investments and jobs at home. The prediction fell short by $3.3 trillion as multinational corporations did what comes naturally: go where profits are greatest, taxes are lowest, and investors are happiest.[7] Nationalist entreaties were no match for corporate lobbyists.[8]

The effort to weaken multilateral economic undertakings also proved counterproductive. Once Trump ended US participation in TPP shortly after taking office, the remaining eleven countries re-formed as the Comprehensive and Progressive Agreement for Trans-Pacific Partnership (CPTPP). (The agreement comes into force when six of the eleven members ratify it.) Under Obama, the TPP had been intended in part to stem Chinese economic influence in Asia, but opting out of the TPP opened the door even wider to China, which already offers Asia-Pacific countries a Regional Comprehensive Economic Partnership, the BRI, and a regional bank. China's total trade with all the CPTPP members nearly exceeds their trade volume with the United States.[9] China was thus positioned to make a credible claim to being the protector of the "global free trade order."[10] In a nutshell, pulling the United States out of the TPP, along with the trade war with China, may have helped Trump's image with his base, but it foreclosed markets and opportunities for further diplomatic engagement to improve environmental and workplace conditions.

Trade with Mexico and Canada may be the exception. Negotiations to revise NAFTA in the fall of 2018 produced a new agreement, known as the United States–Mexico–Canada Agreement (USMCA), that looked like a win for Trump. The agreement immediately ran into trouble in Congress. Democrats found much to dislike, including weak enforcement provisions (which unions found especially problematic), tariffs on Canadian and Mexican steel and aluminum exports, and increased market power for the biggest pharmaceutical firms. Just when it seemed the USMCA was doomed, Democrats, in the midst of impeachment proceedings against Trump, negotiated major concessions from the administration late in 2019 that met most union demands. Republican leaders in the Senate were chagrined, but Trump knew he could count on their support for passage of the agreement. He signed the agreement in January 2020.

Underlying all these steps, and missteps, were policies and priorities that, far from being populist, were pro–big business, anti-consumer, and (except for the USMCA, thanks to the Democrats) anti-labor. Just when competing with China should have called for greater investments in the security of ordinary Americans, every government agency toed the line on privileging corporate interests with regard to taxation, budgeting, regulations, data collection, and penalties.[11] Simultaneously, the Trump administration sought major cuts in social welfare spending. For example, the Department of Education emphasized privatization, as with student loans; the Consumer Protection Bureau virtually dismantled itself, dramatically reducing investigation and punishment of producers of dangerous products; and the Department of Justice failed to pursue corporate polluters. Perhaps worst of all was the pro-corporate agenda of the Environmental Protection Agency (EPA) and Interior Department, detailed in the next section. In virtually every one of these offices, conflicts of interest abounded, since the top staff came from or lobbied for the industries they now oversaw.[12] In short, Trump did precisely the opposite of what he promised, repopulating "the swamp" with lobbyists and Wall Street executives.

BETRAYING FUTURE GENERATIONS

> You owe the earth a pardon.
>
> —Joan Baez, "Nasty Man"

Playing politics with science has a long history, and helps account for why a climate crisis whose origins, consequences, and remedies were well known in the 1970s has never been treated as a matter of national security.[13] Specialists on climate change have come and gone in Washington, and even in the best of times their reports have never created the sense of urgency necessary for a national effort to prevent worst cases. Under Trump, science itself had a bad name, and any government report suggesting a crisis or emergency was sure to be buried. His administration drastically limited the role of scientific inquiry in climate change and other environmental issues. Facts became the enemy of "truth" as politics replaced science.[14] Trump claimed to have "a natural instinct for science," which led him to believe that on climate change "you have scientists on both sides of the picture." That was an inexcusable falsehood, for as is well known, 97 percent of climatologists believe climate change is mainly human caused and an imminent danger to the planet.

As president, Trump abandoned environmental responsibility and put environmental decisions at the service of corporate interests. "What I'm not willing to do is sacrifice the economic well-being of our country for something that nobody really knows," he said.[15] Clean air and clean water laws were overridden when they got in the way of corporate interests.[16] The Office of the Science Advisor was eliminated. Media access to the tens of thousands of scientists working for the government was severely restricted, as was their ability to present their research at scientific meetings and even to work in Washington, DC.[17] The EPA's science advisory board, which included Trump appointees, expressed opposition to some environmental deregulation decisions as being contrary to proven science, but to no avail.[18] Even weather reporting was subject to Trump's whim.[19] As Christine Todd Whitman, who led the EPA under George W. Bush, said, "Whoever is a bigger donor gets to tell [the Trump administration] what the environmental policy should be, it seems."[20]

Personnel choices advanced corporate control of Trump's environment agenda. He gave the fossil fuel industry, and climate-change deniers, new life by appointing first Scott Pruitt and then Andrew Wheeler to head the EPA, and Ryan Zinke and then David Bernhardt to lead the Interior Department. They and their pro-industry staffs were riddled with conflicts of interest.[21] These appointees became the gateway to oil, gas, and coal industries' lobbyists, lawyers, state government supporters, and financial backers (such as the Koch brothers' foundation), who sought to soften or roll back Obama-era environmental regulations and carve up public lands to suit energy interests. Together, the two agencies did as their sponsors wished—opening the Arctic National Wildlife Refuge and national monuments to oil drilling and mining,[22] loosening restrictions on methane and other greenhouse gas emissions, eviscerating air and water quality protections, promoting a dying coal industry at the expense of Obama's Clean Power Plan, weakening safety regulations for offshore drilling, rolling back auto fuel efficiency rules, and reducing protections for wetlands, streams, and endangered species.[23]

Trump's decision to pull the United States out of the 2015 Paris accords on climate change in 2020 could not have come at a worse moment. The key objective of the accords—keeping global warming to 1.5 degrees Celsius—is very unlikely to be met, whereas an increase to 2 or even 3 degrees Celsius is quite possible. By late spring 2019, for the first time in human history the concentration of carbon dioxide in the atmosphere reached 415 parts per million, a widely recognized red line. The year 2019 was also record setting for total fossil fuel emissions worldwide, with the United States contributing about 14 percent, even as coal use declined. Despite some reductions in US and other countries' emissions, and progress by many cities worldwide in moving toward complete reliance on renewable energy, numerous reports by international scientific bodies concluded it is already too late to keep the Paris promise.[24] In October 2018, for instance, the Intergovernmental Panel on Climate Change (IPCC) issued its fifth report, representing the contributions of thousands of scientists from eighty countries. The report was a stunning warning of dire consequences—greatly increased famine and poverty, destruction of coral reefs and the Arctic ice shelf—if remedial action on an historically unprecedented scale were not taken by 2030.[25] The report essentially told governments that had signed on in Paris that they were well behind the curve for preventing catastrophic climate change. And experience on the ground—the more frequent hurricanes, floods, temperature records, Arctic melting, and disappearing Great Barrier Reef—only confirmed the science.

If there was any doubt as to the administration's misdirection, three studies by Trump's own agencies in 2018 made clear that willful ignorance in the executive branch was guiding environmental policy making. The first was a 500-page study on automobile pollution. It assumed no change in policy and a *seven*-degree increase in global temperature by 2100. Yet rather than argue for extraordinary measures to help prevent this increase, the study assumed politics as usual and essentially argued that *restricting auto emissions wouldn't help, so why bother.*[26] The second study, the *Fourth National Climate Assessment* (FNCA), to which some 300 scientists contributed, followed the IPCC's conclusion pretty much to the letter. Its main observations, completely at odds with Trump's thinking, were as follows:

> Observations collected around the world provide significant, clear, and compelling evidence that global average temperature is much higher, and is rising more rapidly, than anything modern civilization has experienced, with widespread and growing impacts. . . . The warming trend observed over the past century can only be explained by the effects that human activities, especially emissions of greenhouse gases, have had on the climate. . . .
>
> The evidence of human-caused climate change is overwhelming and continues to strengthen, . . . the impacts of climate change are intensifying across the country, and . . . climate-related threats to Americans' physical, social, and economic well-being are rising. These impacts are projected to intensify—but how much they intensify will depend on actions taken to reduce global greenhouse gas emissions and to adapt to the risks from climate change now and in the coming decades.[27]

The third study, by the National Oceanic and Atmospheric Administration (NOAA), reported a 95 percent loss of the thickest and oldest Arctic ice. The study warns that this loss of heat-deflecting ice will probably contribute to an ice-free Arctic Ocean in summers and thus to global warming.[28] A follow-up study in 2019 confirmed the worst: It found that warming in the Arctic is having dramatic impacts now. Sea and land ice is disappearing at unprecedented rates as surface temperatures are the second-highest on record. The ice cover is "now more vulnerable to melting out in summer, thereby increasing the likelihood of a continuing decrease in minimum ice extent into the future."[29] In Antarctica, surface temperatures reached 65 degrees in February 2020, another new record.

The Trump administration not only chose to ignore the scientific findings of international and federal government studies; it also actively sought to discredit them. At a G-20 meeting and then at the COP24-Katowice (Poland) and COP25 (Madrid) follow-ups to Paris in 2018 and 2019, the administration went from buyers to sellers, seeking to persuade one and all that the world would have to rely well into the future on fossil fuels. Russia and Saudi Arabia, as major oil producers and exporters, were quick to support the US view. The US representative to the COP24 worked hard to ensure that the meeting merely "noted" the IPCC report, arguing instead that "no country should have to sacrifice their economic prosperity or energy security in pursuit of environmental sustainability."[30] At Madrid the US representative helped insure that carbon trading would not gain approval despite another UN report that it would take an annual 7.6 percent reduction in greenhouse gas emissions to meet the aims of the Paris climate accord. It was an extraordinary display of global irresponsibility.

Trump personally never referred publicly to any of the scientific studies. He kept denying that climate change was human caused and found a cockamamie explanation for every natural disaster—such as poor forest management for California's horrendous fires in November 2018. The best rationale he could come up with was this statement in a nationally televised interview: "I think something's happening. Something's changing and it will change back again."[31] Andrew Wheeler, ignoring the work of his own EPA scientists, persisted with the ignorant claim that "most of the threats from climate change are 50 to 75 years out."[32] At least Trump backed off on the China "hoax" thesis, but then again, he found equally absurd substitutes, such as attacking "windmills" (he meant wind turbines), flush toilets, and LED lightbulbs. A hundred years ago such nonsense coming from a US president, or his leading appointees in the EPA, could be excused, but today?

The cumulative effect of all the science-based reports on global warming since the 1980s is to underscore how little time remains to take remedial action that would head off the worst scenarios. The decade 2010–2020 was the warmest on record, each year meeting or exceeding the previous year's average temperature. We're meandering in unknown and hostile territory, facing a situation that (in the words of the IPCC report) has "no documented historic precedent."[33] Any truly meaningful action involves sacrifice both by the major economies responsible for carbon emissions today—China and the United States—and by developing economies—starting with India and Indonesia—whose energy demands are rapidly escalating. Sacrifice is a political issue, however: It doesn't sell in the United States, even among many liberal politicians. And it doesn't sell in developing countries, whose populations want autos and shopping malls. The next generation thus gets a handoff of one of the world's most urgent security problems.

Chapter Nine

Racism at the Border

The Democrats, the longer they talk about identity politics, I got 'em. I want them to talk about racism every day. If the left is focused on race and identity, and we go with economic nationalism, we can crush the Democrats.

—Steve Bannon [1]

KEEPING PEOPLE OUT

In 2015 Donald Trump began his campaign for the presidency on a racist note, using incendiary language that he would repeat throughout his tenure:

When Mexico sends its people, they're not sending their best. They're sending people that have lots of problems, and they're bringing those problems with us. They're bringing drugs. They're bringing crime. They're rapists. And some, I assume, are good people. [2]

"Some." He followed up those lines by calling for "a total and complete shutdown of Muslims entering the United States." [3] Thus began his camp's reliance on an anti-immigration platform that it believed would be a winning issue in many parts of the United States. It was 1920s-era politics—blaming immigrants for unemployment, stereotyping immigrants as actual or potential criminals, decrying "chain migration" that allows families of new citizens to apply for admission. On occasion he used the language of far-right demagogues, referring to an "invasion" of immigrants who "infest" the country and include gangs of "animals." He warned supporters that immigrants vote Democratic. "This will be the last election that the Republicans have a chance of winning," Trump warned during his campaign, "because you're going to have people flowing across the border" who become eligible to vote. "You just have to look at the maps," he said. [4] Thanks to a political adviser, building a 1,000-mile long wall along the border with Mexico emerged as Trump's signature anti-immigration idea—actually a "memory trick for an undisciplined candidate."[5]

The candidate was indeed "undisciplined," and when it came to immigration, Donald Trump was virtually apoplectic—willing to go to extraordinary lengths to satisfy his goal of keeping migrants out, especially nonwhite people from south of the border and elsewhere in the developing world. Separating children from their parents at the Mexico border, closing the border altogether, defying international law on asylum, excusing away the most deplorable conditions of detention, limiting migrants' ability to seek asylum, and using the military to build a wall with Mexico on spurious national security grounds—Trump carried out all these steps. Within a few months of taking office, he signed the first of many efforts to limit immigration without going through Congress. One was the "Buy American, Hire American" executive order, signed in April 2017, and designed, Trump said, to enable native-born workers to have a "level playing field" with skilled foreigners. A second measure was a cap on refugee resettlement—from 45,000 to 18,000 in the latter half of 2019, marking the lowest level of refugee admissions since the program was established in 1980.[6] There followed several more executive orders that chipped away at the ability of people with the wrong race, country of origin, and financial circumstances to enter the United States. By design, Donald Trump ensured that the United States would no longer be the beacon of hope for the world's refugees.

The main efforts to reduce the number of immigrants and refugees targeted Muslims and Latinos. This clear bias, deplored by some conservative Congress members, ran up against legal resistance and a series of failed court cases in which judges repeatedly cited Trump's tweets directed at travelers from Middle East countries. Eventually, Trump found support for his cause in the Supreme Court, which bowed to his spurious argument on national security grounds. But a federal court in San Francisco turned aside another anti-immigrant executive action, this time directed at the Latino population: an attempt by Commerce Secretary Wilbur Ross to illegally insert a citizenship question in the 2020 census. The judge found that Ross had engaged in a "cynical search to find some reason, any reason" to keep Latinos out of the census count and thus probably reduce the representation of Latino communities in Congress and the electoral college, as well as reduce federal grants to those communities.[7] The Supreme Court reviewed the administration's case and likewise found it "contrived." The administration wisely dropped the attempt.

A NATIONAL DISGRACE

Nothing aroused greater national resentment than Trump's decisions on immigration from Mexico and Central America. These had been foreshadowed during the campaign by his racist comments directed at a Latino judge who presided over a suit against Trump University and by Trump's insistence on building a wall at Mexico's expense. Once it became apparent that neither Mexico nor the US Congress would fund a wall—which led Trump to lie that he had never demanded that of Mexico—he upped the ante. Despite considerable public and congressional support for finding a comprehensive solution to the immigration problem—or, barring that, at least for granting legal residence to the now-grown DACA children, numbering perhaps 1.8 million enrolled and not enrolled in the program—Trump would not budge from his wall-building project. In fact, despite asserting that he supported these so-called Dreamers, *and having in hand a bipartisan proposal to trade protection of DACA for $25 billion to build the wall*, Trump backtracked.

With the virulently anti-immigrant Stephen Miller guiding official policy and the right-wing media pushing hard,[8] Trump was persuaded to seek a drastic reduction in immigration via Mexico altogether, including eliminating so-called chain migration. On various occasions he threatened to "shut down" the government "and finally go to system of Immigration based on MERIT! We need great people coming into our Country!"[9] (Trump's infamous reference to barring people from "shithole countries" such as Haiti occurred during debate in the White House over the DACA deal.)[10] But judges in Texas and elsewhere kept turning aside the administration's effort to end DACA, though it did win on denying law enforcement funds for sanctuary cities, where local police forces were barred from cooperating with federal immigration officials looking for migrant workers to deport. In December 2018 Trump did shut down most federal government offices for thirty-five days, essentially holding some 800,000 workers hostage to his wall demand.

Trump followed up the failure of Congress to find a solution he could support by pushing a "zero tolerance" policy toward immigrants from Central America and Mexico who were crossing the border in rising numbers. The policy was supposed to criminally prosecute everyone who crossed illegally. In reality it was a hostage policy: children, numbering more than 4,000 in 2019,[11] were separated from their parents and placed in prison-like camps. Their parents, if determined to have illegally entered the United States, would be detained or deported, without any plan to reunite them with their children. Attempts by some families to apply for asylum were typically denied or put off without a hearing. The result? An unconscionable inability of immigration authorities to find the separated children, leading them to maintain that, with limited government resources, it would be best to leave the children in the hands of people other than their parents. Kirstjen Nielsen, secretary of homeland security and a hard-liner on immigration, was unable to say at a 2019 congressional hearing how many separated children were being held in custody.[12] Senators like Jeff Merkley of Oregon, who closely tracked these children, struggled to get answers from the administration to the most basic questions, such as the identities of each child and length of stay in detention.[13] A subsequent government statement in response to a lawsuit admitted it might take two years to locate those children.[14]

So widely criticized was the separation and detention of families and the national disgrace it engendered that Trump implied he would abandon it. But it was all pretense. A court order gave the administration a deadline for reuniting families—an arduous task that showed that Immigration and Customs Enforcement (ICE) was far better at seizing, sequestering, and deporting people than at bringing them back together. In quite a few cases, ICE did not know where children or their parents were, including whether or not some parents had been deported.[15] But Trump would not acknowledge a policy failure. On June 20, 2018, the same day he issued an executive order to keep families together, Trump said, "We are keeping a very powerful border, and it continues to be a zero tolerance. We have zero tolerance for people that enter our country illegally."[16] (Among the unannounced exceptions: undocumented workers who served without benefits for low wages at Trump's Mar-a-Lago and other properties.)[17] But the actual policy was "Remain in Mexico," which required people seeking asylum to be deported back to Mexico pending a hearing, an obstacle rarely overcome.[18]

According to David Miliband, former British foreign minister and head of the International Rescue Committee, "People, from mainly El Salvador, Guatemala and Honduras, are exercising their right to claim asylum in the U.S. They're not 'illegal.' It's a right under international law."[19] Contrary to Trump's constant assertion that the United States was being flooded with illegal immigrants, Miliband went on, the vast majority of refugees—he estimated 85–86 percent—went to poor countries, with the United States accounting for only 1 percent. But facts did not stop Trump's most outspoken anti-immigrant voices, led by Miller, from pushing for draconian regulations and berating officials who hesitated to flout the law, such as banning migrants from even seeking asylum.[20] From the administration's viewpoint, adherence to international rules on immigration was "globalist" and a violation of US sovereignty.[21]

International law on asylum is clear: All people have a right to apply for asylum when they have a "well-founded fear of persecution." Those fleeing repression and poverty in Central America certainly qualified. By Trump's time, the profile of migration from south of the border to the United States had changed, from undocumented workers seeking work (economic migrants) to families and unaccompanied children fleeing Central American gangs, civil conflict, government oppression, and climate change that made it virtually impossible to live in safety, much less make a living.[22] The refugees sometimes arrived at the border in large numbers at one time—so-called caravans—but, contrary to Trump's claims, most sought asylum and had nothing to do with terrorists, gangs, or drug trafficking, which was going through legal ports of entry.[23] The real problem was Trump's characterization of asylum as "a big con job."

Early in 2019 there was a backlog of 850,000 asylum cases—200,000 more than when Trump took office—and only 450 judges to handle their applications.[24] Trump responded with a show of force, deploying National Guard troops and then regular army troops to the border, taking away the passports of US citizens of Mexican heritage born in the border area, and characterizing the border situation as a "national emergency" to justify a partial government shutdown until he got his $5.7-billion wall allocation. The shutdown actually cost the US economy double his demand for a wall.[25]

The wall was ultimately all about winning for Trump: "We have to get a win or I'll have to go national security, one or the other," he said at a news conference on January 10, 2019.[26] Numerous lawsuits were filed by states, nongovernmental organizations, and US representatives in Congress to stop the wall. Fifty-eight former senior US foreign policy officials joined in a declaration that "under no plausible assessment of the evidence is there a national security emergency" that warranted building a wall.[27] But Trump was unrelenting, and his threat to veto a bill passed by both houses of Congress to deny funds for the wall won out. He then proceeded to divert more than $13 billion in military construction and drug enforcement funds during 2019 and 2020 for wall construction.

As the numbers of refugee families seeking asylum became unmanageable in the spring of 2019, Trump went even further, cutting off assistance to three countries for programs actually designed by Washington to fight violence and poverty so as to *prevent* migration northward.[28] Then, in characteristic fashion, he backed down on the border closure, giving Mexico a year to improve things. "I'd rather do tariffs," he said. Mexico would either have to stop migrants from reaching the US border or face higher US tariffs. The Mexican government did try, but the increased detention of migrant families both on the Mexico side of the US border and along Mexico's border with Guatemala only added to the humanitarian crisis.[29] Numerous travel advisories issued by the State Department pointed to the dangers of travel in Mexico. Nevertheless, the Supreme Court once again stepped in on the administration's side, overriding lower courts in ruling that immigrants could only seek asylum in the United States if they had been denied it by another country through which they passed. Only the most hardened white nationalist could take pride in such suffering—and he did.[30] And when the coronavirus hit the United States, Trump seized on the opportunity to close the border to all comers, at least temporarily "solving" the immigration problem.

Chapter Ten

Retreat and Advance

A METHOD TO HIS MADNESS

Foreign policy ordinarily rests on a strategic approach to international relations—if not a full-fledged doctrine, then at least a set of ideas offering a direction, priorities, and a match between objectives and capabilities. Trump's thinking was nowhere near so systematic, and even seemed to resist being so. He brought two priorities to his presidency: stop subsidizing other countries' military spending, including that of wealthy allies, and start winning on trade. On election, Trump refined that agenda to include drastically reducing immigration, promoting economic nationalism, and limiting international commitments. The media struggled to categorize America First, calling it "populist," "unconventional," "transactional," and "isolationist." At different times it was all of the above, as policy pronouncements often bore the mark of Trump's unpredictability, insensitivity, and inexperience—qualities that embarrassed many of Trump's advisers and led the more internationalist among them to attempt to deflect the president's worst instincts and rein in chaos.

Franklin D. Roosevelt once said, "Unless there is [human] security here at home there cannot be lasting peace in the world." He recognized that protecting and promoting social well-being is a critical component of real national security. Over the years, many people with extensive government experience have expressed the same sentiment.[1] But Trump wasn't listening. Corruption, violations of law and ethics, intolerance, and indifference to American ideals were commonplace in his administration, and they weakened the president's hand internationally. Announced policies lost credibility, US commitments to treaties and agreements came into question, and the US bargaining position was undermined.[2] The US role as a mediator between disputing parties such as Japan and South Korea, Russia and Ukraine, and India and Pakistan was no longer taken for granted abroad as allies saw Trump reduce international relations to a matter of return on investment or going it alone.

When Barack Obama stepped down, he left Donald Trump a handwritten letter that said, "American leadership in this world really is indispensable. It's up to us, through action and example, to sustain the international order that's expanded steadily since the end of the Cold War, and upon which our own wealth and safety depend."[3] Trump clearly did not share that belief. In one sense, that is not a bad thing: The idea of US international leadership, making national security synonymous with global security, has long been a justification for interventions and interferences abroad to keep threats from American shores, maintain or emplace friendly governments in power, and preserve access to oil and other vital resources. Other than an interest in preserving access to oil, as in Saudi Arabia and Syria, and keeping the military's pump primed, Trump made no connection between national and global security.

And indeed, that was one of the greatest flaws in Trump's thinking. For him, both international security and human security at home were burdens he refused to bear. This view had an internal consistency: It reflected Trump's lifelong distaste for government regulation, lack of interest in democracy and inequality, and disregard for whole classes of Americans. His political agenda was extremely narrow: gain support among the (mainly white) people (mostly men) who elected him and, he hoped, would reelect him; use the belief that other countries needed the United States more than the United States needed them as leverage to win them over on trade and other transactions; and provide fuel for race-based politics in Europe and beyond.[4] There was no place on that white nationalist agenda for protecting democracy, the rule of law, and the environment, or for seeing them as fundamental to America's security.

THE COSTS OF TRUMPISM

Perhaps the most damaging legacy of the Trump years is the disservice he and his associates did to Americans' sense of self and nation. Under Trump, identity politics came to the fore, pushing aside the fundamental tenets of liberal democracy and respect for diversity. This retreat from core values actually began in the 1990s, when America turned inward in self-satisfaction at the Soviet collapse, the supposed "end of history," and the "unipolar moment" of unquestioned US global leadership.[5] Conspiracy theories and the Big Lie took their place—a page out of an autocrat's playbook. From calling facts "hoaxes" to attacking political enemies with outrageous claims, Trump found a ready audience for every baseless (but calculated) statement he chose to make. His ideas often borrowed from or echoed the incendiary language and smear campaigns of the far-right worldview of Fox News, *The National Enquirer*, *Infowars*, QAnon, Proud Boys, Sinclair, and Breitbart.[6] Trump frequently gave direct support to these outlets, repeating their distorted views in tweets and welcoming some of their leaders in the White House.[7] In fact, the FBI considered these conspiracy theories "domestic terrorism."[8]

Second, the Trump administration seriously undermined respect for and protection of human rights abroad.[9] Every postwar US administration has had a very inconsistent record in that regard, but Trump's was the worst, for he did not even pretend to be concerned about human rights. The United States not only withdrew from the UN Commission on Human Rights; Pompeo in essence narrowed those rights by putting the job of overseeing them in the hands of a new group separate from the State Department's own human rights office. No one should have been surprised, however, since Trump openly admired dictators on the left or right, excused their excesses, and believed flattery would win their favor. Not once did he say a critical word about repression in China, Saudi Arabia, Turkey, India, or Russia, for instance. Such actions signaled to the world that violators of human rights could expect no meaningful response from Washington. But then again, how could they? The administration consistently flouted basic rights at home with its racist immigration policies, efforts to limit press freedom, destruction of the environment, and undermining of universal access to health care.

A third cost of Trumpism was to diplomacy and the art of compromise. Give-and-take had no place in Trump's decision-making; photo ops in support of the Trump brand often substituted.[10] Threats and personal attacks to extract concessions were central to his administration's conduct of relations with friends and foes alike, a practice that was very much in accord with Trump's business history. Before the Pompeo-Bolton crew came aboard, people like McMaster and Mattis—his so-called globalist advisers—were sometimes able, with support from military leaders, to prevail upon Trump to take into account the contributions of allies to US security and economy. Once these so-called guardrails were replaced, Trump sidelined the State Department and National Security Council. *Pay to play* became the new normal in several instances: South Korea, the NATO countries, Japan, and Iraq. In stark contrast with the way Trump treated leaders of authoritarian regimes such as Russia, Saudi Arabia, and Turkey, who had valuables to offer him personally as well as politically, Trump raised the "rent" on longtime security partners and on occasion interfered in their politics. (Only in the case of Israel was such interference welcomed.) Some observers worried that the US alliance system would gradually disintegrate as allies responded to Trump's demands by reducing dependence on the United States for security, trade, and environmental leadership.[11]

Chapter 10

To be sure, Trump officials did introduce an Israel-Palestine peace plan, but it was (appropriately) dead on arrival. He talked about negotiating with Iran, replacing Maduro with Guaidó in Venezuela, reaching a denuclearization agreement with North Korea, resolving the trade war with China, and supporting a peace deal with the Taliban in Afghanistan. But *it was all talk and more threats*. There was no serious conflict resolution proposal, no incentives to dialogue for the adversary. Sanctions and other pressure tactics were Trump's preferred approach, and in these and other conflicts—Venezuela, Nicaragua, Syria—*threats never worked* and sanctions never led to changes in an adversary's behavior, just as studies had predicted.[12] Had he been willing to modify or gradually reduce sanctions in return for tension-reducing steps by the other side, he might not only have kept North Korea from continuing refinement and testing of nuclear weapons and long-range missiles, and kept Iran within the framework of the nuclear deal. Trump might also have set the United States on a positive, trust-building arc with these countries that would have payoffs throughout East Asia and the Middle East. Instead, all the sanctioned governments defiantly went about doing what they had been doing before: Iran broke away from the nuclear deal, North Korea developed new strategic missiles, and Moscow continued to interfere in US elections and in Ukraine. Syria continued (with Russian help) to bomb cities and other civilian targets, and eventually won out in its quest to remove US and Kurdish forces. Venezuela's and Nicaragua's authoritarian leaders continued their repression.

A CRIMINAL REGIME

As Americans, we should be frightened—deeply afraid for the future of the nation. When good men and women can't speak the truth, when facts are inconvenient, when integrity and character no longer matter, when presidential ego and self-preservation are more important than national security—then there is nothing left to stop the triumph of evil.
—Admiral William H. McRaven[13]

Finally, Trump's conduct as a national leader probably left a deeper mark on the US reputation than any specific foreign policy. He stained the presidency with his crimes (the payment of hush money, withholding of funds for Ukraine, and obstruction of justice), constant lying, indecent language, ignorance of other countries and cultures, and indifference to the Constitution and the rule of law. The resignation, firing, and indictments of so many of his officials and advisers over Russian interference, corruption, and conflicts of interest raised serious questions about his reliability, strategic thinking, leadership, and soundness of mind, all essential to foreign-policy effectiveness. So did the personal assaults on "disloyal" intelligence officials both before and after the Ukraine scandal. His order to assassinate a key Iranian official established a dangerous precedent and risked war. Trump's carelessness with official secrets was a well-known concern in the Pentagon; whenever he could hope to enhance his stature with supporters and foreign officials by revealing them, he did so. Overruling, or simply ignoring, intelligence and law enforcement agencies, relying on loyal political appointees to carry out his wishes, treating personally damaging communications as top-secret information, diverting the Department of Homeland Security's mission from terrorist threats to immigration, and accepting and encouraging foreign countries' electoral interference did not merely degrade the national security bureaucracy. Such behavior rendered the analytical arms of the government superfluous, leaving national security in the hands of partisan amateurs.

By 2020 a number of observers were likening Trump to another "imperial president." His autocratic tendencies became apparent virtually from day one of taking office. The presidency was all about him, not just in terms of lining his and the largest corporations' pockets but also expanding presidential power. He seemed to presume that presidents are untouchable, loyalty must be absolute, and the law is meant for others. As Trump said on July 23, 2019, "Then I have an Article Two [of the Constitution] where I have the right to do whatever I want as president."[14] Trump took a page out of Louis XIV: *l'état c'est moi.* Policy making was personal, and political appointees, enablers like Giuliani, legislative managers like McConnell, and family members like Kushner—all reliably loyal to Trump—were recruited to do the dirty work that bureaucratic leaders would not. Senior people around the president, including Pence, Barr, and Pompeo, and Republican leaders in the Senate, were sycophants: They may have disagreed with Trump in private, but publicly they indulged his every whim and covered for Trump's lies and misdeeds, up to and including his Senate trial. The few people who understood the need to check his abnormal demands sometimes succeeded by disobeying or delaying the execution of orders, leaking alternative views on national security issues, producing intelligence findings that contradicted his claims, and testifying before Congress at great risk to their careers. But most of them were fired or forced out.

Trump's irascible behavior prompted questions never before raised about US leaders: Does it take impeachment proceedings to force a president to obey Congress' lawful use of countervailing power? How can a president's reliance on social media to lie and evade be overcome? How can US alliances be sustained against a president who doesn't believe in them? What can be done about a president who profits from his businesses while in office, who regularly ignores scientific, military, and economic reports and advice, or who comes to be regarded by many as a national security threat?

TRUMP'S NATIONALISM—AND REALISM

The notion that Trump "revolutionized" US foreign policy is, frankly, absurd. He *disrupted* policy rather than innovated it. His thinking was a jumble of extremist ideas—unilateralism, nativism, right-wing populism—added to which was overweening egotism and an obsession with overturning Barack Obama's diplomatic and legislative achievements. These were not the ingredients of a consistent or sustainable replacement for liberal internationalism. Instead, as the Ukraine scandal showed, they were cause for alarm. In consequence, chaos and confusion frequently reigned in the bureaucracy and in US relations with other countries. Far from being an administration governed by "realism, restraint, and respect" in foreign affairs, as Pompeo once claimed, Trump's time amounted to aides' "put[ting] Humpty Dumpty back together." [15]

Within Congress, Trump's foreign policy and national security directions were looked at askance by plenty of Republicans as well as Democrats. His uncritical view of autocracies, belittling of allies in Europe and Asia, disdain for diplomacy, racially motivated immigration policies, and disputes with Mexico and Canada all bewildered lawmakers. His unilateral decisions on Syria, Saudi Arabia, Turkey, and Afghanistan led to an outpouring of criticism from senators on both sides of the aisle. He failed to see the virtues of international agreements and distanced the United States from international organizations—indeed, made every effort to hobble them—even when those clearly served US interests. He fought against the Bretton Woods system that established US economic hegemony after World War II—a system that really did put America first, and therefore certainly warrants substantial reform in the interest of working people and environments everywhere. But using tariffs and sanctions to bludgeon partners and rivals in disputes was hardly a substitute for a progressive trade policy. [16]

There were times when Trump's thinking reflected "pure realism, devoid of ideals and sentiment," as Robert Kagan wrote, though often that realism was less a personal preference than the result of persuasion by his handpicked internationalist advisers. [17] Toward China, for instance, Trump adopted what amounted to containment and deterrence in addition to economic pressure. He supported high military spending, which is nearly as great as the next fifteen leading countries' expenditures combined, and strategically focused arms sales, such as to India, as the centerpiece of an effort to contain China in the "Indo-Pacific" region. [18] On human rights under authoritarian regimes, his administration acted consistent with US foreign policy tradition in putting strategic and economic interests first. Like all previous presidents, Trump one-sidedly supported Israel, oblivious to the human-security costs for Palestinians and many Israelis. As for developing countries,

Trump showed little interest, even disdain, often choosing sanctions and drone warfare over aid programs.

Even the internationalism (or right-wing globalism) that Trump so detested survived in his administration—specifically, the pivotal role of the US economy and the dollar in world commerce, both of which were central to Trump's use of trade and sanctions as leverage. For the time being, the dollar's ascendance is secure.[19] But China's rise and the alternative development model it represents present a formidable challenge that Trump completely misread. The Chinese were rapidly creating their own global network of trade, finance, and investment partners and institutions, founded on promises of political noninterference, economic nonconditionality, and ample credit. Trump's willingness to cede leadership of globalization to Beijing, glaringly obvious in the COVID-19 crisis, may prove to be the most decisive strategic failure of his tenure, particularly as China uses its economic clout to woo not just developing countries but also US allies in Europe and Asia. Actually, if Trump had been *more* transactional, he would have stayed in the TPP and the Paris climate change accord, joined the Asia Infrastructure Investment Bank initiated by China, avoided promiscuous tariff raises, and proposed cooperation with China on the pandemic. Doing so would have produced greater gains for US consumers and industry, maintained US reliability as a trade and environment partner, and posed a stronger challenge to China.[20] The cost of deal breaking exceeded the cost of deal making, in short.

Trump did take some positive steps in foreign policy, though with important qualifications. He was no neocon: He rejected the notion of American exceptionalism and the universality of American values, beliefs that have been enormously costly when put into practice. Nor did Trump put much confidence in the military's opinion. But like a neocon, Trump preempted military displeasure with him by supporting major increases in military spending that detracted from vital domestic needs such as education, health care, and scientific research. He did try to avoid war, but he was no noninterventionist. As happened with Iran and Venezuela, he ignored his national security team's advice to intervene directly while being perfectly agreeable to using threats, sanctions, and mercenaries to promote regime change. Trump also was quite willing to support others' interventions (Saudi Arabia in Yemen) and continue secret warfare (in Africa and Afghanistan). His inclination to dramatically reduce the US military presence in the Middle East was sensible, yet in 2020 the United States still had 65,000 soldiers in the Middle East. In Syria and Afghanistan, Trump waffled on US troop withdrawals, never clarified their mission, and failed to link them to a diplomatic strategy that would protect allies and civilian populations.[21] These unilateral moves undercut the notion that this president was a dyed-in-the-wool transactionalist.

Trump was right to insist that the Europeans pay more for their defense, though previous presidents had made the same demand with some success, and without the accompanying threat to withdraw from or downgrade NATO. Going to the summit with North Korea was commendable but amateurish, done without proper preparation or understanding of the process needed to end Kim Jong-un's reliance on nuclear weapons for deterrence. Bringing home US jobs rather than seeing them continue to be exported via multinational corporations was welcome, though it was contradicted by tax policies favorable to multinational corporations and their CEOs. Finally, Trump's critique of trade agreements such as the TPP, NAFTA, and with China actually had support from liberals and progressives, but was arrogantly and clumsily carried out. "Tariff man" proved to be a cure worse than the disease.

DAMAGE CONTROL

Contrary to the worst fears about Trump's foreign policy, nothing he did cannot be undone.[22] Neither his bizarre (or, if you like, unique) behavior nor his policy inclinations are permanent. *What America most needs is a normal president with "a decent respect for the opinions of mankind."* The real test for a new president will be restoring faith in democracy, starting with respect for the system of checks and balances, the independence of the judicial system, the right to vote, freedom of the press, and civil liberties.[23] He or she is likely to heed certain lessons of Trump's term, such as avoiding compromising situations with foreign countries, honoring cultural diversity, and not mixing personal and public business. After Trump, the president will also take care to appoint people with proven competence and without conflicts of interest, restore generosity to immigration policy and foreign aid, and bring dignity back to relations with allies and international bodies. Recognition of the nuclear danger will return, and therefore preparedness to engage Russia in a new round of arms talks.[24] Opinion polls show that despite Trump's nativism, or perhaps in response to it, strong majorities among the American public are internationalist—far more open than his administration (or Republicans) to nonwhite immigration, action on climate change, US activism in world affairs, and support for NATO and international trade, for instance.[25] Trump's successor can therefore expect public opinion to endorse a return to liberal positions on those issues.

Overturning Trump's approach to international relations will require an understanding, however, that world leadership is no longer the special province of the United States. A return to earlier US-led strategies—Cold War containment and liberal hegemony—is neither possible nor desirable. Nor is it likely that with Trump gone, US allies will be willing and able to step into the breach and perform the system-maintaining tasks Washington had once undertaken.[26] Besides, the old order was already passé before Trump took office. The United States had failed to craft an Israeli-Palestinian peace, China was already starting to dominate Pacific trade, the United States and Russia were on Cold War terms, the Europeans were going beyond the US position on mitigating climate change, and sanctions had failed to force Iran, North Korea, and others to change course. Furthermore, the United States found itself overextended, still fighting wars and terrorism on multiple fronts. The notion of a "rules-based international order," with the United States leading in the making of the rules, was fast eroding. The time for new rules consistent with *common* security is at hand.

TOWARD A PROGRESSIVE US FOREIGN POLICY

At this writing early in 2020, the outcome of the presidential election is likely to be determined by the public's verdict on Donald Trump's leadership during the coronavirus pandemic. One might think that his failures on that score—inattention to the warnings of his own scientists and advisers, cover-up of mistakes, deflection of blame onto China, dismantling of Obama's pandemic preparedness system, absurd advice on treatments, and chaotic planning to fight the pandemic—would sink his reelection hopes, especially with historic numbers of unemployed and deaths from the virus.[27] His priority to politics and economic recovery over public health and a social safety net—to Wall Street over Main Street, as various commentators put it—was shockingly in evidence. Still, the reelection of Donald Trump remains a possibility. Having been acquitted in his Senate trial, Trump doubled down on two of his trademark characteristics—lack of restraint and vindictiveness. Within a few days of acquittal he interfered in a court case and raised questions about the judge's politics, fired two officials who had testified as to his corrupt intent in the Ukraine scandal, and indicated that a further sell-off of public lands to fossil fuel companies was in the offing.[28]

After acquittal, some Republican senators said they hoped Trump had been chastened by the process and would be more cautious in his actions, but this proved to be wishful thinking—as demonstrated by his false claim that he was now "the chief law enforcement officer of the country" his closing of the Mexico border, and his advocacy of force against anti-racism protesters. In a second term, unless Democrats take control of the Senate, we can therefore expect a further erosion of democratic norms, expansion of Trump's anti-environmental agenda, and a full-blown purge of "disloyal" officials.

In foreign policy, Trump, unlike Nixon—who, according to Henry Kissinger, "went through the motions of governing" once the Watergate crisis broke out, and essentially ceded full control to Kissinger[29]—can be expected to be even more unrestrained in a second term. His policy positions will only be reinforced, and taking unwarranted risks in the name of national security are certainly possible with a president who believes he is not accountable to anyone, including the military. At the least, Trump will continue the US retreat from involvement in alliances and international organizations. Critical issues such as climate change, peace with justice in the Palestinian-Israeli dispute, global health epidemics, and nuclear arms control are likely to find the United States standing alone and often inconsequential. Russia will remain free to interfere in US elections. China will have an easier path to satisfying its global ambitions, contrary to Trump's belief.[30]

But what if a *liberal* Democrat, meaning Joe Biden, were to be elected in 2020? He would probably be an articulate spokesperson for human rights, democracy building, a humane immigration policy (including honoring amnesty requests), freedom of the press, and science-based decision-making.[31] He would surely arouse the public to the dangers of radical nationalism in Europe and beyond and perhaps distance the United States from relations with far-right nationalist governments. He would restore foreign aid programs, revitalize US ties to NATO and other treaty partners, and reaffirm the US commitment to the Paris accord. Renewed respect for the role of congressional oversight and for public opinion could also be expected. Biden would surely seek to restore Obama-era environmental regulations and the removal of industry lobbyists, lawyers, and others who went to work for Trump's EPA. Under Biden, we will not find a US representative to an international conference on climate change saying, as happened under Trump at COP24, that "no country should have to sacrifice their economic prosperity or energy security in pursuit of environmental sustainability."

But Biden's foreign policy agenda would probably preserve some highly questionable directions, in some instances with Cold War coloration. High on the list would be military spending, for which most Democrats in recent years (Obama included) have consistently voted major increases. Like liberals before him, Biden would probably be unable to resist right-wing pressure to keep modernizing the nuclear weapons inventory. He would probably continue US involvement in and financing of multilateral institutions such as the WTO and IMF, and support of "free trade" agreements like the TPP and the USMCA, despite all their deficiencies in governance and inattention to labor conditions and environmental protection. As an establishment Democrat, Biden would still promote arms sales abroad, even to friendly authoritarian governments. Relations with Russia and China might well plummet to new lows, perhaps even back to a containment strategy.[32]

Joe Biden would probably embrace American exceptionalism. He might also be more inclined than Trump to intervene abroad with force. Obama, after all, had planned to withdraw from Iraq and Afghanistan, only to reverse gears and restore US involvement in those "endless wars." Biden, however, seems to have learned from that experience, at least with respect to the Middle East.[33] But he might also depart from Obama's central idea of engagement with adversaries, and thus be unlikely to pursue normalizing relations with North Korea and possibly not even willing to revitalize Obama's signature achievements—restoring relations with Cuba and the nuclear deal with Iran. In fact, Biden might reaffirm Trump's pro-Israel policies rather than take the political risk of challenging them.

A *progressive* administration, by contrast, would be defined by a deeper relationship between domestic and foreign policy—that is, domestic priorities would not merely shape but would significantly *dictate* foreign policy priorities.[34] Fighting authoritarianism, inequality, and environmental irresponsibility abroad begins by promoting democracy, social justice, and environmental protection at home. The military budget would be substantially trimmed, with much of the savings transferred to pay for social needs that bear on human security. Protecting the environment and public health would be elevated to the top of the national security agenda. A progressive US president would take the lead in creating a global coalition on mitigating and reversing climate change and promoting scientific collaboration on pandemics. And on economic globalization, "free trade" would come in for major revision, with an eye to whether or not agreements promote social well-being at home and abroad. The privileged position of multinational corporations would be reduced by removing their numerous tax advantages.

On immigration, a progressive Democrat would immediately restore normal border security measures, meaning focusing specifically on illegal entries and known criminals while reaffirming asylum protections and welcoming all comers without regard to ethnicity or religion. A progressive would also propose a path to citizenship for undocumented workers and adopt a visa program for seasonal workers. Most importantly, a progressive president would adopt policies that give priority to the "push" side of immigration, assisting Central American governments that are committed to providing their people with jobs, education, and peace, and thus a future in their own country. Finally, a progressive administration would educate the populace to the positive contributions migrant workers and refugees make, and have always made, to society.

Among the specific foreign and national security policy shifts a progressive president would be likely to endorse is reducing and ultimately eliminating reliance on nuclear weapons. The president would not be satisfied with arms control measures such as New START, which still leaves thousands of nuclear warheads and missiles in the hands of US and Russian leaders. Rather, he or she would seek a new international agreement to reduce nuclear weapons to the absolute minimum, preliminary to signing and ratifying the TPNW to *eliminate* them;[35] would establish clearer protocols on nuclear weapon deployment to prevent misguided use; and would adopt a national policy of no-first-use of nuclear weapons.

A progressive president would also support a just peace in the Middle East. In the Israel-Palestine conflict, that would mean reaffirming a two-state solution, rejecting Israeli land grabs, urging dual sovereignty in Jerusalem, and in general promoting a "culture of peace."[36] Elsewhere, a new US policy would end military relations with autocracies such as Saudi Arabia and uphold engagement with Iran and other adversaries.[37] Idealistic? In present circumstances, of course; but a change of administration may well present opportunities for major policy shifts that liberals have often avoided.[38]

A return to diplomacy and, specifically, dialogue with adversaries would be high on the list of a progressive president's priorities, though in 2020 it is hard to find any politician willing to talk about trying a new approach to Russia or challenging the demonizing of China.[39] How do we know dialogue would work with, say, Iran or North Korea? We don't, but we do know this much for sure: Dialogue worked with Iran, producing a breakthrough nuclear deal that combined incentives with rigorous verification; and it worked with North Korea to produce, among other agreements, acceptance of the principle of "action for action" rather than (as Trump and previous presidents had it) disarmament first and rewards second. Whether or not serious talks—meaning substantive, verifiable agreements undertaken with mutual respect, incentives for peace, and sensitivity to history—could work now cannot be predicted. We only know that it was rarely even considered under Donald Trump.

WHERE ARE WE HEADED?

In American politics, the deep divisions, whose history goes back well before Trump, portend huge obstacles for any president looking to restore sense and consensus in policy making. Divided government will remain the norm for a long time to come. A very conservative Supreme Court will rule well into the future, with a strong tendency to endorse expansion of presidential power. The demographic and geographic lines between the parties are more clear cut than ever.[40] Political extremism is well entrenched; anger and retribution are primary emotions these days. Racism, authoritarianism, and white nationalism may go back underground with a liberal or progressive president in charge, but they will fester and look for a comeback. Attacks on the media and the president will still be ferocious and personal. The two parties are themselves divided into contending blocs—the Democrats between establishment liberals and progressives, the Republicans between the far right, the "moderate" conservatives, and the Never Trumpers.[41]

Domestic political disarray will set the stage for fierce battles over foreign policy—for instance, over Russia and China policy, immigration, sovereignty or multilateralism, and military involvement abroad. The most contentious topic, however, may be climate change, whose up-front costs in any serious effort are likely to be very high on everything from public health and safety to protection of military installations.[42] The payoffs from a green economy, however—in savings on energy and waste, creation of new jobs, and resource protection, for instance—should more than compensate, and a progressive president will want to push for a strong version of a Green New Deal bill.[43] Especially with the cratering of its economy caused by the coronavirus pandemic, the United States is likely to be hard put to afford a global foreign policy commensurate with traditional notions of great-power responsibility.

In short, the dysfunctions of American politics will weigh heavily on foreign policy regardless of who is president. Donald Trump accelerated the triumph of tribalism over bipartisanship, but that doesn't mean the political system is headed for collapse.[44] But it is in grave danger. The nationwide protests that followed the murder of a black man by Minneapolis police in May 2020 led Trump to label the protesters "domestic terrorists" and deploy regular army units instead of calling for national unity. It was America's Tiananmen, showing how thin the line is between a constitutional leadership and despotism. To former intelligence officials with experience in authoritarian countries, Trump's use of the dictator's playbook was familiar.[45] His successor will have an opportunity to reaffirm America's moral leadership, in keeping with the founders' belief in the nation as a "shining example" of democracy and liberty. That president's challenge will be to demonstrate that a foreign policy based on engaging adversaries, nonintervention abroad, human and environmental rights, social justice, and a path to citizenship for immigrants is in the national interest and global interest—a proper response to rising nativism and far-right nationalism.

Before Senator McCain died, he wrote a letter to Americans aimed at reassuring them that better times lay ahead. Without naming Donald Trump, McCain took aim at Trump's disheartening leadership—his divisiveness, lack of interest in social equality, and serious ethical lapses. McCain, though generally a hard-liner on foreign policy, also stood for bipartisan cooperation in Congress, a sensible immigration policy, and devotion to American ideals. His appeal harkened back to another America, one where effective leadership meant civility, fairness, a unifying, empathetic voice. Donald Trump's presidency failed the leadership test. Joe Biden may have his chance to make America whole again.

Notes

1. WE WERE WARNED

1. Peter Baker and Maggie Haberman, "For Trump, 'A War Every Day,' Waged Increasingly Alone," *New York Times*, December 22, 2018. (Hereafter, *NYT*. Reference is to the online edition unless otherwise noted.)

2. On Trump's mindset, see Dana Milbank, "Trump Seems to Be Transparently Mad," *Washington Post*, May 22, 2019. (Hereafter, *WaPo*. Reference is to the online edition unless otherwise noted.) As of May 2019, twenty-eight federal, state, and Congressional investigations of Trump, members of his family, business associates, and the Trump Organization were underway. See Larry Buchanan and Karen Yourish, "Tracking 29 Investigations Related to Trump," *NYT*, May 13, 2019.

3. "A Letter from G.O.P. National Security Officials Opposing Donald Trump," *NYT*, August 8, 2016.

4. Bob Woodward and Robert Costa, "Transcript: Donald Trump Interview with Bob Woodward and Robert Costa," *WaPo*, April 2, 2016.

5. Robert Kagan, "'America First' Has Won," *NYT*, September 24, 2018.

6. Michael Gove and Kai Diekmann, "Full Transcript of Interview with Donald Trump," *The Times* (London), January 16, 2017, https://www.thetimes.co.uk/article/full-transcript-of-interview-with-donald-trump-5d39sr09d.

7. See Jan-Werner Müller, "False Flags: The Myth of the Nationalist Resurgence," *Foreign Affairs*, vol. 98, no. 2 (March–April 2019), pp. 35–41.

8. I define that perspective in several books, most recently in the introductory chapter of *Engaging Adversaries: Peacemaking and Diplomacy in the Human Interest* (Lanham, MD: Rowman & Littlefield, 2018). In short, writing in the human interest means assessing world affairs from the standpoint of a global citizen, divorced from any particular national interest and instead seeing issues of security in terms of economic and social inequality, military excesses, and human rights violations. Cooperative values such as empathy, nonviolence, and win-win outcomes underlie human-interest analyses.

9. Jonathan Chait, "Will Trump Be Meeting with His Counterpart—Or His Handler?," *New York Magazine*, July 2018, https://nymag.com/intelligencer/2018/07/trump-putin-russia-collusion.html.

10. Trump singled out Japan and Saudi Arabia. See Michael Kranish and Marc Fisher, *Trump Revealed: The Definitive Biography of the 45th President* (New York: Scribner, 2016), p. 275.

11. Glenn Plaskin, "The Playboy Interview with Donald Trump," *Playboy*, March 1, 1990, http://www.playboy.com/read/playboy-interview-donald-trump-1990.

12. Woodward and Costa, "Transcript: Donald Trump Interview."

13. Plaskin, "The Playboy Interview."

14. Jennifer M. Miller, "Let's Not Be Laughed at Anymore: Donald Trump and Japan from the 1980s to the Present," *Journal of American-East Asian Relations*, vol. 25 (2018), pp. 138–68.

15. Woodward and Costa, "Transcript: Donald Trump Interview."

16. Woodward and Costa, "Transcript: Donald Trump Interview."

17. Woodward and Costa, "Transcript: Donald Trump Interview." Newt Gingrich, the former U.S. House of Representatives majority leader, said this of Trump: "He has to win. His entire reputation, his entire relationship with the base, it's all a function of being committed on big things and not backing down." Robert Costa et al., "'In the White House Waiting': Inside Trump's Defiance on the Longest Shutdown Ever," *WaPo*, January 12, 2019.

18. See David Cay Johnston, *The Making of Donald Trump* (New York: Melville House, 2017), pp. 9–23, 33–39; David Frum, *Trumpocracy: The Corruption of the American Republic* (New York: HarperCollins, 2018), pp. 99–100; Kranish and Fisher, *Trump Revealed*; Plaskin, "The Playboy Interview"; Woodward and Costa, "Transcript: Donald Trump Interview"; Gove and Diekmann, "Full Transcript of Interview with Donald Trump." Regarding Trump's wealth, a *New York Times* investigation revealed that the president was anything but a self-made billionaire. He inherited at least a half-billion dollars from his father's real estate holdings and, during the 1990s, used both "dubious tax schemes and outright fraud" to avoid paying more than the minimum on his earnings. See David Barstow, Susanne Craig, and Russ Buettner, "Trump Engaged in Suspect Tax Schemes as He Reaped Riches from His Father," *NYT*, October 2, 2018.

19. Plaskin, "The Playboy Interview."

20. The leading countries with Trump companies were India (16), United Arab Emirates (13), Canada (12), and China (9). Indonesia, Panama, and Saudi Arabia all had eight. Drew Harwell and Anu Narayanswamy, "A Scramble to Assess the Dangers of President-Elect Donald Trump's Global Business Empire," *WaPo*, November 20, 2016.

21. According to one investigation, Donald Trump, his daughter, and his wife have around 1,200 trademark applications, most filed before 2017. Since then, "Trump-related entities have filed at least 40 trademark applications . . . , with a further 51 being officially registered [in a total of thirteen countries]. By our count, there are at least 132 applications in eight jurisdictions filed since 2015 that remain in the examination phase." "The Trump Trademarks: The 'America First' President's Truly Global IP Portfolio Revealed," *World Trademark Review*, October 24, 2019.

22. An investigation by *Forbes* magazine found that Trump's personal wealth actually dropped after he took office, due partly to lying about his net worth but mainly to his growing unpopularity. Customers and investors jumped ship as Trump's irascible behavior became apparent, and Trump's wealth was estimated to have dropped from $4.5 billion to $3.1 billion, thus making him only the 386th richest American. Dan Alexander and Chase Peterson-Withorn, "How Trump Is Trying—and Failing—to Get Rich Off His Presidency," *Forbes*, October 2, 2018, https://www.forbes.com/sites/danalexander/2018/10/02/how-trump-is-tryingand-failingto-get-rich-off-his-presidency. See also Jonathan O'Connell and Justin Vicory, "Trump's Sons Are Running the Business—and Their Big Hotel Expansion Is at a Standstill," *WaPo*, January 4, 2019.

23. Colum Lynch, "Trump's 'Unbridled, Egotistical Narcissism Defines White House Summits," *Foreign Policy*, July 20, 2018, https://foreignpolicy.com/2018/07/20/trumps-unbridled-egotistical-narcissism-thomas-pickering_helsinki-summit-putin-u-s-russiadefines-white-house-summits.

24. The Clapper and Brennan quotes are both in Tim Weiner, "The 'Witch Hunters,'" *New York Review of Books*, August 16, 2018.

25. Quoted by Chris Cillizza, "The Greatest Trick Donald Trump Ever Pulled," CNN, January 7, 2019.

26. Michael Lewis, "'This Guy Doesn't Know Anything': The Inside Story of Trump's Shambolic Transition Team," *The Guardian*, September 27, 2018.

27. From his former position as director of White House message strategy, Cliff Sims, in his memoir, *Team of Vipers: My 500 Extraordinary Days in the White House* (New York: Thomas Dunne Books, 2019), recounts the "out of control" chaos and fighting inside the White House.

2. PRESIDENT TRUMP, IN PERSON

1. Aaron Blake, "President Trump's Full Washington Post Interview Transcript, Annotated," *WaPo*, November 27, 2018.

2. The *New York Times* investigation cited above exploded that myth. Barstow, Craig, and Buettner, "Trump Engaged in Suspect Tax Schemes."

3. For example, Karen Tumulty, "Trump's Tweets on Children Dying in U.S. Custody Are a New Low," *WaPo*, December 29, 2018. Throwing rolls of paper towels to Puerto Rican hurricane victims is another example. Another is the many times during the coronavirus crisis when he failed to acknowledge the victims, consistently giving priority to reviving the economy.

4. Trump never could forgive Sessions for recusing himself from the Mueller investigation. The recusal allowed the investigation to proceed under Sessions's deputy attorney general, Rod J. Rosenstein. Time and again Trump criticized Sessions for failing to "take control" of the Justice Department and inadequately supporting him, at one point even saying, "I don't have an attorney general." Trump publicly urged Sessions to reverse his recusal, without success. Yet, inasmuch as Sessions took a hard line on immigration, Trump repeatedly delayed firing Sessions while looking around for someone loyal to the president to replace him.

5. Such agreements are considered unenforceable, which is apparently why Trump paid off certain people who left his administration with what is essentially hush money. See Maggie Haberman, "Trump Appears to Admit White House Aides Signed Nondisclosure Agreements," *NYT*, August 14, 2018.

6. When McCain died in August 2018, America mourned, but not Trump, who rejected a White House statement on McCain's service in favor of a brief tweet, refused to answer reporters' repeated questions about McCain, and for days ordered the White House's flag flown at full staff until public outrage forced Trump to lower the flag.

7. Peter Baker, "Trump Lashes Out at Impeachment Foes and Pelosi Hits Back," *NYT*, February 6, 2020.

8. Bandy X. Lee and Robert Jay Lifton, eds., *The Dangerous Case of Donald Trump: 27 Psychiatrists and Mental Health Experts Assess a President* (New York: Macmillan, 2017). I am indebted to Dr. Fred Sierles, professor emeritus of psychiatry at the Rosalind Franklin School of Medicine and Science, for enlightenment on psychiatric disorders. Dan P. McAdams draws an excellent psychological profile of Trump, emphasizing his "sky-high extroversion combined with off-the-chart low agreeableness," in "The Mind of Donald Trump," *The Atlantic*, June 2016, https://www.theatlantic.com/magazine/archive/2016/06/the-mind-of-donald-trump/480771.

9. See also Chris Cillizza, "Donald Trump's LaVar Ball Tweets Cross a Line—Even for Him," CNN, November 23, 2017.

10. Fred Turner writes that Trump's success with his core stemmed from his having "mastered the politics of authenticity for a new media age." "He is the personification of his supporters' grievances," much like Hitler and Mussolini—"the living embodiment of the nation." Fred Turner, "Machine Politics," *Harper's*, January 2019, p. 31.

11. Chris Cillizza, "Donald Trump Is Laying the Groundwork to Delegitimize the 2020 Election," CNN, March 6, 2019.

12. Ashley Parker, "'Totally Dishonest': Trump Asserts Only He Can Be Trusted Over Opponents and 'Fake News,'" *WaPo*, August 30, 2018.

13. Greg Sargent, "As New Questions on Trump's Corruption Emerge, His Lawless Threats Escalate," *WaPo*, April 26, 2019.

14. Ellen Nakashima and Aaron Gregg, "Pentagon's Inspector General Finds No Evidence of Undue Influence in $10 Billion Cloud Computing Contract," *WaPo*, April 15, 2020.

15. Bob Woodward, *Fear: Trump in the White House* (New York: Simon & Schuster, 2018), p. 175.

16. Marc Fisher, "'Grab That Record': How Trump's High School Transcript Was Hidden," *WaPo*, March 5, 2019.

17. Woodward, *Fear*, pp. 34, 242–44, 247, provides examples.

18. Josh Dawsey and John Wagner, "'A Total Loser': Trump Lashes Out at George Conway," *WaPo*, March 19, 2019.

19. Jeremy W. Peters, "Charles Koch Takes on Trump. Trump Takes on Charles Koch," *NYT*, July 31, 2018.

20. CNN, September 16, 2016.

21. Woodward, *Fear*, p. 244.

22. David E. Sanger, "Vague on Details, Trump Is Betting on 'Special Bond' with Kim to Deliver Deal," *NYT*, June 12, 2018.

23. Tim Elfrink, "Trump Lashes Out after Paul Ryan Slams Him in New Book," *WaPo*, July 12, 2019.

24. Mike Mullen, "Adm. Mike Mullen on Ex-intel Officials Keeping Clearances," interview by Chris Wallace, Fox News, August 19, 2018, https://www.foxnews.com/transcript/adm-mike-mullen-on-ex-intel-officials-keeping-clearances-mulvaney-on-potential-storm-clouds-ahead-for-trump-economy.

25. Greg Miller and Greg Jaffe, "In Aftermath of Ukraine Crisis, a Climate of Mistrust and Threats," *WaPo*, December 25, 2019; Dana Milbank, "For Trump, the Name of the Season Is Treason," *WaPo*, April 12, 2019.

26. Rebecca Savransky, "Trump: Tillerson a 'World Class Player and Dealmaker,'" *The Hill*, December 11, 2016, https://thehill.com/homenews/administration/309879-trump-tillerson-a-world-class-player-and-dealmaker; Carol Morello, "Tillerson Calls Trump Undisciplined; Trump Calls Tillerson 'Dumb as a Rock,'" *WaPo*, December 7, 2018.

27. Philip Rucker, Don Lamothe, and Josh Dawsey, "Trump Forces Mattis Out Two Months Early, Names Shanahan Acting Defense Secretary," *WaPo*, December 23, 2018.

28. James Comey, *A Higher Loyalty* (New York: Macmillan, 2018).

29. Sharon LaFraniere, Kenneth P. Vogel, and Peter Baker, "Trump Said Ukraine Envoy Would 'Go Through Some Things.' She Has Already," *NYT*, September 27, 2019.

30. "We are united in the conviction that the Fed and its chair must be permitted to act independently and in the best interests of the economy, free of short-term political pressures and, in particular, without the threat of removal or demotion of Fed leaders for political reasons." Paul Volcker, Alan Greenspan, Ben Bernanke, and Janet Yellen, "America Needs an Independent Fed," *Wall Street Journal*, August 5, 2019, online ed.

31. Devlin Barrett, Shane Harris, and Matt Zapotosky, "Barr Personally Asked Foreign Officials to Aid Inquiry into CIA, FBI Activities in 2016," *WaPo*, September 30, 2019. Australia, Britain, and Italy are the countries mentioned in the article. As for Flynn, even though he had admitted to two counts of lying to the FBI about conversations with the Russian ambassador, the Department of Justice abandoned the case against him in May 2020, clearly in response to Trump's aim to remove all vestiges of Robert Mueller's Russia investigation.

32. Neal K. Katyal and Joshua A. Geltzer, "The Appalling Damage of Dropping the Michael Flynn Case," *NYT*, May 8, 2020.

33. David Von Drehle, "Trump's Résumé Is Rife with Mob Connections," *WaPo*, August 10, 2018.

34. Mark Landler, "With a Vocabulary from 'Goodfellas,' Trump Evokes His Native New York," *NYT*, August 23, 2018.

35. The dinner took place at the Trump International Hotel on April 30, 2018, and included two men who worked with Rudy Giuliani in what became the Ukraine scandal, discussed in chapter 3. See Rosalind S. Helderman, Tom Hamburger, and Josh Dawsey, "Listen: Trump Tells Associates to 'Get Rid of' U.S. Ambassador to Ukraine," *WaPo*, January 25, 2020.

36. The interview is recounted in Peter Baker and Nicholas Fandos, "Trump Equates Taking Dirt from Russia with Presidential Diplomacy," *NYT*, June 13, 2019.

37. Cohen's public testimony before Congress, February 27, 2019. The transcript is available from *Lawfare* at https://www.lawfareblog.com/house-intelligence-committee-releases-cohen-transcripts .

38. Comey, *A Higher Loyalty*, p. 221.

39. Ashley Parker, Josh Dawsey, and Carol D. Leonnig, "'Very Much Counter to the Plan': Trump Defies Advisers in Embrace of Putin," *WaPo*, July 16, 2018.

40. Trump took Putin at his word when Putin assured Trump at their Helsinki summit that Russia had not interfered in US elections. "I have President Putin [at my side]; he just said it's not Russia. I will say this: I don't see any reason why it would be." Days later, facing a great deal of criticism for his comment, Trump said he meant to say "why it *wouldn't* be." Kevin Liptak and Jeff Zeleny, "Trump, Facing Fury, Says He Misspoke with Putin," CNN, July 18, 2018. Sure. He took Kim Jong-un at his word when Kim told Trump he knew nothing about the death of an American student, Otto Warmbier, who had been in North Korean detention and died shortly after being returned to the United States with severe brain damage. The student was imprisoned for seventeen months on a frivolous charge, and Trump in his 2018 State of the Union address condemned the "depraved character of the North Korean regime." Donald J. Trump, "President Donald J. Trump's State of the Union Address," January 30, 2018, https://www.whitehouse.gov/briefings-statements/president-donald-j-trumps-state-union-address . But after Trump's second summit meeting with Kim in 2019, the president used the same words he had used with Putin: "He [Kim] tells me that he didn't know about it and I will take him at his word," and that Kim "felt badly about it. He felt very badly." (Chris Cillizza, "Donald Trump's Shocking, Shameful About-Face on Otto Warmbier," CNN, February 28, 2019.) It later emerged that the North Koreans had billed Washington $2 million for treatment of Warmbier, evidently the price of his release. The young man's parents called it "ransom"; Trump denied a payment was ever made. (Anna Fifield, "North Korea Issued $2 Million Bill for Comatose Otto Warmbier's Care," *WaPo*, April 25, 2019.)

41. "Where's my favorite dictator?" Trump was heard saying as he awaited a meeting with el-Sisi. Nancy A. Youssef, Vivian Salama, and Michael C. Bender, "Trump, Awaiting Egyptian Counterpart at Summit, Called Out for 'My Favorite Dictator,'" *Wall Street Journal*, September 13, 2019.

42. Felicia Sonmez, "Putin Is 'Probably' Involved in Assassinations and Poisonings, but 'It's Not in Our Country,' Trump Says," *WaPo*, October 14, 2018.

43. David D. Kirkpatrick, "Trump Endorses an Aspiring Libyan Strongman, Reversing Policy," *NYT*, April 19, 2019.

44. Donald Trump, interview by Chris Wallace, Fox News, August 22, 2018. Chris Wallace tweet @FoxNewsSunday.

45. Donald Trump, speech at the United Nations, September 25, 2018, video available at "Trump Addresses World Leaders at United Nations, CNN, September 25, 2018, https://www.cnn.com/videos/politics/2018/09/25/trump-un-general-assembly-reaction-speech-nr-vpx.cnn. In another interview, Trump said, "I've had the most successful two years in the history of this country as a president. . . . Nobody has done what I've done," except for George Washington. Aaron Blake, "Trump's Fanciful, Falsehood-Filled AP Interview, Annotated," *WaPo*, October 17, 2018.

46. Reporters Without Borders, which ranks 180 countries on press freedom, ranked the United States forty-eighth in 2019, just below Romania. It was the third straight year of a drop in the US ranking. Paul Farhi, "Report: U.S. Declines Again in Press-Freedom Index, Falls to 'Problematic' Status," *WaPo*, April 18, 2019.

47. Ashley Parker and Philip Rucker, "'I Could Really Tone It Up': Trump Shows Little Interest in Uniting the Nation during Crises," *WaPo*, October 26, 2018.

48. See also James Comey's impressions in *A Higher Loyalty*, pp. 239–43.

49. Katie Rogers, "Trump's Book Club: A President Who Doesn't Read Promotes Books That Promote Him," *NYT*, November 30, 2018.

3. TAKING SIDES

1. John Gans, "At the National Security Council, Trump Loyalists Are at War with Career Aides," *WaPo*, November 21, 2019.
2. Ronan Farrow, *War on Peace: The End of Diplomacy and the Decline of American Influence* (New York: W. W. Norton, 2018), p. xv.
3. Woodward, *Fear*, pp. 206–7, 262.
4. Woodward, *Fear*, provides numerous examples. See, for instance, pp. 262, 264–65, 271, and 276 on Trump's lack of knowledge about governing, his determination to withdraw from three major international agreements, and his inability (and unwillingness) to pay attention to details about them.
5. Kaitlan Collins, Kevin Liptak, and Zachary Cohen, "Bolton-Pompeo Relationship Hits New Low as Foreign Policy Tests Mount," CNN, September 6, 2019.
6. Woodward, *Fear*, p. 237.
7. Woodward, *Fear*, p. 145.
8. Kushner's interview with Axios in 2019 (Isaac Stanley-Becker, "'I Wasn't Involved in That': Kushner Is Mum on Trump's Birther Conspiracy Theory," *WaPo*, June 3, 2019) revealed not just incompetence when it came to dealing with foreign policy issues, specifically the Israeli-Palestinian conflict and refugees, but also disingenuousness regarding his father-in-law. Secretary of State Tillerson said he clashed with Kushner over Kushner's infrequent consultations with the State Department. Tillerson also decried Kushner's unfamiliarity with history. John Hudson and Josh Dawsey, "Putin Out-Prepared Trump in Key Meeting, Rex Tillerson Told House Panel," *WaPo*, May 22, 2019.
9. The two top White House aides were Donald F. McGahn, counsel to the president, and Chief of Staff John Kelly, both of whom reportedly wrote internal memoranda to clarify that the security clearances were granted despite their opposition. Maggie Haberman et al., "Trump Ordered Officials to Give Jared Kushner a Security Clearance," *NYT*, February 28, 2019. A whistleblower in the White House long involved in the clearance process confirmed the news reports, saying that twenty-five people (Kushner and Ivanka Trump among them) were cleared for top-secret access despite conflicts of interest and other grounds for denial. Rachael Bade, "Whistleblower Says 25 Security Clearance Denials Overturned During Trump Administration," *WaPo*, April 1, 2019.
10. Woodward, *Fear*, p. 286.
11. Sophie Tatum, "Trump's Future Chief of Staff Calls Him 'Terrible Human Being' in Video from 2016," CNN, December 16, 2018.
12. Kelly said he had warned Trump not to appoint a "yes-man" as his successor because the president might be impeached. Trump went ahead and did just that, and paid the price when, in the Ukraine scandal, Mulvaney inadvertently admitted that there had been a quid pro quo for Trump to release military aid to Ukraine. Caroline Kelly and Nikki Carvajal, "Trump Is Disputing Kelly Said 'Don't Hire a Yes-Man' or 'You Will Be Impeached,'" CNN, October 26, 2019.
13. For examples, see Aaron Blake, "Trump Congratulates Poland as It Commemorates Nazi Invasion," *WaPo*, September 3, 2019.
14. See the account of Guy Snodgrass, who was present as General Mattis's speechwriter: "Inside Trump's First Pentagon Briefing," *Politico*, October 21, 2019, https://www.politico.com/magazine/story/2019/10/21/inside-trumps-first-pentagon-briefing-229865.
15. Tina Nguyen, "Leaked Documents Confirm the Worst-Kept Secret of Trump's Presidency," *Vanity Fair*, February 4, 2019, https://www.vanityfair.com/news/2019/02/the-worst-kept-secret-of-trumps-presidency.
16. Hudson and Dawsey, "Putin Out-Prepared Trump in Key Meeting." Trump's response to Tillerson's criticism was typical of the president: "I don't think I have to prepare very much. It's about attitude, it's about willingness to get things done."
17. Ashley Parker, Josh Dawsey, and Carol D. Leonnig, "'Very Much Counter to the Plan': Trump Defies Advisers in Embrace of Putin," *WaPo*, July 16, 2018.
18. Katie Glueck, "Donald Trump's Man on Israel," *Politico*, August 4, 2016, https://www.politico.com/story/2016/08/donald-trump-israel-jason-greenblatt-226651.

19. Alex Horton and John Hudson, "'Very Telling' That Trump Didn't Know His Own Anti-ISIS Point Man, Former Official Says," *WaPo*, December 24, 2018.

20. The most public proof of this came in January 2019 when the intelligence chiefs produced a "worldwide threat assessment" that contradicted Trump on North Korea, Iran, ISIS, and the Mexico border wall. Daniel R. Coats, *Worldwide Threat Assessment of the US Intelligence Community*, Senate Select Committee on Intelligence, January 29, 2019, https://www.dni.gov/files/ODNI/documents/2019-ATA-SFR---SSCI.pdf.

21. As with Trump's response to the *Worldwide Threat Assessment*: see Shane Harris and John Wagner, "In Latest Attack on Intelligence Agencies, Trump Ignores Where They Actually Agree," *WaPo*, January 31, 2019. In an interview with CBS News, Trump seemed to rest his case for ignoring intelligence findings by citing the intelligence failure concerning weapons of mass destruction in Iraq under George W. Bush. Josh Dawsey, "Trump Refuses to Comment on Whether Mueller Report Should Be Made Public," *WaPo*, February 3, 2019.

22. Veronica Stracqualursi, "Former Intelligence Leaders: Trump Attempting to 'Stifle Free Speech by Revoking Brennan's Clearance," CNN, August 17, 2018.

23. See the graphic by Kevin Schaul, Reuben Fischer-Baum, and Kevin Uhrmacher in "It's Been 43 Days since a High-Profile Departure from the Trump Administration," *WaPo*, September 10, 2019, https://www.washingtonpost.com/graphics/2018/politics/trump-turnover.

24. "Tracking How Many Key Positions Trump Has Filled So Far," *WaPo*, updated Monday of each week, https://www.washingtonpost.com/graphics/politics/trump-administration-appointee-tracker/database.

25. For a profile of the former US ambassador to Panama, see Jon Lee Anderson, "Behind the Wall," *The New Yorker*, May 28, 2018, pp. 24–30. The former ambassador to Mexico, Roberta S. Jacobson, a thirty-year veteran of the foreign service, wrote of her experience in "My Year as a Trump Ambassador," *NYT*, October 20, 2018. The US envoy on ISIS, Brett McGurk, had been appointed by Obama and reappointed under Trump. He resigned in apparent outrage over Trump's decision to withdraw US forces from Syria, arguing that declaring victory over ISIS was unwarranted. John Hudson, Ellen Nakashima, and Karen DeYoung, "U.S. Envoy to Coalition Fighting ISIS Resigns in Protest of Trump's Syria Decision," *WaPo*, December 22, 2018. Also see Julian Borger, "US State Department's Top Official for Latin America Resigns," *The Guardian*, August 8, 2019.

26. William J. Burns, "The Lost Art of American Diplomacy," *Foreign Affairs*, vol. 98, no. 3 (May–June 2019), pp. 98–107.

27. Under Trump, 40 percent of ambassadors were political (as opposed to career diplomat) appointees, well above the 30 percent average for previous ambassadors. Trump's political appointees paid an average of more than $189,000 to his 2016 campaign, compared to an average of under $85,000 for all presidents since 1980. Ryan Scoville, "Troubling Trends in Ambassadorial Appointments: 1980 to the Present," *Lawfare*, February 20, 2019, https://www.lawfareblog.com/troubling-trends-ambassadorial-appointments-1980-present.

28. Marie L. Yovanovitch, "Opening Statement of Marie L. Yovanovitch to the House of Representatives Permanent Select Committee on Intelligence, Committee on Foreign Affairs, and Committee on Oversight and Reform," October 11, 2019.

29. Yovanovitch, "Opening Statement of Marie L. Yovanovitch."

30. Trump made that difference quite explicit in an address to the UN General Assembly on September 23, 2019. Donald Trump. "Remarks by President Trump to the 74th Session of the United Nations General Assembly," The White House, September 29, 2019, https://www.whitehouse.gov/briefings-statements/remarks-president-trump-74th-session-united-nations-general-assembly.

31. According to Woodward's account (*Fear*, pp. 304–7), Trump was prepared to scrap the trade agreement known as KORUS, refusing to listen to arguments from Tillerson, Mattis, McMaster, and others about the security as well as the economic benefits to the United States of the alliance with South Korea. Trump had little patience for instruction, though eventually the KORUS agreement was renewed on somewhat better terms for the United States. Trump threatened to withdraw the United States from NAFTA as a way to force the Democrats in Congress to vote to approve the new United States–Mexico–Canada Agreement, which critics found wanting on labor standards and environmental protection and which contained a $5

billion provision to build his Mexico wall. Once again Trump's "globalist" faction reportedly opposed US withdrawal, which could have left the three countries without any agreement. Glenn Thrush, "Trump Plans to Withdraw from Nafta," *NYT*, December 2, 2018.

32. As the trade war showed no signs of easing in the fall of 2018, the Chinese reportedly grew angry and bewildered by Trump's rejection of various proposals his team had put forward and by his raising of the ante rather than sitting down and talking. David J. Lynch and Gerry Shih, "Crossed Wires: Why the U.S. and China Are Struggling to Reach a Trade Deal," *WaPo*, October 24, 2018.

33. As Peter Navarro wrote in describing the Trump administration's negotiating strategy, walking away from a deal shows "unwavering resolve." Peter Navarro, "The Trump Guide to Diplomacy," *NYT*, October 15, 2019.

34. John Gans, "Col. Vindman and the Trumpification of the National Security Council," *NYT*, February 7, 2020.

35. Seung Min Kim, Josh Dawsey, and Damian Paletta, "Trump Defies Close Advisers in Deciding to Threaten Mexico with Disruptive Tariffs," *WaPo*, May 31, 2019.

36. Dexter Filkins, "On the Warpath," *The New Yorker*, May 6, 2019, pp. 32–45.

37. Prior to his firing (or resignation, depending on whose story one believes), Bolton's clashes with Pompeo were well publicized. See Collins, Liptak, and Cohen, "Bolton-Pompeo Relationship Hits New Low as Foreign Policy Tests Mount."

38. House Permanent Select Committee on Intelligence, *The Trump-Ukraine Impeachment Report*, U.S. House of Representatives, 2019, https://www.documentcloud.org/documents/6566093-House-impeachment-report-PDF.html.

39. As Michelle Goldberg ("'The Beacon Has Gone Out': What Trump and Giuliani Have Wrought," *NYT*, October 12, 2019) succinctly wrote, "In Giuliani's fevered alternative reality, Ukraine's most stalwart foes of corruption are actually corruption's embodiment." Parallel to their actions was an attempt by Trump's energy secretary, Rick Perry, to place oil and gas associates on the board of Ukraine's state-owned gas company, Naftogaz. Kenneth P. Vogel, Matina Stevis-Gridneff, and Andrew E. Kramer, "Rick Perry's Focus on Gas Company Entangles Him in Ukraine Case," *NYT*, October 7, 2019.

40. Shane Harris, Josh Dawsey, and Carol D. Leonnig, "Former White House Officials Say They Feared Putin Influenced the President's Views on Ukraine and 2016 Campaign," *WaPo*, December 19, 2019. The authors of this important article wrote that it was based on "interviews with 15 former administration and government officials."

41. David Ignatius, "In Ukraine, the Quid Pro Quo May Have Started Long before the Phone Call," *WaPo*, October 31, 2019.

42. Ben Protess, William K. Rashbaum, and Michael Rothfeld, "Lev Parnas Adds New Details on Push to Oust U.S. Ambassador to Ukraine," *NYT*, January 15, 2020.

43. Those valuables, said Parnas, included *all* US aid (not just military aid), an official visit by Zelensky to Washington, and Vice President Pence's attendance at the inauguration. Pence, apparently on orders from Trump, did not attend and would not meet Zelensky in Kyev until September 1. Rachel Maddow, "Rachel Maddow Interviews Lev Parnas," MSNBC, January 15, 2020.

44. The person in question is Dmytro Firtash; see Franklin Foer, "The Kremlin Inches Closer to the Biden Plot," *The Atlantic*, January 18, 2010, https://www.theatlantic.com/ideas/archive/2020/01/firtash-kremlin-biden/605188.

45. According to Bolton's memoir, Trump instructed him to call Zelensky and arrange a meeting between the Ukraine president and Giuliani. Bolton wrote that the conversation with Trump was witnessed by Giuliani, Mulvaney, and Pat A. Cipollone, a White House counsel who would represent Trump at his impeachment trial. Bolton wrote that he never made the call. Maggie Haberman and Michael S. Schmidt, "Trump Told Bolton to Help His Ukraine Pressure Campaign, Book Says," *NYT*, January 31, 2020.

46. Fiona Hill used that term when testifying before Congress. Her statement is at Fiona Hill, "Opening Statement of Dr. Fiona Hill to the House of Representatives Permanent Select Committee on Intelligence," *NYT*, November 21, 2019. Russian efforts to turn attention to Ukraine as the source of election interference are detailed by Julian E. Barnes and Matthew Rosenberg, "Charges of Ukraine Meddling? A Russian Operation, U.S. Intelligence Says,"

NYT, November 22, 2019. In 2017 a Republican-led Senate Intelligence Committee briefly investigated the charge and concluded there was nothing to it. Justin Wise, "Senate Intel Found No Evidence of 2016 Ukraine Interference: Report," *The Hill*, December 2, 2019, https://thehill.com/homenews/senate/472721-senate-intel-committee-found-no-evidence-of-top-down-ukraine-interference.

47. Neither Ukraine's prosecutor general nor any other source found evidence to support the charge that the senior Biden interfered to prevent an investigation of his son. See Daryna Krasnolutska, Kateryna Choursina, and Stephanie Baker, "Ukraine Prosecutor Says No Evidence of Wrongdoing by Bidens," *Bloomberg News*, May 16, 2019, https://www.bloomberg.com/news/articles/2019-05-16/ukraine-prosecutor-says-no-evidence-of-wrongdoing-by-bidens; Michael Birnbaum, David L. Stern, and Natalie Gryvnyak, "Former Ukraine Prosecutor Says Hunter Biden 'Did Not Violate Anything,'" *WaPo*, September 26, 2019.

48. Giuliani told a *New Yorker* interviewer, "I believed that I needed Yovanovitch out of the way. She was going to make the investigations difficult for everybody." MSNBC broadcast, December 16, 2019. That view coincides with Trump's private remarks, quoted in chapter 2, to "get rid of" and "take out" the ambassador. Documents later released by Lev Parnas suggested that the ambassador's anti-corruption efforts rankled Ukraine's top prosecutor, prompting an American offer to remove her in exchange for information on the Bidens. Aaron Blake, "Lev Parnas Reveals a New Quid Pro Quo," *WaPo*, January 15, 2020. Deputy Assistant Secretary of State George Kent, responsible for Ukraine, testified that Giuliani's "assertions and allegations against former Ambassador Yovanovitch were without basis, untrue, period." Colby Itkowitz, John Wagner, and Felicia Sonmez, "House Investigators Subpoena Mulvaney; State Department Official Says Giuliani Was Engaged in a Campaign 'Full of Lies and Incorrect Information' about Former Ambassador," *WaPo*, November 7, 2019. While Yovanovitch was testifying in open hearing before the House judiciary committee on November 15, Trump attacked her record in a number of tweets, raising another impeachable offense: witness tampering.

49. Trump actually agreed to release the transcript of his conversation with Zelensky. The transcript and the whistleblower's complaint are available in *NYT*: "Full Document: Trump's Call with the Ukrainian President," *NYT*, September 25, 2019; "Document: Read the Whistle-Blower Complaint," *NYT*, September 26, 2019. Most of the witnesses, like Bolton, had listened in on the call. Trump also reportedly delayed granting Ukraine a tariff-reducing trade agreement, and he urged Zelensky to find a way to make peace with Putin, despite Russia's seizure of Crimea and its continuing support of rebel Ukraine forces in the Donbass region of the country. The trade agreement was pulled from Trump's desk when Bolton told the US trade negotiator that the president wouldn't sign anything of benefit to Ukraine. David J. Lynch and Josh Dawsey, "White House Delayed Ukraine Trade Decision in August," *WaPo*, October 24, 2019. The agreement was finally signed off on in October 2019.

50. It later came to light that Trump had also asked China's leader, Xi Jinping, to investigate the Bidens as well as Senator Elizabeth Warren, another top presidential candidate, again with the conversation buried in a top-secret server. Kylie Atwood et al., "Trump Raised Biden with Xi in June Call Housed in Highly Secure Server," CNN, October 3, 2019. A China specialist and adviser to Trump, Michael Pillsbury, told the *Financial Times* of London on October 10, 2019, that he had gone to China and received "quite a bit" of information on Joseph Biden, Jr. Pillsbury then denied the account, but he was too late; the *Financial Times* produced the relevant e-mails. See Colin Kalmbacher, "Trump Adviser Admits He Got Background Info on Hunter Biden, Then Tells Falsehood on Air about It," *Law & Crime*, October 10, 2019, https://lawandcrime.com/high-profile/trump-advisor-admitted-he-got-background-info-on-hunter-biden-from-china-then-lied-on-air-about-it.

51. Peter Baker and Michael S. Schmidt, "Sondland Says 'We Followed the President's Orders' on Ukraine," *NYT*, November 20, 2019.

52. Edwin Wong, "Officials Discussed Hold on Ukraine Aid after Trump Spoke with Country's Leader," *NYT*, December 21, 2019.

53. "White House Budget Official Told Pentagon That Order to Hold Ukraine Aid Came from Trump, National Security Site Reports," CNN, January 2, 2020.

54. In a January 2020 report, the Government Accountability Office found that the White House budget office "withheld funds for a political reason" in violation of the 1974 Impound-

ment Control Act. Jeremy Herb, "Government Watchdog Concludes Trump Administration Broke Law by Withholding Ukraine Aid," CNN, January 16, 2020.

55. William B. Taylor, "Opening Statement of Ambassador William B. Taylor, October 22, 2019," https://www.washingtonpost.com/context/opening-statement-of-ambassador-william-b-taylor/6b3a6edf-f976-4081-ba7f-bce45468a3ff. Taylor said, "I have a particular interest in and respect for the importance of our country's relationship with Ukraine. Our national security demands that this relationship remain strong. However, in August and September of this year [2019], I became increasingly concerned that our relationship with Ukraine was being fundamentally undermined by an irregular informal channel of U.S. policy-making [*sic*] and by the withholding of vital security assistance for domestic political reasons."

56. Besides Taylor's own "Opening Statement," his opposing views on the Ukraine deal are in messages he exchanged with Sondland. Sondland worked with Giuliani and at first proclaimed there was no quid pro quo—after discussing the matter with Trump. See Charlie Savage and Josh Williams, "Read the Text Messages between U.S. and Ukraine Officials," *NYT*, October 4, 2019. But after reviewing his own and others' testimony, Sondland changed his testimony, agreeing that US military aid was indeed the quid pro quo. He so testified publicly on November 20, 2019 (Jeremy Herb and Marshall Cohen, "Key Diplomat Changes Testimony and Admits Quid Pro Quo with Ukraine," CNN, November 5, 2019), adding that all the other top US officials, from Trump and Pence on down, were "in the loop" on using an official visit by Zelensky to extract a public statement of intent to investigate the Bidens.

57. McKinley said under oath that he asked Pompeo for a statement of support of Ambassador Yovanovitch. Pompeo did not provide one and even denied McKinley had ever requested it. Stephen Collinson, "New Impeachment Disclosures Lay Bare Trump's Power Game," CNN, November 5, 2019.

58. Hill, "Opening Statement of Dr. Fiona Hill"; and Greg Miller and Greg Jaffe, "At Least Four National Security Officials Raised Alarms about Ukraine Policy Before and after Trump Call to Ukrainian President," *WaPo*, October 10, 2019.

59. Vindman's testimony said, "'I stated to Ambassador Sondland that his statements were inappropriate' and that the 'request to investigate Biden and his son had nothing to do with national security, and that such investigations were not something the N.S.C. was going to get involved in or push.'" Danny Hakim, "Army Officer Who Heard Trump's Ukraine Call Reported Concerns," *NYT*, October 28, 2019. The day after the July 25 phone call, David Holmes, a foreign service officer, overheard Sondland promising Trump in a phone call from Kyev that the Ukrainians were going ahead with investigation of the Bidens. Sondland told Holmes that Trump "didn't give a shit about Ukraine," caring only about an investigation. Rachel Maddow, *The Rachel Maddow Show*, MSNBC, November 15, 2019.

60. Barr handpicked two investigators in hopes of undermining the FBI's initial probe of Russian interference and uncovering Ukraine's role in the 2016 election. Both investigations turned up some irregularities but nothing that changed the conclusion of the Mueller Report. See Matt Zebotosky and Devlin Barrett, "Barr's Handpicked Prosecutor Tells Inspector General He Can't Back Right-Wing Theory That Russia Case was U.S. Intelligence Setup," *WaPo*, December 4, 2019.

61. Speaking at the trial on January 21, 2020, Congressman Hakeem Jeffries (D-NY) stated that Trump had prevented twelve key officials from testifying, produced zero documents requested by House Democrats, rejected seventy-one other requests for information, and blocked nine subpoenaed individuals from testifying. "Rep. Jeffries Says Impeachment Trial Without Witnesses Would Be 'Stunning Departure,'" *PBS NewsHour*, January 21, 2020, https://www.youtube.com/watch?v=QHTA542K7rs.

62. Andrew E. Kramer, "Ukraine Knew of Aid Freeze in July, Says Ex-Top Official in Kyev," *NYT*, December 3, 2019; Andrew E. Kramer and Kenneth P. Vogel, "Ukraine Knew of Aid Freeze by Early August, Undermining Trump Defense," *NYT*, October 23, 2019; Michael S. Schmidt, Julian E. Barnes, and Maggie Haberman, "Trump Knew of Whistle-Blower Complaint When He Released Aid to Ukraine," *NYT*, November 26, 2019.

63. In September 2019 Zelensky announced that he favored elections in Donbass, and in December he met with Putin in Paris under French and German auspices. But without the

United States in attendance, Ukraine and Russia could only agree to an exchange of prisoners and a cease-fire in Donbass.

64. A Ukrainian oligarch with ties to Putin provided $2 million to the wife of one of Giuliani's associates, almost certainly to facilitate production of "proof" of the Bidens' corruption in Ukraine. The oligarch had clear political interests, akin to Moscow's, in making the payment. See Jo Becker et al., "Why Giuliani Singled Out 2 Ukrainian Oligarchs to Help Look for Dirt," *NYT*, November 25, 2019; Editorial Board, "How a Putin Ally Is Aiding Giuliani in Ukraine," *WaPo*, December 21, 2019.

65. The UN Security Council responded to the Israeli occupation by passing resolution 497. It declares that "the Israeli decision to impose its laws, jurisdiction, and administration in the occupied Syrian Golan Heights is null and void and without international legal effect." See Stephen Zunes, "U.S. Recognition of Israel's Golan Annexation a Threat to World Order," *The Progressive*, March 25, 2019, https://progressive.org/dispatches/us-recognition-golan-annexation-a-threat-to-world-order-zunes-190325.

66. Yuval Shany, "Israel's New Plan to Annex the West Bank: What Happens Next?," *Lawfare*, May 6, 2019, https://www.lawfareblog.com/israels-new-plan-annex-west-bank-what-happens-next.

67. See the excellent critique of the plan by Rashid Khalidi, "The Neocolonial Arrogance of the Kushner Plan," *New York Review of Books*, June 12, 2019, https://www.nybooks.com/daily/2019/06/12/the-neocolonial-arrogance-of-the-kushner-plan.

68. John Hudson and Loveday Morris, "Exclusive: Pompeo Delivers Unfiltered View of Trump's Middle East Peace Plan," *WaPo*, June 2, 2019.

69. In August 2019 Trump prevailed on Netanyahu to deny entry to two Muslim-American Democratic congresswomen who were strong supporters of the Palestinian cause, tweeting that Israel would "show great weakness" if it allowed in two anti-Israel, Jew-hating women. This lie, coupled with the outrageous effort to harm his political enemies, backfired when both leaders were heavily criticized even by some right-wing allies. The criticism multiplied when Trump followed up by vocalizing an old anti-Semitic trope that Jewish Americans who vote for Democrats are disloyal to Israel and "the Jewish people." Eileen Sullivan, "Trump Again Accuses American Jews of Disloyalty," *NYT*, August 21, 2019.

70. The Israeli public prefers the two-state option by 52 percent, whereas the Palestinian public prefers it by 42 percent. Geneva Initiative, Two-State Index, December 26, 2019, via TSI@genevainitiative.org. The Arab states generally responded with praise for Trump's "efforts" but disappointment that the Palestinians' "legitimate rights" had yet to be acknowledged.

71. Mark Mazzetti, Ronen Bergman, and David D. Kirkpatrick, "Trump Jr. and Other Aides Met with Gulf Emissary Offering Help to Win Election," *NYT*, May 19, 2018. Whether or not the plan was actually implemented remains unclear.

72. Sharon LaFraniere, Maggie Haberman, and Adam Goldman, "Trump Inaugural Fund and Super PAC Said to Be Scrutinized for Illegal Foreign Donations," *NYT*, December 13, 2018.

73. Peter Finn, ed., *The Mueller Report* (New York: Scribner, 2019), pp. 124–231. (Hereafter, *Mueller Report*.) See also Karen Yourish and Larry Buchanan, "Trump and His Associates Had More than 100 Contacts with Russians Before the Inauguration," *NYT*, January 26, 2019; Sharon LaFraniere, "Prodded by Putin, Russians Sought Back Channels to Trump through the Business World," *NYT*, April 20, 2019.

74. Prior to Trump's inauguration, Kushner, along with Flynn, met with the Russian ambassador to set up a secret back channel to Moscow within the Russian embassy in Washington. Kushner also had contact with the head of the state-owned Vnesheconombank (VEB), which had ties to Wall Street investors and New York banks; it also had convicted spies among its employees. Ben Protess, Andrew F. Kramer, and Mike McIntire, "Bank at Center of U.S. Inquiry Projects Russian 'Soft Power,'" *NYT*, June 4, 2017. The Obama administration sanctioned VEB in 2016, and the banker with whom Kushner spoke had close ties to Putin and a past history with Russian intelligence.

75. Rosalind S. Helderman and Tom Burger, "Coincidence or Coordination?," *WaPo*, December 9, 2018.

76. When Putin announced that Russia would not retaliate, Trump tweeted, "Great move on delay (by V. Putin)." *Mueller Report*, pp. 228–30.

77. *Mueller Report*, p. 131.

78. Craig Unger, "Trump's Businesses Are Full of Russian Dirty Money," *WaPo*, March 29, 2019. As Unger observes, the arrangement was perfectly legal.

79. As CNN was first to report on December 18, 2018, Trump actually signed an October 2015 letter of intent, which CNN produced, to build the hotel, contrary to his previous insistence otherwise. See also the *Mueller Report*, pp. 128–29, which indicates just how lucrative the hotel project would have been for Trump. On the thirty-year history of Trump's interest in building a hotel in Moscow, see Rosalind S. Helderman and Tom Hamburger, "'We Will Be in Moscow': The Story of Trump's 30-Year Quest to Expand His Brand to Russia," *WaPo*, November 29, 2018. Worth noting is that Michael Cohen was convicted in part for also lying to Congress about the hotel project, claiming Trump stopped work on it in January 2016. He later amended the date to June 2016, but Rudy Giuliani quoted Trump as giving a new timeline of January 2017. See Maggie Haberman and Michael S. Schmidt, "Giuliani Says Talks for Trump Tower in Moscow Lasted through 2016 Election," *NYT*, January 20, 2019. Days later, Giuliani retracted the quote—a typical move of his, probably after being scolded by Trump.

80. As detailed in volume 1 of the *Mueller Report*, the social media campaign was run by the Internet Research Agency based in St. Petersburg, and hacking was under Russian military intelligence: the Main Intelligence Directorate of the General Staff (GRU).

81. Matthew Rosenberg, Adam Goldman, and Michael S. Schmidt, "Obama Administration Rushed to Preserve Intelligence of Russian Election Hacking," *NYT*, March 1, 2017.

82. "I never worked for Russia," Trump said in January 2019 when the FBI probe became known. News of the probe was the result of a lengthy *New York Times* investigation: Adam Goldman, Michael S. Schmidt, and Nicholas Fandos, "F.B.I. Opened Inquiry into Whether Trump Was Secretly Working on Behalf of Russia," *NYT*, January 11, 2019.

83. Shane Harris et al., "Kushner's Overseas Contacts Raise Concerns as Foreign Officials Seek Leverage," *WaPo*, February 27, 2018.

84. The lavish reception given by the Saudis to Trump and Kushner in May 2017, when Trump made his first overseas trip as president, may have set the stage for Crown Prince Mohammed bin Salman's reported view that he had Kushner "in his pocket." Mohamad Bazzi, "The Heart of the US-Saudi Relationship Lies in the Kushner-Prince Friendship," *The Guardian*, March 10, 2019, online ed.

85. *Mueller Report*, p. 340.

86. Once Michael Cohen confessed to having lied about Trump's business contacts with Russia, Trump, put on the defensive, tweeted, "I decide to run for President & continue to run my business—very legal & very cool, talked about it on the campaign trail. Lightly looked at doing a building somewhere in Russia. Put up zero money, zero guarantees and didn't do the project. Witch Hunt!" Philip Rucker and John Wagner, "'Very Legal & Very Cool': Trump Dismisses Criticism of His 2016 Business Project in Russia," *WaPo*, November 30, 2018.

87. *Mueller Report*, pp. 306, 324–39, 359–82. For example, Trump pressured Comey to "let Flynn go" and then fired Comey, and told the White House counsel, Don McGahn, to fire Mueller, which McGahn refused to do more than once.

88. The *New York Times* counted 1,100 times that Trump had publicly denounced the investigation only two years into his presidency. See Mark Mazzetti et al., "Intimidation, Pressure and Humiliation: Inside Trump's Two-Year War on the Investigation Encircling Him," *NYT*, February 19, 2019.

89. Mary McCord, a former head of the National Security Division of the Justice Department, said, "There is no way you could come away from [the Mueller] report without recognizing that there was a high level of interest and encouragement by people associated with the [Trump] campaign in Russia continuing with its interference activities, particularly in the release of emails." Sharon LaFraniere , "Mueller Report Leaves Unanswered Questions about Contacts between Russians and Trump Aides," *NYT*, April 18, 2019.

90. *Mueller Report*, p. 60.

91. "Statement by Former Federal Prosecutors," May 6, 2019, https://medium.com/ @dojalumni/statement-by-former-federal-prosecutors-8ab7691c2aa1. More than 900 individu-

als who served in both Democratic and Republican administrations signed the statement, which reads in part, "Each of us believes that the conduct of President Trump described in Special Counsel Robert Mueller's report would, in the case of any other person not covered by the Office of Legal Counsel policy against indicting a sitting President, result in multiple felony charges for obstruction of justice."

92. *Mueller Report*, p. 264.

93. Katya Tubman, "Trump Flips on Fox News Analyst after He Calls President's Actions 'Criminal,'" *Yahoo News*, April 28, 2019, https://www.aol.com/article/news/2019/04/28/trump-flips-on-fox-news-analyst-after-he-calls-presidents-actions-criminal/23718500.

4. FOREIGN POLICY BY IMPROVISATION

1. Luke Baker, "With Trump Sitting Nearby, Macron Calls Nationalism a Betrayal," Reuters, November 11, 2018, https://www.reuters.com/article/us-ww1-centenary-macron-nationalism/with-trump-sitting-nearby-macron-calls-nationalism-a-betrayal-idUSKCN1NG0IH.

2. Quoted in Quint Forgey, "Trump: 'I'm a Nationalist,'" *Politico*, October 22, 2018, https://www.politico.com/story/2018/10/22/trump-nationalist-926745.

3. H. R. McMaster and Gary D. Cohn, "America First Doesn't Mean America Alone," *Wall Street Journal*, May 30, 2017.

4. Donald Trump, "Remarks by President Trump to the 73rd Session of the United Nations General Assembly, New York," September 25, 2018, https://www.whitehouse.gov/briefings-statements/remarks-president-trump-73rd-session-united-nations-general-assembly-new-york-ny.

5. Aaron Blake, "Rex Tillerson on Trump: 'Undisciplined, Doesn't Like to Read' and Tries to Do Illegal Things," *WaPo*, December 7, 2018.

6. At CNN town hall, March 29, 2016, quoted in Glenn Kessler, "Trump's Claim That the U.S. Pays the 'Lion's Share' for NATO," *WaPo*, March 30, 2016.

7. New York Times Editorial Board, "Transcript: Donald Trump Expounds on His Foreign Policy Views," *NYT*, March 26, 2016.

8. John Swaine and Julian Borger, "Trump Set to Benefit as Qatar Buys $6.5m Apartment in New York Tower," *The Guardian*, May 4, 2018; Gardiner Harris and Mark Landler, "Qatari Charm Offensive Appears to Have Paid Off, U.S. Officials Say," *NYT*, April 9, 2018; Julie Bykowicz, "The New Lobbying: Qatar Targeted 250 Trump 'Influencers' to Change U.S. Policy," *Wall Street Journal*, August 25, 2018.

9. Frum, *Trumpocracy*, pp. 148–58.

10. Richard Falk, "Wider Consequences of U.S. Withdrawal from the UN Human Rights Council," *Global Justice in the 21st Century* (blog), June 21, 2018, https://richardfalk.wordpress.com/2018/07/07/wider-consequences-of-u-s-withdrawal-from-the-un-human-rights-council. On foreign aid, Trump twice (in 2018 and 2019) proposed eliminating most of it, about $4 billion in the latter year. But he withdrew the idea when it aroused a great deal of opposition, even in the State Department.

11. The reality is that these breaks cost taxpayers and tax-dependent organizations, such as public schools, a great deal of money, since the promise of jobs is rarely met and the actual cost per employee vastly exceeds the subsidy. See Robert Reich, "Almost 80% of US Workers Live from Paycheck to Paycheck. Here's Why," *The Guardian*, July 29, 2018.

12. Michael J. Mazarr, "The Real History of the Liberal Order: Neither Myth nor Accident," *Foreign Affairs*, August 7, 2018, https://www.foreignaffairs.com/articles/2018-08-07/real-history-liberal-order?cid=nlc-fa_twofa-20180809; Robert Kagan, "Trump's America Does Not Care," *WaPo*, June 14, 2018.

13. Christopher Layne and Benjamin Schwarz, "American Hegemony—Without an Enemy," *Foreign Policy*, no. 92 (Fall 1993), pp. 1–8.

14. Michael J. Mazarr, "Summary of the Building a Sustainable International Order Project," RAND Corporation, 2018, https://www.rand.org/pubs/research_reports/RR2397.html.

15. Regarding international law, when the International Criminal Court, of which the United States is not a member, considered trying US soldiers for war crimes committed in Afghanistan, Trump threatened sanctions against the judges. John Bolton, in his first speech as national security adviser, said, "The United States will use any means necessary to protect our citizens and those of our allies from unjust prosecution by this illegitimate court." Steve Holland, "Trump Administration Takes Aim at International Criminal Court, PLO," Reuters, September 9, 2018, https://www.reuters.com/article/us-usa-trump-icc/trump-administration-to-take-tough-stance-against-international-criminal-court-idUSKCN1LQ076. Trump also lifted restrictions on the US military's use of land mines, which are almost universally banned in keeping with the 1997 Ottawa Treaty. Ben Doherty, "Human Rights Groups Call on Scott Morrison to Confront Trump over Landmines," CNN, February 15, 2020.

16. Michelle Ye Hee Lee and John Wagner, "'A Total Joke': Trump Lashes Out at Koch Brothers," *WaPo*, July 31, 2018.

17. Robert Kraychik, "Japan CPAC: In Searing Defense of 'Trump Miracle,' Bannon Calls Out Chinese Regime," *Breitbart News*, December 16, 2017, https://www.breitbart.com/radio/2017/12/16/bannon-in-tokyo-america-and-japan-enter-the-valley-of-decision.

18. In 2019 Bannon resuscitated the Ronald Reagan–era Committee on the Present Danger, which in the 1980s had aimed at the Soviet threat. Now it was China, at a time when even many liberals had hopped on the anti-China bandwagon. See Ana Swanson, "A New Red Scare Is Reshaping Washington," *NYT*, July 20, 2019.

19. Nate Cohn and Alicia Parlapiano, "How Broad, and How Happy, Is the Trump Coalition?," *NYT*, August 9, 2018. The authors point out, however, that 40 percent of white Trump supporters held college degrees, and nearly as many women as men voted for him in 2016.

20. Frum, *Trumpocracy*, p. xii.

21. "I think that's their [the Trump administration's] kind of governing," said retiring Republican senator Bob Corker of Tennessee. "I think that's how they think they stay in power, is to divide." Ashley Parker, Seung Min Kim, and Robert Costa, "'I'm Not Going There': As Trump Hurls Racial Invective, Most Republicans Stay Silent," *WaPo*, August 18, 2018.

22. David Brooks, "Morality and Michael Cohen," *NYT*, February 28, 2019.

23. Thomas L. Friedman, "A President with No Shame and a Party with No Guts," *NYT*, July 18, 2018.

24. Senator John Thune, Republican of South Dakota, quoted by Parker, Kim, and Costa, "'I'm Not Going There.'"

25. Woodward, *Fear*, p. 265.

26. Julian E. Barnes, Eric Schmitt, and Katie Benner, "Trump Doubles Down on Russia," *NYT*, July 20, 2018.

27. Caroline Kelly and Nikki Carvajal, "Trump Is Disputing Kelly Said 'Don't Hire a Yes-Man' or 'You Will Be Impeached,'" CNN, October 26, 2019.

28. Among these advisers were Roger Stone and Jerome Corsi, both of whom became involved in the investigation of WikiLeaks' publication of e-mails hacked by the Russians. Jeffrey Toobin, "Roger Stone's and Jerome Corsi's Time in the Barrel," *The New Yorker*, February 18, 2019, https://www.newyorker.com/magazine/2019/02/18/roger-stones-and-jerome-corsis-time-in-the-barrel.

29. Jim Acosta, "Mulvaney Slams 'Deep State' of Government Employees Undermining Trump," CNN, February 21, 2020.

30. Frum, *Trumpocracy*, pp. 162–63. Stephen Miller, Trump's chief adviser on immigration, used the deep-state myth to try to debunk the whistleblower who reported on Trump's Ukraine cover-up. Miller said the whistleblower was a "deep-state operative," another in the group of "unelected bureaucrats who think they need to take down this president." Sheryl Gay Stolberg, Maggie Haberman, and Peter Baker, "Trump Was Repeatedly Warned That Ukraine Conspiracy Theory Was 'Completely Debunked,'" *NYT*, September 29, 2019.

31. Chuck Park, "I Can No Longer Justify Being Part of Trump's 'Complacent State,' So I'm Resigning," *WaPo*, August 8, 2019. Park wrote, "The Complacent State sighs when the president blocks travel by Muslim immigrants; shakes its head when he defends Saudi Crown Prince Mohammed bin Salman; averts its gaze from images of children in detention camps. Then it complies with orders."

32. Comey, *A Higher Loyalty*, p. 221.

33. Greg Miller, "Trump Has Concealed Details of His Face-to-Face Encounters with Putin from Senior Officials in Administration," *WaPo*, January 13, 2019. According to the article, the Helsinki summit was one of five occasions where the record of Trump-Putin talks was kept from other US officials.

34. Comey, *A Higher Loyalty*, p. 237.

35. A particularly egregious example occurred in February 2020 when the Office of the Director of National Intelligence (DNI)'s Joseph Maguire briefed members of the House Intelligence Committee on the ongoing Russian election threat, specifying that the committee's conclusion was that Russia's intention was to get Trump reelected. Trump was reportedly furious: Democrats would use the finding against him. It could hardly be coincidental that days later, Maguire was replaced as acting DNI with a Trump loyalist, US ambassador to Germany Richard Grenell, as was Maguire's chief deputy. Both replacements had no experience in intelligence.

36. Philip Bump, "Trump Relies on Acting Cabinet Officials More Than Most Presidents," *WaPo*, April 8, 2019; Barbara Starr, "19 Senior Pentagon Roles Are Currently Filled by Temporary Officials or Vacant," CNN, July 8, 2019.

37. His initial pardons included lawbreakers such as Sheriff Joe Arpaio, the racial profiler in Arizona, and the far-right writer Dinesh D'Souza. Then, in 2020, Trump pardoned or commuted the sentences of eleven individuals convicted of corruption, including the former Democratic governor of Illinois Rod Blagojevich. Trump actually promised a *future* pardon to anyone in his administration who broke the law in order to hasten construction of the wall with Mexico. Greg Sargent, "Trump Is 'Joking' about Pardons? How Is This a Defense?," *WaPo*, August 29, 2019.

38. Trump tweeted on October 7, 2019, "If Turkey does anything that I, in my great and unmatched wisdom, consider to be off limits, I will totally destroy and obliterate the Economy of Turkey."

39. Anne Gearan, Josh Dawsey, and John Hudson, "'They Screwed This Whole Thing Up': Inside the Attempt to Derail Trump's Erratic Syria Policy," *WaPo*, January 13, 2019; John Hudson and Kareem Fahim, "Trump's Vow to 'Devastate' Turkey Rattles Negotiations over Syria Withdrawal," *WaPo*, January 14, 2019. Trump's reversal on Turkey came when Erdogan decided to buy an air defense missile system from Russia rather than from the United States. While the Pentagon and State Department threatened sanctions, Trump sympathized with Erdogan. The sanctions were never imposed, preserving Trump's supposed friendship with Erdogan, but a pending US sale of fighter jets to Turkey was canceled. Amie Ferris-Rotman and Kareem Fahim, "Russia Readies S-400 Missiles for Turkey amid Warnings of U.S. Sanctions on NATO Ally," *WaPo*, July 5, 2019; Katie Rogers and Thomas Gibbons-Neff, "U.S. Punishes Turkey by Canceling Sale of Jets," *NYT*, July 17, 2019. On the decision to withdraw from northeastern Syria, see Karen DeYoung, Missy Ryan, Kareem Fahim, and Karen Dadouch, "Republicans Assail Trump's Decision to Pull Troops from Northern Syria as Turkey Readies Offensive," *WaPo*, October 8, 2019.

40. That weak posture showed up when Trump invited Erdogan to visit Washington in November 2019. Erdogan used the occasion to call Kurdish forces "terrorists" and refused to back down on Turkey's purchase of Russian missiles.

41. Anonymous, "I Am Part of the Resistance Inside the Trump Administration," *NYT*, September 5, 2018.

42. Amazingly, the author or authors of the op-ed were never identified, at least not publicly, and the matter disappeared from public attention within a few weeks.

43. Stephen Collinson, "Trump's Impeachment Defense Has Come to This," CNN, October 24, 2019.

44. David Leonhardt and Ian Prasad Philbrick, "Donald Trump's Racism: The Definitive List," *NYT*, January 15, 2018; Emily Jane Fox, "Michael Cohen Says Trump Repeatedly Used Racist Language before His Presidency," *Vanity Fair*, November 2, 2018, https://www.vanityfair.com/news/2018/11/michael-cohen-trump-racist-language.

45. Chris Cillizza, "The 35 Most Mind-Blowing Lines from Donald Trump's Las Vegas Speech," CNN, September 21, 2018, https://www.cnn.com/2018/09/21/politics/donald-trump-las-vegas-speech/index.html.

46. "Trump Tells US Jews That Netanyahu Is 'Your Prime Minister,'" *Times of Israel*, April 7, 2019, https://www.timesofisrael.com/trump-tells-us-jews-that-netanyahu-is-your-prime-minister/amp.

47. Felicia Sonmez and Mike DeBonis, "Trump Tells Four Liberal Congresswomen to 'Go Back' to Their Countries, Prompting Pelosi to Defend Them," *WaPo*, July 14, 2019.

48. Woodward, *Fear*, p. 15. The other two themes were bringing manufacturing jobs back home and withdrawing from "pointless foreign wars."

49. Tom Kertscher, "Donald Trump's Racial Comments about Hispanic Judge in Trump University Case," *Politifact*, June 8, 2016, https://www.politifact.com/wisconsin/article/2016/jun/08/donald-trumps-racial-comments-about-judge-trump-un.

50. See the account in Woodward, *Fear*, pp. 238–44.

51. Jack Dawsey, "Trump Derides Protections for Immigrants from 'Shithole' Countries," *WaPo*, January 12, 2018.

52. Joe Palazzolo et al., "Donald Trump Played Central Role in Hush Payoffs to Stormy Daniels and Karen McDougal," *Wall Street Journal*, November 9, 2018,

53. Charles M. Blow, "President Dumb and Dumber," *NYT*, August 5, 2018. One of Trump's favorite targets was Senator Elizabeth Warren, whom Trump called "Pocahontas" numerous times, arguing she had falsely claimed Native American heritage. Warren had DNA tests run that proved her claim. Instead of apologizing, Trump repeated the racist word multiple times. Trump also attacked Congresswoman Maxine Waters, whom he called an "extraordinarily low IQ person," and Congresswoman Ilhan Omar, one of two Muslim women in the House, whom Trump viciously tried to link to being unconcerned about the 9/11 attack. During and immediately after a news conference in November 2018, Trump called three different CNN black reporters "loser," "racist," someone who "asks stupid questions." Their questions were legitimate inquiries regarding the Mueller investigation. A final example: Trump called Carmen Yulín Cruz, the mayor of San Juan, Puerto Rico, "crazed and incompetent" for criticizing his disaster relief effort.

54. Arwa Mahdawi, "Trump's N-Word Tape Is Going to Be Pussygate All Over Again," *The Guardian*, August 11, 2018, online ed.

55. Polls showed that white, working-class people who voted for Trump regarded discrimination against them as equal to or greater than discrimination against blacks or any other group. Philip Bump, "How to Understand Trump's Condemnation of 'All Types of Racism,'" *WaPo*, August 12, 2018.

56. Fox, "Michael Cohen Says Trump Repeatedly Used Racist Language before His Presidency."

57. A *New York Times* investigation of Trump's tax returns for 1985–1994 found that he was deeply in debt, having accumulated business losses totaling $1.17 billion. Susanne Craig and Russ Buettner, "5 Takeaways from 10 Years of Trump Tax Figures," *NYT*, May 7, 2019.

58. "Testimony of Michael D. Cohen," Committee on Oversight and Reform, U.S. House of Representatives," February 27, 2019.

59. Again, see David Cay Johnston's *The Making of Donald Trump*, for these and many other examples.

60. Maggie Haberman et al., "Trump Ordered Officials to Give Jared Kushner a Security Clearance," CNN, March 6, 2019.

61. Behind the scenes, Trump, through an intermediary, may have offered WikiLeaks' founder, Julian Assange, a pardon in return for covering up Russia's role in the hacking of the Democratic National Committee's e-mails. The claim was made by Assange's lawyer during an extradition hearing in London. See Nico Hines, "Trump Offered Assange Pardon if He Covered Up Russian Hack," *Daily Beast*, February 19, 2020, https://www.thedailybeast.com/trump-offered-assange-pardon-if-he-covered-up-russian-hack-court-hears.

62. E. J. Dionne, Jr., "Trump Lies. And Lies. And Lies," *WaPo*, July 25, 2018.

63. Donald Trump, "Remarks by President Trump at the Veterans of Foreign Wars of the United States National Convention, Kansas City, MO," July 24, 2018, https://www.whitehouse.

gov/briefings-statements/remarks-president-trump-veterans-foreign-wars-united-states-national-convention-kansas-city-mo.

64. Karen DeYoung and Josh Dawsey, "White House Drafts More Clearance Cancellations Demanded by Trump," *WaPo*, August 18, 2018.

65. Aliza Nadi and Ken Dilanian, "In Closed-Door Meeting, Trump Told Christian Leaders He Got Rid of a Law. He Didn't," NBC News, August 28, 2018, https://www.nbcnews.com/politics/elections/trump-told-christian-leaders-he-got-rid-law-he-didn-n904471.

66. Shawn Boburg and Spencer S. Hsu, "Ex-Congressional IT Staffer Reaches Plea Deal That Debunks Conspiracy Theories," *WaPo*, July 3, 2018.

67. Salvador Rizzo, "Trump Falsely Claims Obama Gave Citizenship to 2,500 Iranians during Nuclear Deal Talks," *WaPo*, July 4, 2018.

68. Lewandowski said, "I have no obligation to be honest with the media because they're just as dishonest as anyone else." Paul Farhi, "Corey Lewandowski Tells the Truth (Gasp!) about Lying to the News Media," *WaPo*, September 18, 2019.

69. Beck Dorey-Stein, "I Was a White House Stenographer. Trump Wasn't a Fan," *NYT*, July 17, 2018.

70. Hannity even stood side by side with Trump during a few campaign rallies in 2018. Fox News was forced to issue a tepid criticism of such conduct.

71. Tom Kludt, "Frenemies with Benefits: A Brief History of the Trump-Murdoch Relationship," CNN, January 17, 2018.

72. For instance, Trump's communications director (Bill Shine) was a former senior Fox executive (who failed to act on sexual misconduct cases while there), his second United Nations ambassador (Heather Nauert) was a Fox News pundit, John Bolton appeared frequently on Fox, and Sarah Huckabee Sanders joined Fox News after leaving the White House as press secretary.

73. David Smith, "Fox News Reportedly Killed Stormy Daniels Story to Help Trump Win," *The Guardian*, March 4, 2019. On the rare occasion when Fox reported adversely on Trump, he responded as though a conspiracy was at work at the network. For example, when a mid-2019 Fox poll found, in agreement with other polls, that Trump was trailing all the Democratic candidates for president, Trump said, "There something going on at Fox, I'll tell you right now. And I don't like it." Chris Cillizza, "Donald Trump's Latest Conspiracy Theory Target? Fox News," CNN, August 19, 2019. The same thing happened in 2020 as Fox News joined with all other polls in finding Trump trailing Joe Biden.

74. Jane Mayer, "Trump TV," *The New Yorker*, March 11, 2019, pp. 40–53; David Roth, "The Man Who Was Upset: Making Sense of Donald Trump's Petulant Reign," *The New Republic*, June 12, 2019, https://newrepublic.com/article/154100/making-sense-donald-trump-petulant-presidency.

75. Paul Farhi and John Wagner, "'Fox Isn't Working for Us Anymore,' Tweets Trump in Another Blast at the Network," *WaPo*, August 28, 2019.

76. Julian Sanchez, "Trump Could Get His Intel from the Government. Instead He Gets It from Fox News," *WaPo*, July 20, 2018.

77. This took place on August 24, 2018. QAnon promotes deep-state conspiracies involving (for example) Hillary Clinton, John McCain, and 9/11, and claims to have Trump's "understanding."

78. The Christchurch Call, signed by eighteen governments, was made following a massacre in New Zealand by a right-wing terrorist who used social media to advertise his rampage. The purpose of the Call was to press Facebook, Google, and other social media to prevent posting of hate messages, but Trump used it to decry limitations on speech.

79. Trump's support of violence against his detractors came out during his campaign and, in one instance of roughing up a protester, resulted in a jury trial of his security guards. Asked in an interview if he was concerned that constant references to "enemy of the people" might lead to assaults on reporters, Trump said, "It's my only form of fighting back. I wouldn't be here if I didn't do that." Jonathan Swan and Jim VandeHei, "Exclusive: Trump Says His Supporters Demand Red-Hot Rhetoric," *Axios*, November 1, 2018, https://www.axios.com/trump-axios-hbo-media-enemy-of-the-people-441ae349-3670-4f7d-b5d5-04d339a15f68.html.

80. Trump tweeted on October 25, "It [the anger] has gotten so bad and hateful . . . Mainstream Media must clean up its act, FAST!" When his insistence that the media was really responsible for the murder of eleven Jews at a synagogue in Pittsburgh led to criticism of Trump's insensitivity, Trump and some of his staff doubled down with further attacks on "the enemy of the people."

81. See the *Axios* interview cited above in note 79: "If they would write accurately about me, I would be the *nicest* president you've ever seen. It's much easier for me to be *nice* than it is for me to be the way I have to be." Swan and VandeHei, "Exclusive: Trump Says His Supporters Demand Red-Hot Rhetoric."

82. Interview with the *Houston Chronicle*, quoted in Aaron Blake, "Rex Tillerson on Trump: 'Undisciplined, Doesn't Like to Read' and Tries to Do Illegal Things," *WaPo*, December 7, 2018.

83. "Trump: 'We're Bucking a Court System That Never Rules for Us,'" *Politico* video, April 9, 2019, https://www.politico.com/video/2019/04/09/trump-immigration-cours-lawsuits-067968.

84. Max Boot, "This Nation Is at the Mercy of a Criminal Administration," *WaPo*, May 3, 2019.

85. Thomas B. Edsall, "Will Trump Ever Leave the White House?," *NYT*, October 2, 2019.

86. John Wagner and Deanna Paul, "Trump Asks Lawyers if Census Can Be Delayed," *WaPo*, June 27, 2019. This article also reported that the Supreme Court had ruled against the administration in that case, leading Trump to call the ruling "totally ridiculous."

87. Kevin Breuninger, "Trump Says Powell and the Fed 'Fail Again'—'No Guts, No Sense, No Vision,'" CNBC, September 18, 2019.

88. Michael S. Schmidt and Maggie Haberman, "Trump Wanted to Order Justice Dept. to Prosecute Comey and Clinton," *NYT*, November 20, 2018.

89. See, for example, Murray Waas, "The Flynn Tapes: A New Tell," *New York Review of Books*, August 29, 2018, https://www.nybooks.com/daily/2018/08/29/the-flynn-tapes-a-new-tell. McCabe, who was deputy director of the FBI under Comey and then acting director when Comey was fired, maintains that he, Rosenstein, and others were so alarmed by the Comey firing that they discussed who among the cabinet and vice president could be counted on to invoke the 25th Amendment to oust Trump. Trump fired McCabe too. Matt Zapotosky, "McCabe Says He Told Lawmakers about Opening an Investigation into Trump, and 'No One Objected,'" *WaPo*, February 19, 2019. James Baker, former general counsel at the FBI, testified before a House of Representatives committee in October 2018 that he and colleagues at the FBI as well as people in the Justice Department and the IC were shocked by Comey's firing and worried that it was a clear case of obstruction of justice. Baker also confirmed McCabe's account of the Rosenstein story, adding that two cabinet members were willing to invoke the 25th Amendment. Kyle Cheney, "Newly Released Testimony: Former Top FBI Lawyer Says Agency Concerned Trump Obstructed Justice," *Politico*, April 9, 2019, https://www.politico.com/story/2019/04/09/fbi-doj-trump-obstructed-justice-james-baker-1264092.

90. See the investigative report by Mazzetti et al., "Intimidation, Pressure and Humiliation."

91. Michael A. Cohen, "Mitch McConnell, Republican Nihilist," *New York Review of Books*, February 28, 2019, https://www.nybooks.com/daily/2019/02/25/mitch-mcconnell-republican-nihilist.

92. A group of conservative lawyers tried to arouse support at the annual Federalist Society convention in 2018 for criticizing Trump's undermining of the rule of law. One of them, Peter D. Keisler, acting attorney general in the George W. Bush administration, said, "It's important that people from across the political spectrum speak out about the country's commitment to the rule of law and the core values underlying it—that the criminal justice system should be nonpartisan and independent, that a free press and public criticism should be encouraged and not attacked. These are values that might once have been thought so basic and universally accepted that they didn't need defending, but that's no longer clearly the case." Adam Liptak, "Conservative Lawyers Say Trump Has Undermined the Rule of Law," *NYT*, November 14, 2018.

93. Deanna Paul, "Colin Powell: 'The Republican Party Has Got to Get a Grip on Itself,'" *WaPo*, October 7, 2019.

94. Richard Hofstadter, *The Paranoid Style in American Politics and Other Essays* (New York: Vintage Books, 1967), p. 65.

95. Johnston, *The Making of Donald Trump*; David Cay Johnston, "How to Make Trump's Tax Returns Public," *NYT*, July 5, 2018; Barstow, Craig, and Buettner, "Trump Engaged in Suspect Tax Schemes as He Reaped Riches from His Father."

96. Peter Wehner, "The Full-Spectrum Corruption of Donald Trump," *NYT*, August 25, 2018.

97. See Adam Davidson, "Is Fraud Part of the Trump Organization's Business Model?," *The New Yorker*, October 17, 2018,https://www.newyorker.com/news/swamp-chronicles/is-fraud-part-of-the-trump-organizations-business-model.

98. As an example, immediately after Trump's election, lobbyists for the Saudi government rented around 500 rooms for groups of American veterans in all-expenses-paid stays at the Trump International Hotel in downtown Washington, DC. The apparent aim was to get veterans to lobby on behalf of the Saudis' interest in avoiding lawsuits stemming from US legislation that would give families of 9/11 attack victims the right to sue the Saudi government. David A. Fahrenthold and Jonathan O'Connell, "Saudi-Funded Lobbyist Paid for 500 Rooms at Trump's Hotel after 2016 Election," *WaPo*, December 5, 2018.

99. Frum, *Trumpocracy*, p. 49.

100. FBI prosecutors dropped their investigation of the case in July 2019, probably at the direction of Attorney General Barr.

101. Some of these foreign sources operated under multiple names, fake addresses, and an assortment of shell companies. See the investigative report of Jon Swaine, "Trump Inauguration Took Money from Shell Companies Tied to Foreigners," *The Guardian*, March 8, 2019.

102. David Enrich, "A Mar-a-Lago Weekend and an Act of God: Trump's History with Deutsche Bank," *NYT*, March 18, 2019.

103. Jesse Drucker and Emily Flitter, "Jared Kushner Paid No Federal Income Taxes for Years, Documents Suggest," *NYT*, October 13, 2018.

104. Vicky Ward, "Exclusive Photos of Giuliani in Spain Show Lev Parnas Has Lots More to Share," CNN, February 7, 2020.

105. Among those conflicts of interest was Bernhardt's support for raising the Shasta Dam in California to benefit the wealthiest farmers, despite scientific research that consistently showed the adverse environmental impact of the project. Coral Davenport, "The Interior Secretary Wants to Enlarge a Dam. An Old Lobbying Client Would Benefit," *NYT*, September 28, 2019.

106. On Ross, see David Leonhardt, "The Wilbur Ross Debacle," *NYT*, January 25, 2019. Scalia represented a number of major US corporations, such as Walmart and Ford, in labor rights cases. On Chao, see Michael Forsythe et al., "A 'Bridge' to China, and Her Family's Business, in the Trump Cabinet," *NYT*, June 2, 2019. Chao promoted her family's shipping operations in China and failed to divest stock, as promised, in a construction business that benefited from Trump's plans to improve US infrastructure.

107. *Moral* corruption was also characteristic of some of Trump's nominees. Wilbur Ross's attempt to insert a citizenship question in the 2020 census is one example. Prior to taking office and to avoid federal prosecution, Labor Secretary Alexander Acosta cut a secret deal with a billionaire businessman accused of sex trafficking. The deal was judged unconstitutional by a court. Other men considered for seats on the Federal Reserve, such as Herman Cain and Stephen Moore, had to be withdrawn because of their attitudes toward women as well as questions about their competence.

108. Greg Sargent, "New Disclosures about Lewd Trump Video Reveal His Mastery of the GOP," *WaPo*, July 10, 2019.

109. Trump takes pride in seeing foreign groups imitate his cries of "fake news" and often uses speeches to arouse anger toward journalists. But as A. G. Sulzberger, publisher of the *New York Times*, warned Trump in a private meeting, his "inflammatory language is contributing to a rise in threats against journalists and will lead to violence." Mark Landler, "New York Times Publisher and Trump Clash over President's Threats against Journalism," *NYT*, July 29, 2018. When a Montana congressman physically assaulted a *Guardian* reporter who had asked a question about health care, Trump said nothing at the time. But some months later during a rally in Montana, Trump endorsed the assault, saying the congressman was "my guy." Ed

Pilkington, "'He's My Guy': Donald Trump Praises Gianforte for Assault on Guardian Reporter," *The Guardian*, October 19, 2018.

110. In the Philippines, for example, the State Department was silent when Duterte jailed Maria Ressa, a renowned journalist and critic of the regime. Duterte often charged newspapers with publishing "fake news," and once said at a press conference, "Just because you're a journalist, you're not exempted from assassination." Frida Ghitis, "The U.S. Is Silent as the Philippines Arrests a Leading Journalist," *WaPo*, February 13, 2019.

111. Mike Isaac and Kevin Roose, "Disinformation Spreads on WhatsApp Ahead of Brazilian Election," *New York Times*, October 19, 2018.

5. THE COSTS OF INEXPERIENCE

1. Quoted in Edward Luce, "Watch Out for an Even More Erratic Donald Trump Abroad," *Financial Times*, November 8, 2018, https://www.ft.com/content/2948b72c-e305-11e8-a6e5-792428919cee.

2. Philip Rucker and Carol D. Leonnig, *A Very Stable Genius: Donald J. Trump's Testing of America* (New York: Penguin, 2020). That meeting revealed to all those present Trump's lack of knowledge or interest in history and geography—and his disrespect for people in uniform.

3. Trump cited rain as the reason for not visiting a cemetery for US war dead while in Paris for a celebration of the one-hundredth anniversary of the end of World War I, and did not visit Arlington National Cemetery on Veterans' Day 2018 (which, in a rare moment, he said he regretted). On Trump's relations with "failed generals," see Eric Schmitt and Maggie Haberman, "Trump to Allow Months for Troop Withdrawal in Syria, Officials Say," *NYT*, December 31, 2018.

4. Leo Shane III, "Half of Active Duty Service Members Are Unhappy with Trump, New Military Times Poll Shows," *Military Times*, December 17, 2019, https://www.militarytimes.com/news/pentagon-congress/2019/12/17/half-of-active-duty-service-members-are-unhappy-with-trump-new-military-times-poll-shows.

5. Eric Schmitt, "Trump's Criticism of Architect of Bin Laden Raid Draws Fire," *NYT*, November 19, 2018.

6. Caroline Kelly, "Trump Attacks McCrystal after Retired General Called Trump Immoral," CNN, January 2, 2019.

7. Helene Cooper, "Fraying Ties with Trump Put Mattis's Fate in Doubt," *NYT*, September 15, 2018.

8. Dan Lamothe and Anne Gearan, "Mattis Departs as Defense Secretary as the Pentagon Faces Period of Uncertainty," *WaPo*, December 31, 2018.

9. Brian Kilmeade, "John Bolton on Iran & Turkey Sanctions, North Korean Denuclearization & President Trump's Press Conference with Vladimir Putin," Fox News Radio, August 7, 2018,https://radio.foxnews.com/2018/08/07/john-bolton-on-iran-turkey-sanctions-north-korean-denuclearization-president-trumps-press-conference-with-vladimir-putin.

10. Helene Cooper and Julian E. Barnes, "U.S. Official Scrambled behind the Scenes to Shield NATO Deal from Trump," *NYT*, August 9, 2018.

11. And not only Europe. While on a trip to Japan for a G-20 meeting, Trump astounded his hosts by dismissing the importance of the security alliance, saying, "If Japan is attacked, we will fight World War III. But if we're attacked, Japan doesn't have to help us at all. They can watch it on a Sony television."

12. Interviewed by Lesley Stahl in 2018, Trump said, "I mean, what's an ally? We have wonderful relationships with a lot of people. But nobody treats us much worse than the European Union. The European Union was formed in order to take advantage of us on trade, and that's what they've done." (Donald Trump, "President Trump on Christine Blasey Ford, His Relationships with Vladimir Putin and Kim Jong Un and More," interview by Lesley Stahl, *60 Minutes*, October 15, 2018, https://www.cbsnews.com/news/donald-trump-full-interview-60-minutes-transcript-lesley-stahl-2018-10-14.) At the start of 2019 the EU mission in Washington

discovered that the State Department had downgraded it from a state to an international organization without notification—a needless slight.

13. Julian E. Barnes and Helene Cooper, "Trump Discussed Pulling U.S. from NATO, Aides Say Amid New Concerns over Russia," *NYT*, January 14, 2019.

14. Ivan Krastev, "Sorry, NATO, Trump Doesn't Believe in Allies," *NYT*, July 11, 2018.

15. Barnes and Cooper, "Trump Discussed Pulling U.S. from NATO."

16. Tom Newton Dunn, "Trump's Brexit Blast: Donald Trump Told Theresa May How to Do Brexit 'But She Wrecked It'—And Says the US Trade Deal Is Off," *The Sun* (London), July 13, 2018, https://www.thesun.co.uk/news/6766531/trump-may-brexit-us-deal-off.

17. Josh Dawsey and Seung Min Kim, "Trump Told Britain to 'Sue' European Union to Speed Brexit, Theresa May Says," *WaPo*, July 15, 2018.

18. Nord Stream 2 is a $10 billion deal that enables Germany and other Western European countries to obtain Russian natural gas directly, bypassing pipelines to Ukraine, Belarus, and Poland. A longtime concern in Europe and the United States has been that Russia might turn off the gas in a crisis.

19. "A Sedate Dinner, but a Bombshell Interview, for Trump's U.K. Visit," *NYT*, July 12, 2018.

20. Nick Wadhams and Jennifer Jacobs, "Trump Seeks Huge Premium from Allies Hosting U.S. Troops," *Bloomberg*, March 8, 2019, https://www.bloomberg.com/news/articles/2019-03-08/trump-said-to-seek-huge-premium-from-allies-hosting-u-s-troops.

21. See, for example, Angela Merkel's speech to the annual Munich Security Conference in February 2019 in which she said (with Vice President Pence in attendance), "What we see as an overall architecture underpinning our world as we know it is a bit of a puzzle now; if you like, it has collapsed into many tiny parts. We have to think of integrated structures and interdependencies." "Angela Merkel Warns of Global Political Disintegration at Munich Security Conference," DW.com, February 16, 2019, https://www.dw.com/en/angela-merkel-warns-of-global-political-disintegration-at-munich-security-conference/a-47546255.

22. On Russia's destabilizing efforts, see Raphael S. Cohen and Andrew Radin, *Russia's Hostile Measures in Europe: Understanding the Threat* (Santa Monica, CA: RAND Corporation, 2019), https://www.rand.org/pubs/research_reports/RR1793.html. Italy's League (Liga) party apparently secretly worked with Russians close to the Kremlin to receive oil money. Jason Horowitz, "Audio Suggests Secret Plan for Russians to Fund Party of Italy's Salvini," *NYT*, July 10, 2019; Alberto Nardelli et al., "Unmasked: The Russian Men at the Heart of Italy's Russian Oil Scandal," *Buzzfeed News*, September 3, 2019, https://www.buzzfeednews.com/article/albertonardelli/russians-matteo-salvini-metropol-meeting-italy-russia-oil. The Russian subversion unit, part of the GRU, that was also responsible for election hacking in the United States, is reported about by Michael Schwirtz, "Top Secret Russian Unit Seeks to Destabilize Europe, Security Officials Say," *NYT*, October 8, 2019.

23. See Jane Mayer, "New Evidence Emerges of Steve Bannon and Cambridge Analytica's Role in Brexit," *The New Yorker*, November 17, 2018, https://www.newyorker.com/news/news-desk/new-evidence-emerges-of-steve-bannon-and-cambridge-analyticas-role-in-brexit. In November 2019 a British intelligence report on Russian interference in British politics was blocked by the Boris Johnson government ahead of a national election. That report is said to have identified Russian contributions to the Conservative Party and the pro-Brexit campaign. Davis Sabbagh, Peter Walker, and Luke Harding, "No. 10 Blocks Russia EU Referendum Report until after Election," *The Guardian*, November 4, 2019.

24. Tina Nguyen, "Steve Bannon's Populist Media Empire Is Funded with Offshore Cash," *Vanity Fair*, November 7, 2017, https://www.vanityfair.com/news/2017/11/steve-bannon-paradise-papers-offshore-cash/amp.

25. Jason Horowitz, "Matteo Salvini Announces New European Alliance of Far-Right Populists," *NYT*, April 8, 2019.

26. Peter Walker and Paul Lewis, "Nigel Farage Discussed Fronting Far-Right Group Led by Steve Bannon," *The Guardian*, May 22, 2019.

27. Katrin Bennhold, "Chemnitz Protests Show New Strength of Germany's Far Right," *NYT*, August 30, 2018. Two other writers (Thomas Meaney and Saskia Schäfer, "The Right-Wing Rot at the Heart of the German State," *NYT*, October 3, 2018) argue that the far right has

infected the political system to a greater extent than commonly realized: "A constellation of forces is now relearning to cooperate: right-wing street movements, right-wing news outlets, a fully fledged political party and a murky portion of the state bureaucracy." That "portion" is the security services: the federal domestic intelligence service and local police. Attacks on immigrants occur more frequently in the former East Germany, whose economy and political voice lag behind the western half of the country.

28. In Hungary, Viktor Orbán's self-styled "Christian democracy" openly opposes liberal democracy and immigration. He has either taken over or shut down news organizations that criticize him. The European Parliament voted in late 2018 to sanction Hungary over its rejection of immigrants. Trump, on the other hand, welcomed Orbán to Washington on an official visit in May 2019 and said not a word about Orbán's antidemocratic policies. Poland's government mimics Hungary's: polarizing, anti-EU, and anti-immigrant, with the far right dominating civic institutions. The European Court of Justice rejected the Polish government's attempt to remove supreme court judges it disliked. The right-wing government that took over in Italy in 2018 openly admires Viktor Orbán's anti-immigrant stance and, led by Matteo Salvini's League party, has close ties with Vladimir Putin. Lorenzo Tondo, "Matteo Salvini and Viktor Orbán to Form Anti-Migrant Front," *The Guardian*, August 28, 2018.

29. See Christopher R. Browning's important essay, "The Suffocation of Democracy," *New York Review of Books*, October 25, 2018, https://www.nybooks.com/articles/2018/10/25/suffocation-of-democracy, which traces the similarities as well as the differences.

30. See, for example, Ronald Inglehart, "The Age of Insecurity," *Foreign Affairs*, vol. 97, no. 3 (May–June 2018), pp. 20–28; Yascha Mounk and Roberto Stefan Foa, "The End of the Democratic Century," *Foreign Affairs*, vol. 97, no. 3 (May–June 2018), pp. 29–36; Peter Beinart, "The New Authoritarians Are Waging War on Women," *The Atlantic*, January–February 2019, https://www.theatlantic.com/magazine/archive/2019/01/authoritarian-sexism-trump-duterte/576382.

31. The main US organizations are the Alliance Defending Freedom and the American Center for Law and Justice. See Mary Fitzgerald and Claire Provost, "Christian 'Fundamentalists' Pour Millions of 'Dark Money' into Europe, Boosting the Far Right," *Open Democracy*, March 27, 2019, https://www.opendemocracy.net/en/5050/revealed-trump-linked-us-christian-fundamentalists-pour-millions-of-dark-money-into-europe-boosting-the-far-right.

32. William J. Burns, former US ambassador to Russia and, under Obama, Undersecretary of State, lists Putin's grievances over US interference in Russian elections in 2009 and 2012 as a major reason for interfering in the US election. See William J. Burns, "How the U.S.-Russian Relationship Went Bad," *The Atlantic*, April 2019, https://www.theatlantic.com/magazine/archive/2019/04/william-j-burns-putin-russia/583255.

33. See the Council on Foreign Relations study by Robert D. Blackwill and Philip H. Gordon, *Containing Russia: How to Respond to Moscow's Intervention in U.S. Democracy and Growing Geopolitical Challenge*, Council Special Report No. 80 (New York: Council on Foreign Affairs, January 2018); Craig Timberg and Tony Romm, "New Report on Russian Disinformation, Prepared for the Senate, Shows the Operation's Scale and Sweep," *WaPo*, December 17, 2018.

34. Tillerson, McMaster, and Mattis were among them. Blackwill and Gordon, *Containing Russia*, p. 28.

35. This eye-opening information only came to light more than two years later. Shane Harris, Josh Dawsey, and Ellen Nakashima, "Trump Told Russian Officials in 2017 He Wasn't Concerned about Moscow's Interference in Election," *WaPo*, September 28, 2019. See also Harris, Dawsey, and Leonnig, "Former White House Officials Say They Feared Putin Influenced the President's Views on Ukraine and 2016 Campaign."

36. Veronica Stracqualursi, "Reporter Says Trump Called Him after Putin Meeting to Side with Russian Explanations for 2016 DNC Hacks," CNN, January 17, 2019, https://www.cnn.com/2019/01/17/politics/nyt-reporter-trump-putin/index.html.

37. Most conspicuous were Clinton's critical comments on the conduct of Russia's parliamentary elections in December 2011—comments that Putin blamed for protests across the country. Michael Isikoff and David Corn, *Russian Roulette: The Inside Story of Putin's War on*

America and the Election of Donald Trump (New York: Twelve, 2018), pp. 35–36. The incident was the beginning of the end of Obama's effort to "reset" US-Russia relations.

38. "SMA TRADOC White Paper Russian Strategic Intentions," NSI, May 2019, https://nsiteam.com/sma-white-paper-russian-strategic-intentions. The white paper was compiled by twenty-three Russia experts drawn mainly from the US army.

39. By "liberalism" Putin meant openness to immigrants and to diverse gender identities. Lionel Barber, Henry Foy, and Alex Barker, "Vladimir Putin Says Liberalism Has 'Become Obsolete,'" *Financial Times*, June 27, 2019, https://www.ft.com/content/670039ec-98f3-11e9-9573-ee5cbb98ed36.

40. Mark Landler and Julie Hirschfeld Davis, "Trump Opens His Arms to Russia. His Administration Closes Its Fist," *NYT*, July 14, 2018. Indeed, what Trump and Putin discussed in their private two-hour meeting at the summit left the bureaucracy high and dry, unable to answer straightforward questions about what Trump said and what commitments he made, if any. In August 2018, five of the top national security officials in the administration convened a news conference out of the blue to reaffirm their view that Russia had interfered and was continuing to interfere with the US election process. They also stated that the president had "directed" them to deal with the problem, yet once more were at pains to defer on the question of what happened at Helsinki and whether or not the president was really on board.

41. Frum, *Trumpocracy*, p. 172; Mark Landler, "There's Trump's Foreign Policy and Then There's His Administration's," *NYT*, August 3, 2018.

42. In an interview with Tucker Carlson of Fox News, Trump said, "Montenegro is a tiny country with very strong people . . . They're very aggressive people. They may get aggressive, and congratulations, you're in world war three." Montenegro only joined NATO in 2016, and its pro-Western government was the object of an attempted coup by Russia. To a number of observers, Trump's remark was yet another sign of his willingness to put Russian interests ahead of Europe's, and even to encourage Russian destabilization of Montenegro. Helena Smith, "How Trump Destabilised Montenegro with a Few Words," *The Guardian*, July 19, 2018.

43. Thomas P. Bossert, Trump's first Homeland Security secretary, told of how Trump simply refused on numerous occasions to listen to any other version of reality even though the theory of Russian noninterference had "no validity." Stolberg, Haberman, and Baker, "Trump Was Repeatedly Warned."

44. Washington Post Staff, "Transcript of Robert S. Mueller III's Testimony before the House Judiciary Committee, *WaPo*, July 24, 2019.

45. Adam Goldman et al., "Lawmakers Are Warned That Russia Is Meddling to Re-elect Trump," *NYT*, February 20, 2020.

46. Nancy Pelosi, at a press conference on December 5, 2019, during the Trump impeachment inquiry.

47. See Elliott Abrams, "Trump Versus the Government," *Foreign Affairs*, vol. 98, no. 1 (January–February 2019), pp. 129–37.

48. Jennifer Hansler, "Lawmaker Petitions Pompeo on Delayed Russia Sanctions," CNN, September 10, 2019.

49. As a result, the then-secretary of Homeland Security dropped the idea of developing a coordinated strategy to prevent foreign hacking. Eric Schmitt, David E. Sanger, and Maggie Haberman, "In Push for 2020 Election Security, Top Official Was Warned: Don't Tell Trump," *NYT*, April 24, 2019.

50. On the latter, see Anders Åslund, "How the United States Can Combat Russia's Kleptocracy," Atlantic Council, July 2018, https://www.atlanticcouncil.org/in-depth-research-reports/issue-brief/how-the-united-states-can-combat-russia-s-kleptocracy. More robust measures are advocated in Blackwill and Gordon, *Containing Russia*.

51. Blackwill and Gordon, *Containing Russia*, pp. 19–27. Containment would involve countermeasures such as a much wider range of sanctions than previously imposed, strengthening of cybersecurity and information warfare, increased military deployments in Europe, full funding of the European Reassurance Initiative, and expanded NATO capabilities. Trump might also have said and done more to clarify NATO's commitment to defend Ukraine or Montenegro.

52. I document all the "treason" accusations in my blog, Mel Gurtov, "Post #212: Some Dare Call It Treason," *In the Human Interest—Mel Gurtov* (blog), July 19, 2018, https://melgurtov.com/2018/07/19/post-212-some-dare-call-it-treason.

53. Following the summit, Trump initially agreed to consider Putin's proposal that in return for allowing US investigators to interview the twelve indicted Russians, Trump would allow them to interview several American critics of Russian affairs, including the former US ambassador to Moscow, Michael McFaul, a Trump critic. Trump said it was "an incredible offer," but later declined, though the White House thanked Putin for his "sincerity"—*four days* after his press secretary said Trump and his cabinet were meeting to consider it.

54. Aaron Blake, "How Just One Republican Could Punish Trump for His Putin Apostasy—and Why No One Will," *WaPo*, July 18, 2018.

55. Deutsche Bank made large loans—anywhere from $300 million to more than $400 million—to the Trump Organization. It was the one big bank that was willing to give Trump loans when others turned him down because of his poor financial record. VTB, the state-owned Russian bank under US and European sanctions, may have underwritten Deutsche Bank's loans. Deutsche Bank had already been penalized $630 million for laundering $10 billion in rubles; US authorities were investigating whose Russian money that was and whether or not the US dollars that the bank converted were tied to Trump. See David Enrich, *Dark Towers: Deutsche Bank, Donald Trump, and an Epic Tale of Destruction* (New York: HarperCollins, 2020); "Deutsche Bank Soll Trump-Kredite Offenlegen," *Zeit Online*, May 24, 2017, https://www.zeit.de/politik/ausland/2017-05/donald-trump-konten-deutsche-bank-us-demokraten-ueberpruefung; Darren Woon, "Deutsche Bank Whistleblower: Russian State-Owned Bank Underwrote Trump's Loans," *The Intellectualist*, January 3, 2020, https://mavenroundtable.io/theintellectualist/news/deutsche-bank-whistleblower-russian-state-owned-bank-underwrote-trump-s-loans-8aSkypIDCUOWj7AKxwASAA.

56. Isikoff and Corn, *Russian Roulette*, pp. 1–18; Seth Abramson, *Proof of Collusion: How Trump Betrayed America* (New York: Simon & Schuster, 2018). The breakthrough reporting on Trump's hotel project is by Anthony Cormier and Jason Leopold, "Trump Moscow: The Definitive Story of How Trump's Team Worked the Russian Deal during the Campaign," *BuzzFeed News*, May 17, 2018, https://www.buzzfeednews.com/article/anthonycormier/trump-moscow-micheal-cohen-felix-sater-campaign. In November 2018, Michael Cohen, Trump's former lawyer, told a court that he had lied to a Senate committee about conversations with Trump concerning the hotel in Moscow. Trump's involvement in seeking Russian help for the hotel project did not end when his presidential campaign began in 2016; Cohen now said the contacts continued for several months, contrary to Trump's public claim that he had no business involvement with the Russians. Rosalind S. Helderman, Matt Zabotosky, and Devlin Barrett, "Michael Cohen, Trump's Former Lawyer, Pleads Guilty to Lying to Congress about Moscow Project," *WaPo*, November 29, 2018. One Trump associate, Felix Sater, claims he had the idea of giving Putin a $50 million suite in Trump Tower Moscow in order to lure Russian oligarchs to take apartments there at $250 million apiece. Sater coordinated with Michael Cohen on trying to bring the deal to fruition. Anthony Cormier and Jason Leopold, "The Trump Organization Planned to Give Vladimir Putin the $50 Million Penthouse in Trump Tower Moscow," *BuzzFeed News*, November 29, 2018, https://www.buzzfeednews.com/article/anthonycormier/the-trump-organization-planned-to-give-vladimir-putin-the.

57. Natasha Bertrand, "Trump's Top Targets in the Russia Probe Are Experts in Organized Crime," *The Atlantic*, August 30, 2018, https://www.theatlantic.com/politics/archive/2018/08/trumps-top-targets-in-the-russia-probe-are-experts-in-organized-crime/569056. It may hardly be accidental that the members of Mueller's team and the FBI, whose resignation Trump regularly called for, all had in common a background in investigating money laundering and organized crime, especially in Russia. Trump's business interests at home and abroad linked him to Russian mobsters as well as oligarchs—all people ultimately in the service of the Russian state.

58. Jennie Neufeld, "Read the Full Transcript of the Helsinki Press Conference," *Vox*, July 17, 2018, https://www.vox.com/2018/7/16/17576956/transcript-putin-trump-russia-helsinki-press-conference.

59. John Hudson and Elise Viebeck, "Testimony from Career Diplomats to Outline Trump's Dark View of Ukraine," *WaPo*, October 30, 2019. The incident involved an attack on three Ukrainian Navy boats in the Kerch Strait entry to the Azov Sea by Russian border guard vessels, with injuries to some Ukrainian sailors and seizure of the boats. It was the first open attack by Russia on Ukraine after years of barely disguised intervention and other pressure tactics. Russia argued that the Ukrainian vessels were in Russian waters, but the area in question is regulated by a Russia-Ukraine treaty that stipulates these are internal waters for both countries. A possible motive for Russia was to undermine Ukraine's presidential elections in April 2019, in which Russia's preferred candidate lost in a landslide. See Anders Åslund, "In Ukraine It's No Longer about Little Green Men," *Politico*, November 27, 2018, https://www.politico.eu/article/in-ukraine-its-no-longer-about-little-green-men-russia-agression-azov-sea-kerch-strait.

60. This section updates two of my articles: "The China Conundrum," *China-US Focus*, September 26, 2018, https://www.chinausfocus.com/foreign-policy/the-china-conundrum, and Gurtov and Mark Selden, "The Dangerous New US Consensus on China and the Future of US-China Relations," *The Asia-Pacific Journal*, vol. 17, no. 5 (July 21, 2019), https://apjjf.org/2019/15/Gurtov-Selden.html.

61. "The Situation Room with Wolf Blitzer: Donald Trump on China, 'These Are Not Our Friends. These Are Our Enemies,'" *CNN Press Room* (blog), January 20, 2011, http://cnnpressroom.blogs.cnn.com/2011/01/20/the-situation-room-with-wolf-blitzer-donald-trump-on-china-these-are-not-our-friends-these-are-our-enemies.

62. See David Nakamura, "After Détente with North Korea, Trump Increasingly Takes Aim at a New Foe—China," *WaPo*, August 18, 2018.

63. Anna Swanson, Jim Tankersley, and Alan Rappeport, "Trump Blasts Fed, China and Europe for Putting U.S. Economy at a Disadvantage," *NYT*, July 20, 2018.

64. David Lynch and Amanda Erickson, "China Declares New Tariffs on $16 Billion Worth of US Products," *The Star* (Toronto), August 8, 2018.

65. Trump, "Remarks by President Trump to the 73rd Session of the United Nations General Assembly." The only evidence Trump offered for the accusation of Chinese interference in elections was a pullout pro-China ad placed by a state-run Chinese newspaper in an Iowa newspaper.

66. On August 23, 2019, Trump tweeted, "We don't need China and, frankly, would be far better off without them. The vast amounts of money made and stolen by China from the United States, year after year, for decades, will and must STOP." He "ordered" US companies to stop investing in China.

67. Anna Fifield, "After Latest Threats, China Sees Trump as a Marvel Villain Out to Destroy Them," *WaPo*, May 6, 2019.

68. Xinhua, the official Chinese news agency, said on May 26, 2019, that "behind the United States' trade war against China, it is trying to invade China's economic sovereignty and force China to damage its core interests." http://www.xinhuanet.com/english.

69. Daniella Zessoules, "China Tariff Costs by Congressional District," Center for American Progress, August 29, 2019, https://www.americanprogress.org/issues/economy/news/2019/08/29/473895/china-tariff-costs-congressional-district. Farm bankruptcies, for instance, increased 20 percent in 2019, largely due to the drop in US-China trade.

70. Andrew J. Nathan, "How China Really Sees the Trade War," *Foreign Affairs*, June 27, 2019, https://www.foreignaffairs.com/articles/china/2019-06-27/how-china-really-sees-trade-war.

71. David J. Lynch and Anna Fifield, "White House Offers First Details of Partial Trade Deal with China," *WaPo*, December 13, 2019. With an election coming up, and the farm vote in doubt, Trump abandoned talk of Chinese structural change, such as on subsidies of major industries, and settled for larger Chinese agricultural imports and a pledge not to coerce technology turnover by US companies. In return, though, China got lower US tariffs and Trump's abandonment of additional tariffs that he had threatened to impose in December. Whether or not a "phase two" agreement will ever be negotiated is very uncertain.

72. Donald J. Trump, *National Security Strategy of the United States of America*, December 2017, https://www.whitehouse.gov/wp-content/uploads/2017/12/NSS-Final-12-18-2017-0905-2.pdf.

73. Anton Troianovski, Anna Fifield, and Paul Sonne, "War Games and Business Deals," *WaPo*, September 11, 2018.

74. Joby Warrick and Simon Denyer, "A 'Massive' Spike in Oil Smuggling Has Eased the Economic Pressure on North Korea," *WaPo*, September 20, 2018.

75. See, for example, Stephen Blank, "The North Korean Factor in the Sino-Russian Alliance," in *Joint U.S.-Korea Academic Studies Journal* (2019), http://keia.org/publication/north-korean-factor-sino-russian-alliance.

76. The reparations issue stems from the era of Japanese colonization of Korea (1910–1945), when the Imperial Army used forced labor. Whereas Japan considers the issue resolved by a 1965 treaty, South Korean courts, supported by the government, agree with plaintiffs that they are entitled to reparations from Japanese firms. In 2019 Japan responded by restricting exports to South Korea of certain high-tech products, and South Korea retaliated by severing intelligence sharing with Japan. "Bound in alliance with the United States for so long, diplomats and politicians in both capitals [Seoul and Tokyo] today seem less interested in relying on Washington to keep their differences in check, and the Trump administration has shown little interest in trying to build bridges." Sheila A. Smith, "Seoul and Tokyo: No Longer on the Same Side," Council on Foreign Relations: *Asia Unbound* (blog), July 1, 2019, https://www.cfr.org/blog/seoul-and-tokyo-no-longer-same-side.

77. Gerry Shih, "In Trump's Trade Wars, China's Unexpected Win: More Friends," *WaPo*, September 14, 2018.

78. China's military buildup in the South China Sea conflicts with Philippine claims and has led to conflict on some occasions. Philippines public opinion and the military view China with suspicion, but China's large investments there have won favor with Duterte, whereas US criticism of his human rights record has caused resentment. See Joshua Kurlantzick, "Is Duterte Trying to End the U.S.-Philippines Alliance?," *World Politics Review*, February 21, 2020, https://www.worldpoliticsreview.com/articles/28549/us-philippines-relations-take-a-hit-as-duterte-axes-a-key-military-pact.

79. Statement of Geng Shuang, foreign ministry spokesman, quoted by Megan Specia, "Iran Says It Has Surpassed Critical Enrichment Level in 2015 Deal," *NYT*, July 8, 2019.

80. Iran's foreign minister talked about establishing a "strategic partnership" with China. Beijing evidently is wary of going that far, but it is Iran's principal trade partner and a major investor in its energy and transportation sectors. Alex Vatanka, "China's Great Game in Iran," *Foreign Policy*, September 5, 2019, https://foreignpolicy.com/2019/09/05/chinas-great-game-in-iran.

81. The administration's move was essentially to blacklist Chinese companies, making it unlawful for a US firm to supply them with components without government approval. Ana Swanson, "U.S. Blacklists 25 Chinese Entities over Abuses in Xinjiang," *WaPo*, October 7, 2019.

82. In July 2019, twenty-two countries, including eighteen in Europe, wrote a letter to the UN High Commissioner for Human Rights sharply critical of China's mass detention of Uyghurs. The United States, having withdrawn from that commission, did not join the letter. Nick Cumming-Bruce, "China Rebuked by 22 Nations over Xinjiang Repression," *NYT*, July 10, 2019.

83. In 2019 Trump was reportedly willing to soften criticism of China in return for progress on trade. But in 2020, when Beijing announced it would impose a new national security law on Hong Kong, the administration reacted harshly, deciding to no longer treat Hong Kong as a special trade and travel zone separate from the rest of China.

84. Wang Jisi, "Did America Get China Wrong?," *Foreign Affairs*, vol. 97, no. 4 (July–August 2018), pp. 183–84. On August 12, 2019, Trump tweeted that Hong Kong was a "very tough situation." "I hope it works out for everybody," he wrote, "including China."

85. Trump said in an October 2018 interview that he believed China was as great a problem as Russia when it came to meddling in US elections. "I'm saying Russia [meddled], but I'm

also saying China." Trump, "President Trump on Christine Blasey Ford, His Relationships with Vladimir Putin and Kim Jong Un and More."

86. Mike Pence, "Remarks by Vice President Pence on the Administration's Policy toward China," October 4, 2018, https://www.whitehouse.gov/briefings-statements/remarks-vice-president-pence-administrations-policy-toward-china.

87. Graham Allison, *Destined for War: Can America and China Escape Thucydides's Trap?* (New York: Houghton Mifflin Harcourt, 2017).

88. Zhang Tuosheng, "Developing a New Type of Major Power Relationship with the U.S.," *China-US Focus*, January 4, 2013, https://www.chinausfocus.com/foreign-policy/developing-a-new-type-of-major-power-relationship-between-china-and-the-u-s.

89. Xi Jinping has pledged billions of dollars in loans to countries that have signed up for the BRI, and more than seventy have—mainly for infrastructure projects. But the money may incur obligations beyond repayment—Sri Lanka's and Greece's ceding of port facilities to China is most often mentioned—though more often than not the Chinese portion of debt is small compared with other donors. For a critical view, see Frida Ghitis, "Grumbling Grows from Guyana to Australia Over China's 'Debt Trap Diplomacy,'" *World Politics Review*, November 8, 2018, https://www.worldpoliticsreview.com/articles/26694/grumbling-grows-from-guyana-to-australia-over-china-s-debt-trap-diplomacy. For positive accounts that stress China's contribution to Africa's economic growth and a more leavened view of its loans to developing countries, see Deborah Bräutigam, "U.S. Politicians Get China in Africa All Wrong," *WaPo*, April 12, 2018, and Deborah Bräutigam, "Is China the World's Loan Shark?," *NYT*, April 26, 2019. The Trump administration's response to BRI was a $60 billion program, called the United States International Development Finance Corporation, that provides loans and insurance to companies willing to invest in developing countries. Doubts exist, especially among American business executives, that they can compete with Chinese state companies. See Edward Wong, "Competing against Chinese Loans, U.S. Companies Face Long Odds," *NYT*, January 13, 2019.

90. Evan Osnos, "Fight Fight, Talk Talk," *The New Yorker*, January 13, 2020, pp. 32–45. Some specialists argue otherwise on China's aim—for example, Oriana Skylar Mastro, "The Stealth Superpower: How China Hid Its Global Ambitions," *Foreign Affairs*, vol. 98, no. 1 (January–February 2019), pp. 31–39.

91. See, for example, David Shambaugh, "All Xi, All the Time: Can China's President Live Up to His Own Top Billing?," *Global Asia*, vol. 13, no. 3 (September 2018), pp. 14–19; and Mel Gurtov, "The Coronavirus and China-U.S. Relations," *Foreign Policy In Focus*, March 31, 2020, https://fpif.org/the-coronavirus-and-china-u-s-relations/.

92. Yan Xuetong, "The Age of Uneasy Peace: Chinese Power in a Divided World," *Foreign Affairs*, vol. 98, no. 1 (January–February 2019), pp. 40–46.

93. See the "Open Letter to the President and Congress on China Policy" by five China specialists, representing more than 130 others, in *WaPo*, July 2, 2019.

94. See David Shambaugh, "U.S.-China Decoupling: How Feasible, How Desirable?," *China-US Focus Digest*, vol. 24 (December 2019), pp. 18–22.

95. See, for example, Working Group on Chinese Influence Activities in the United States, *Chinese Influence & American Interests: Promoting Constructive Vigilance* (Stanford, CA: Hoover Institution Press, 2018), https://www.hoover.org/sites/default/files/research/docs/chineseinfluence_americaninterests_fullreport_web.pdf; and Peter Waldman, "As China Anxiety Rises in U.S., Fears of New Red Scare Emerge," *Bloomberg*, December 31, 2019, https://www.bloomberg.com/news/articles/2019-12-31/as-china-anxiety-rises-in-u-s-fears-of-new-red-scare-emerge.

96. Sebastian Mallaby, "Trump Is Rising to the China Challenge in the Worst Way Possible," *WaPo*, September 30, 2018. More than 133,000 Chinese graduate students and 148,000 undergraduates were enrolled in US colleges and universities in 2017–2018, by far the largest contingent of foreign enrollees.

97. China's military expenditures are second only to the United States, but US spending in 2019 (about $684 billion) was more than 3.5 times China's ($181 billion). US spending on military research and development and procurement was also nearly three times China's spending. Lucie Béraud-Sudreau, "Global Defence Spending: The United States Widens the Gap,"

International Institute for Strategic Studies: *Military Balance Blog*, February 14, 2020, https://www.iiss.org/blogs/military-balance/2020/02/global-defence-spending.

98. Kurt Campbell and Ely Ratner, "The China Reckoning," *Foreign Affairs*, vol. 97, no. 1 (March–April 2018), p. 70.

6. THE (LOST) ART OF THE DEAL

1. Evan Osnos, "On the Brink," *The New Yorker*, September 18, 2017, pp. 36–53.

2. Andrei Lankov, "Kim Jong Un Is a Survivor, Not a Madman," *Foreign Policy*, April 26, 2017, http://foreignpolicy.com/2017/04/26/kim-jong-un-is-a-survivor-not-a-madman.

3. Alexandre Y. Mansourov, "Kim Jong Un's Nuclear Doctrine and Strategy: What Everyone Needs to Know," Nautilus Institute: NAPSNet Special Reports, December 16, 2014, https://nautilus.org/napsnet/napsnet-special-reports/kim-jong-uns-nuclear-doctrine-and-strategy-what-everyone-needs-to-know.

4. A State Department spokeswoman, quoted in Zachary Cohen et al., "Trump Advisers Clash Over 'Bloody Nose' Strike on North Korea," CNN, February 1, 2018. Vice President Pence, speaking in Japan, said on February 7, 2018, "We will continue to isolate North Korea until it abandons its nuclear and ballistic missile programs once and for all. . . . We will continue to intensify our maximum pressure campaign until North Korea takes concrete steps toward complete, verifiable, and irreversible denuclearization." Ashley Parker and Anna Fifield, "North Korea to Face Harshest U.S. Sanctions Yet, Pence Vows," *WaPo*, February 7, 2018. Pence used the word "dismantlement" a few days later while attending the Winter Games in Seoul.

5. Dunford stalled for time. Woodward, *Fear*, pp. 99–100.

6. Woodward, *Fear*, p. 302.

7. Woodward, *Fear*, p. 281; see also pp. 282, 300.

8. Andrei Lankov, "The Best Deal Trump Can Hope for from North Korea Is a Flawed One. Here's Why That's Okay," *WaPo*, April 9, 2018.

9. See my *Engaging Adversaries: Peacemaking and Diplomacy in the Human Interest* (Lanham, MD: Rowman & Littlefield, 2018).

10. Suzanne DiMaggio and Joel S. Wit, "How Trump Should Talk to North Korea," *NYT*, November 7, 2017.

11. See United Nations Security Council, "Report of the Panel of Experts Established Pursuant to Resolution 1874 (2009)," S/2019/691, August 30, 2019, https://undocs.org/s/2019/691. On North Korea's evasion of oil sanctions, see a report, based on US military intelligence, by Courtney Kube and Dan De Luce, "Top Secret Report: North Korea Keeps Busting Sanctions, Evading U.S.-Led Sea Patrols," NBC News, December 14, 2018, https://www.nbcnews.com/news/north-korea/top-secret-report-north-korea-keeps-busting-sanctions-evading-u-n947926.

12. In a tweet of July 9, 2018, Trump said, "I have confidence that Kim Jong Un will honor the contract we signed &, even more importantly, our handshake. We agreed to the denuclearization of North Korea. China, on the other hand, may be exerting negative pressure on a deal because of our posture on Chinese Trade-Hope Not!" Susan Heavy, "Trump Suggests China Might Be Interfering in N. Korea Talks," aol.com, July 9, 2018, https://www.aol.com/article/news/2018/07/09/trump-suggests-china-might-be-interfering-in-n-korea-talks/23477924.

13. Joel S. Wit, "You Can Negotiate Anything—Even North Korea," *Foreign Affairs*, April 27, 2016, http://foreignpolicy.com/2016/04/27/north_korea_negotiations_kim_jong_un_agreed_framework.

14. Anne Gearan, "Tillerson Calls for 'Painful' Measures to Punish North Korea," *WaPo*, April 28, 2017; Rex Tillerson and James Mattis, "We're Holding Pyongyang to Account," *Wall Street Journal*, August 13, 2017.

15. Trump said Tillerson was "wasting his time" talking about negotiating with the North Koreans. Peter Baker and David E. Sanger, "Trump Says Tillerson Is 'Wasting His Time' on North Korea," *NYT*, October 1, 2017. See also Mark Landler, "White House Corrects Tillerson on Whether U.S. Will Talk to North Korea," *NYT*, December 13, 2017; Tracy Wilkinson,

"Trump Administration Fans Confusion over Its Stand on Talks with North Korea," *Los Angeles Times*, December 15. 2017.

16. "North Korea has proposed 'relief from military threat and guaranteed safety of the regime,'" according to a member of the ROK Advisory Committee for the Office of National Security. Cho Seong Ryoul, "Accomplishments of Korea's Special-Envoy Diplomacy and Future Tasks," *ROK Angle*, No. 76 (April 6, 2018).

17. Choe Sang-Hun, "Kim Says He'd End North Korea Nuclear Pursuit for U.S. Truce," *NYT*, April 29, 2018.

18. "Joint Statement of President Donald J. Trump of the United States of America and Chairman Kim Jong Un of the Democratic People's Republic of Korea at the Singapore Summit," June 12, 2018, https://www.whitehouse.gov/briefings-statements/joint-statement-president-donald-j-trump-united-states-america-chairman-kim-jong-un-democratic-peoples-republic-korea-singapore-summit.

19. He repeatedly referred to "process" at a June 1, 2018, news conference. See Donald J. Trump, "Remarks by President Trump after Meeting with Vice Chairman Kim Yong Chol of the Democratic People's Republic of Korea," June 1, 2018, https://www.whitehouse.gov/briefings-statements/remarks-president-trump-meeting-vice-chairman-kim-yong-chol-democratic-peoples-republic-korea.

20. As Trump said after the summit broke up, "I think having a fake hearing like that and having it in the middle of this very important summit is really a terrible thing." Edward Wong, "Trump's Talks with Kim Jong-un Collapse over North Korean Sanctions," *NYT*, February 28, 2019.

21. See John Bolton's "The Legal Case for Striking North Korea First," *Wall Street Journal*, February 28, 2018.

22. Lesley Wroughton and David Brunnstrom, "With a Piece of Paper, Trump Called on Kim to Hand Over Nuclear Weapons," Reuters, March 29, 2019, https://www.reuters.com/article/us-northkorea-usa-document-exclusive/exclusive-with-a-piece-of-paper-trump-called-on-kim-to-hand-over-nuclear-weapons-idUSKCN1RA2NR.

23. Carla Freeman and I have written on what a US-DPRK deal might include. See our "Unpacking a US Decision to Engage North Korea: What It Entails and What It Could Achieve," *38 North* Special Report, April 2018, https://www.38north.org/reports/2018/04/cfreemanmgurtov041618. Also see Michael Fuchs, "The North Korea Deal: Why Diplomacy Is Still the Best Option," *Foreign Affairs*, December 21, 2017, https://www.foreignaffairs.com/authors/michael-fuchs, and Lynn Ruston and Richard Johnson, *Building Security through Cooperation: Report of the NTI Working Group on Cooperative Threat Reduction with North Korea*, Nuclear Threat Initiative, 2019, https://media.nti.org/documents/NTI_DPRK2019_RPT_FNL.pdf.

24. David C. Kang, for instance, wrote, "North Korea has imposed a moratorium on missile tests and nuclear tests. It has dismantled entrances to a nuclear test site (at Punggye-ri) and a satellite-launching site (at Sohae). There's evidence of a shutdown of an I.C.B.M.-assembly facility near Pyongyang. It has returned what it says are the remains of 55 United States soldiers killed during the Korean War and has released three American citizens arrested in North Korea as a condition for the summit meeting. Pyongyang has also reduced domestic anti-American propaganda. The United States has canceled one war game." David C. Kang, "Why Should North Korea Give Up Its Nuclear Weapons?," *NYT*, August 22, 2018. Shortly after the Hanoi summit and citing cost rather than tension reduction with North Korea, the Pentagon indicated it would do away with the two annual, large-scale, joint US-ROK military exercises.

25. At a Communist party meeting, Kim emphasized self-reliance on the economy, indicating he was prepared to do without sanctions relief, and he gave the United States a year to "abandon its current calculation and approach us with a new one." Choe Sang-Hun, "Kim Jong-un Says He's Open to Another Trump Meeting, with Conditions," *NYT*, April 12, 2019.

26. Exactly who had been executed or purged was the subject of much speculation. See Ivan Watson and Brad Lendon, "US' Top North Korea Diplomat 'Doesn't Know' if Kim Executed Official over Trump Summit," CNN, May 31, 2019.

27. Text at "Pyongyang Declaration," *Korea Times*, September 10, 2018, https://www.koreatimes.co.kr/www/nation/2018/09/103_255848.html.

28. Choe Sang-Hun, "South Korea Backtracks on Easing Sanctions after Trump Comment," *NYT*, October 11, 2018. On human rights in North Korea, see United Nations General Assembly, "Situation of Human Rights in the Democratic People's Republic of Korea: Report of the Secretary-General," Document A/74/268, August 2, 2019. The UN's special rapporteur for human rights in the DPRK, in a later report, noted continued widespread malnutrition, which he linked to the lack of agreement on denuclearization. United Nations Human Rights, Office of the High Commissioner, "North Korea: UN Expert Calls for Engagement Amid Continuing Rights Violations," October 24, 2019.

29. Mel Gurtov, "Summit Misdirection: Trump's North Korea Ploy to Tackle Iran," *Global Asia*, September 21, 2018, https://globalasia.org/v13no3/focus/summit-misdirection-trumps-north-korea-ploy-to-tackle-iran_mel-gurtov.

30. Nicola Smith, "Trump Praises 'Beautiful' Letter from Kim as He Relaxes Nuclear Weapons Demands," *The Telegraph* (London), September 27, 2018.

31. John Hudson, "Russia Edges into Nuclear Talks Ahead of Kim-Trump Summit," *WaPo*, February 27, 2019.

32. Lena H. Sun, "Report Identifies Another Secret North Korea Missile Site, One of 20," *WaPo*, January 21, 2019. A still-secret, mid-2018 US intelligence finding was that North Korea had hidden nuclear bombs and research facilities that remained operational despite the Trump-Kim summit. Ellen Nakashima and Joby Warrick, "North Korea Working to Conceal Key Aspects of Its Nuclear Program, U.S. Officials Say," *WaPo*, June 30, 2018. Published in late 2018, another report based on satellite observations showed at least thirteen previously undisclosed missile sites in North Korea. Trump dismissed the report as "fake news," saying he had known about the sites and "nothing happening out of the normal." John Wagner and Adam Taylor, "Trump Says 'Nothing New' in Report on Hidden Missile Bases in North Korea," *WaPo*, November 13, 2018. When the Pentagon's 2019 *Worldwide Threat Assessment* stated that North Korea would probably never give up its nuclear weapons, Trump insisted, "North Korea relationship is best it has ever been with U.S. No testing, getting remains, hostages returned. Decent chance of Denuclearization." Harris and Wagner, "In Latest Attack on Intelligence Agencies, Trump Ignores Where They Actually Agree."

33. Kim urged the United States to "abandon its calculation," adding, "We don't like—and we are not interested in—the United States' way of dialogue, in which it tries to unilaterally push through its demands. We don't welcome—and we have no intention of repeating—the kind of summit meeting like the one held in Hanoi." Choe Sang-Hun, "Kim Jong-un Says He's Open to Another Trump Meeting, with Conditions," *NYT*, April 12, 2019.

34. "Some of my people" probably referred to Bolton, and "others" probably to the Japanese, since Trump's tweet came on the first day of a visit to Tokyo where both Bolton and Prime Minister Shinzo Abe condemned the missile tests as violations of the UN Security Council's ban. Trump, agreeing with Kim Jong-un, denied that the missiles tested were ballistic; they were. Annie Karni and Katie Rogers, "Trump Opens Tokyo Visit with a Tweet Sure to Unnerve the Japanese," *NYT*, May 25, 2019; Ashley Parker and Simon Denyer, "Still Angling for a Deal, Trump Backs Kim Jong Un over Biden, Bolton and Japan," *WaPo*, May 27, 2019.

35. An official North Korean statement in November 2019 said, with reference to the resumption of joint US-ROK drills, "We, without being given anything, gave things the U.S. president can brag about but the U.S. side has not yet taken any corresponding step. Now, betrayal is only what we feel from the U.S. side." Simon Denyer, "North Korea Threatens Military Escalation as Clock Ticks on Year-End Deadline," *WaPo*, November 13, 2019. In December a vice foreign minister also spoke of US betrayal and said the US negotiating strategy was "nothing but a foolish trick hatched to keep the DPRK bound to dialogue and use it in favor of the political situation and election in the U.S." Simon Denyer, "North Korea Warns United States of an Unwelcome 'Christmas Gift,'" *WaPo*, December 3, 2019.

36. At the end of 2019 Kim said, with what seemed like resignation, that DPRK aims had not been achieved and therefore that more sacrifice, rather than increased prosperity, lay ahead. "If the US persists in its hostile policy toward the DPRK, there will never be denuclearization on the Korean Peninsula. The scope and depth of bolstering our deterrent will be properly coordinated depending on the US future attitude to the DPRK." Kim did not rule out further talks, but he did promise to unveil a "new strategic weapon." Kim Jong-un, "Report on 5th

Plenary Meeting of 7th C.C. [Central Committee], WPK [Korean Workers Party]," January 1, 2020, https://kcnawatch.org/newstream/1577829999-473709661/report-on-5th-plenary-meet ing-of-7th-c-c-wpk.

37. Aaron Blake, "What Trump Said about Obama and War with Iran—And What It Means Now," *WaPo*, January 3, 2020.

38. On this background, see Adam Entous, "Donald Trump's New World Order," *The New Yorker*, June 18, 2018, https://www.newyorker.com/magazine/2018/06/18/donald-trumps-new-world-order.

39. On the nuclear deal, see Scott Ritter, *Dealbreaker: Donald Trump and the Unmaking of the Iran Nuclear Deal* (Atlanta, GA: Clarity Press, 2018); and Trita Parsi, *Losing an Enemy: Obama, Iran, and the Triumph of Diplomacy* (New Haven, CT: Yale University Press, 2017).

40. When Trump announced the withdrawal, he referenced a presentation on April 30, 2018, by Netanyahu, who attempted to prove Iranians' lying about a nuclear weapon program. Netanyahu in fact presented old information that the International Atomic Energy Agency (IAEA) under the UN already knew and took into account in determining that Iran was in compliance with the nuclear agreement. Ritter, *Dealbreaker*, pp. 273–79. Trump said Israeli intelligence had provided "definitive proof" of an active Iranian nuclear weapon program—which was untrue, as Ritter documents.

41. Gurtov, *Engaging Adversaries*, pp. 46–47.

42. Michael R. Pompeo, "After the Deal: A New Iran Strategy," U.S. Department of State, May 21, 2018, https://www.state.gov/after-the-deal-a-new-iran-strategy.

43. Ritter, *Dealbreaker*, pp. 299–307.

44. Michael R. Pompeo, "Confronting Iran: The Trump Administration's Strategy," *Foreign Affairs*, vol. 97, no. 6 (November–December 2018), pp. 60–70.

45. See, for example, John Bolton's op-ed, "To Stop Iran's Bomb, Bomb Iran," *NYT*, March 26, 2015. In a later article, Bolton reverted to advocating a "full-court [diplomatic] press" on Iran following abrogation of the nuclear agreement. See John R. Bolton, "How to Get Out of the Iran Nuclear Deal," *National Review*, August 28, 2017, https://www.nationalreview.com/2017/08/iran-nuclear-deal-exit-strategy-john-bolton-memo-trump.

46. Patrick Wintour, "US Ready to Drive Iranian Oil Exports to Zero, Says National Security Adviser," *The Guardian*, August 22, 2018. The following month Bolton was even more hawkish: "Let my message today be clear: we are watching, and we will come after you. If you cross us, our allies, or our partners; if you harm our citizens; if you continue to lie, cheat, and deceive, yes, there will indeed be hell to pay." Julian Borger, "John Bolton Warns Iran Not to Cross the US or Allies: 'There Will Be Hell to Pay,'" *The Guardian*, September 25, 2018.

47. Dion Nissenbaum, "White House Sought Options to Strike Iran," *Wall Street Journal*, January 13, 2019. According to this report, nothing is known about exactly who made the request or what came of it. The State Department and Pentagon were said to have been "rattled" by it.

48. In January 2019, after the Director of National Intelligence delivered the *Worldwide Threat Assessment* that disputed Trump's view of Iran's nuclear weapon plans, Trump angrily tweeted, "The Intelligence people seem to be extremely passive and naive when it comes to the dangers of Iran. . . . Be careful of Iran. Perhaps Intelligence should go back to school." Harris and Wagner, "In Latest Attack on Intelligence Agencies, Trump Ignores Where They Actually Agree."

49. Major General Chris Ghika, deputy head of the US-led coalition fighting ISIS, said, "There has been no increased threat from Iranian-backed forces in Iraq or Syria." Anonymously, some US officials agreed. Helene Cooper and Edward Wong, "Skeptical U.S. Allies Resist Trump's New Claims of Threats from Iran," *NYT*, May 14, 2019.

50. Erin Cunningham and Carol Morello, "Iran Vows to 'Break' U.S. Sanctions and Resist 'Psychological Warfare,'" *WaPo*, November 5, 2018. Iran's foreign minister, Javad Zarif, later said, "We are used to pressure and we are used to resisting pressure. Sanctions always hurt and they hurt ordinary people, but sanctions seldom change policy, and that has been the problem with US sanctions all the time. They do not take people back to the negotiating table. In fact, they strengthen the resolve to resist." Patrick Wintour, "Iran Will Thrive Despite US Sanctions, Says Foreign Minister," *The Guardian*, November 19, 2018.

51. Ben Hubbard, "As U.S. Tightens Iran Sanctions, Militant Groups and Political Allies Feel the Pain," *NYT*, March 28, 2019.

52. The SPV will have a bartering system based on credits, thereby disconnecting from the dollar-denominated international banks. Washington mocked the SPV concept, saying it would have minimal impact on its sanctions strategy but would "create still more distance between Europe and America." Patrick Wintour and Saeed Kamali Dehghan, "European 'Clearing House' to Bypass US Sanctions against Iran," *The Guardian*, November 6, 2018; Carol Morello and Anne Gearan, "Pence Urges Europeans to Withdraw from Iran Nuclear Deal, Warns of More Sanctions," *WaPo*, February 14, 2019.

53. Edward Wong and Clifford Krauss, "U.S. to Stop Exempting Major Buys of Iranian Oil from Biting Sanctions," *NYT*, April 22, 2019.

54. John A. Mathews and Mark Selden, "China: The Emergence of the Petroyuan and the Challenge to US Dollar Hegemony," *The Asia-Pacific Journal*, vol. 16, no. 3 (November 10, 2018), https://apjjf.org/2018/22/Mathews.html.

55. China has also been vocal in its support for the Iran nuclear deal, sharply criticizing US "military adventurism" for the attack (discussed later) that killed Iran's top general, Qassim Soleimani. China is also among the top three arms suppliers to Iran; it exported $270 million in arms to Iran between 2008 and 2018. Iran also participated in a naval exercise with China and Russia in December 2019. Helena Lagarda, "China Rhetoric Meets Reality: Beijing Caught Out by the Iran Crisis," *International Institute for Strategic Studies,* no. 6 (July–September 2019), https://www.iiss.org/blogs/research-paper/2020/02/china-security-tracker-n6.

56. David D. Kirkpatrick and Isabel Kershner, "Iran Disparages U.S. Over Sanctions," *NYT*, June 25, 2019.

57. Mark Landler, Maggie Haberman, and Eric Schmitt, "Trump Tells Pentagon Chief He Does Not Want War with Iran," *NYT*, May 16, 2019; John Wagner, "Trump Characterizes Alleged Attacks by Iran on Oil Tankers as 'Very Minor,'" *WaPo*, June 18, 2019.

58. Trump said he canceled the attack because it would not be "proportionate." But by one account, he was mainly persuaded by concern over starting a war with Iran that would ruin his reelection chances. Peter Baker, Maggie Haberman, and Thomas Gibbons-Neff, "Urged to Launch an Attack, Trump Listened to the Skeptics Who Said It Would Be a Mistake," *NYT*, June 21, 2019.

59. Speaking on *Face the Nation* on September 22, 2019, Pompeo said, "We hope the Iranian people, who we think are demanding that their country stop this kind of behavior, act in a way that causes the Iranian regime's behavior to change. That's our mission sense."

60. Steven Simon and Jonathan Stevenson, "Iran: The Case against War," *New York Review of Books*, August 15, 2019,https://www.nybooks.com/articles/2019/08/15/iran-case-against-war.

61. Adel Abdul Mahdi said he was to meet with Soleimani, who was bringing to Baghdad a message in response to a Saudi offer of talks. Other sources doubt the story. Peter Baker et al., "Seven Days in January: How Trump Pushed U.S. and Iran to the Brink of War," *NYT*, January 11, 2020.

62. Trump claimed, without support from his own aides, that Soleimani had targeted four US embassies for attack. Pompeo, pressed for evidence, could only say (on Fox News, January 10, 2020), "There is no doubt that there were a series of imminent attacks being plotted by Qassim Soleimani. We don't know precisely when and we don't know precisely where, but it was real." Defense Secretary Mark Esper said he "didn't see" evidence of a coming attack on US embassies, and merely *assumed* they would be targets. Peter Baker and Thomas Gibbons-Neff, "Esper Says He Saw No Evidence Iran Targeted 4 Embassies, As Story Shifts Again," *NYT*, January 12, 2020. Days later, Trump essentially admitted to lying when he tweeted that "it doesn't really matter" whether or not the threat was imminent "because of his [Soleimani's] horrible past." And the media found that Trump had Soleimani on a hit list several months before using the option—in other words, well before the militia attack that killed a US contract worker.

63. With an impeachment trial hanging over him, moreover, Trump may have been especially anxious in an election year to avoid what would have been a very unpopular war triggered by

an unpopular assassination decision. See Andrew Payne, "Trump Just De-escalated in the Middle East," *WaPo*, January 11, 2020.

64. The House of Representatives passed a war powers resolution to restrain Trump on Iran; it got support from four Republicans and was sent to the Senate in January 2020, where a slightly different bill won support. But Trump was set to veto the bill. Other steps envisioned on Iran were repeal of the 2002 authorization to use military force (AUMF) in the Middle East and a prohibition on use of funds for military action in Iran without congressional approval.

65. See Susan E. Rice, "How Did We Get Ten Minutes from War with Iran?," *NYT*, June 23, 2019.

66. Germany's defense minister said the threat entailed a 25 percent tariff on European autos. Patrick Wintour, "Germany Confirms Trump Made Trade Threat to Europe over Iran Policy," *The Guardian*, January 16, 2020.

67. Parsi, *Losing an Enemy*, pp. 369–73; Gurtov, *Engaging Adversaries*, p. 42.

68. Philip Rucker, Josh Dawsey, and Damian Paletta, "Trump Slams Fed Chair, Questions Climate Change," *WaPo*, November 27, 2018.

69. Woodward, *Fear*, pp. 115, 312–13.

70. Brown University's Costs of War Project (https://watson.brown.edu/costsofwar) provides figures. They include an estimated 147,000 people killed since 2001, including more than 38,000 civilian deaths.

71. The history is fully told by Steve Coll, *Directorate S: The C.I.A. and America's Secret Wars in Afghanistan and Pakistan* (New York: Penguin Press, 2018).

72. Woodward, *Fear*, p. 315.

73. A longtime US ambassador to Afghanistan was among those who criticized the agreement for failing to include the Afghan government at the outset, thus abandoning it to an uncertain fate and exposing Afghani women to renewed oppression. Ryan Crocker, "I Was Ambassador to Afghanistan; This Deal Is a Surrender," *WaPo*, January 29, 2019. From the Taliban's point of view, negotiating with a government it considered illegitimate could only occur after the Americans departed.

74. See Luke Mogelson, "The Afghan Way of Death," *The New Yorker*, October 28, 2019, pp. 32–53; and Peter Baker, Mujib Mashal, and Michael Crowley, "How Trump's Plan to Secretly Meet with the Taliban Came Together, and Fell Apart," *NYT*, September 8, 2019. At this writing early in 2020, US talks with the Taliban have resumed and a violence-reduction agreement was reached. But talks between the Taliban and a deeply divided Afghan government were going nowhere, undermined by the resumption of fighting.

75. Charles Glass, "'Tell Me How This Ends,'" *Harper's*, February 2019, pp. 51–61.

76. Seth Harp, "Is the Trump Administration Pivoting the Fight in Syria toward War with Iran?," *The New Yorker*, November 26, 2018, https://www.newyorker.com/news/dispatch/is-the-trump-administration-pivoting-the-fight-in-syria-toward-a-war-with-iran.

77. Senator Bob Corker, for example, tweeted that there was no "interagency process" at all behind Trump's decision. *The Rachel Maddow Show*, MSNBC News, December 19, 2018. General Joseph Votel, head of the US Central Command, said he was not consulted and "it would not have been my military advice" to withdraw from Syria in view of the strength and influence of ISIS there. Barbara Starr, "Top US General Disagrees with Trump over Syria Troop Pullout," CNN, February 15, 2019.

78. See the eloquent appeal by Kareem Shaheen, "3 Million People with Nowhere to Go," *NYT*, September 8, 2018.

79. Reportedly, Trump decided not to impose sanctions after saying he would, a reversal that caught his UN ambassador, Nikki Haley, who had announced the sanctions, by surprise. Maggie Haberman, "Nikki Haley Resigns as U.S. Ambassador to the United Nations," *NYT*, October 9, 2018.

80. I rely here on Federico Pieraccini, "The Deeper Story behind the Assassination of Soleimani," *Strategic Culture*, January 8, 2020, https://www.strategic-culture.org/news/2020/01/08/the-deeper-story-behind-the-assassination-of-soleimani; and F. William Engdahl, "Unintended Consequences: Did Trump Just Give the Middle East to China and Russia?," *Global Research*, January 15, 2020, https://www.globalresearch.ca/did-trump-just-give-middle-east-china-russia/5700660.

81. Steven Simon, "The Middle East: Trump Blunders In," *New York Review of Books*, February 13, 2020, https://www.nybooks.com/articles/2020/02/13/middle-east-trump-blunders-in.

82. John Hudson and Sudarsan Raghavan, "Pompeo Uses Obama as Foil in Sweeping Middle East Speech," *WaPo*, January 10, 2019.

83. John R. Bolton, "Remarks by National Security Advisor Ambassador John R. Bolton on the Trump Administration's New Africa Strategy," December 13, 2018, https://www.whitehouse.gov/briefings-statements/remarks-national-security-advisor-ambassador-john-r-bolton-trump-administrations-new-africa-strategy.

84. Steven Metz, "Trump Seems to Be Writing Off African Security, but Will It Matter to the U.S.?," *World Politics Review*, September 7, 2018, https://www.worldpoliticsreview.com/articles/25794/trump-seems-to-be-writing-off-african-security-but-will-it-matter-to-the-u-s.

85. As Reuben Brigety writes, when Trump hosted nine African leaders in September 2017, he began by mistakenly referring to "Nambia" and then lauded Africa's business potential by citing "so many friends going to your countries, trying to get rich." Reuben Brigety, "A Post-American Africa," *Foreign Affairs*, August 28, 2018, https://www.foreignaffairs.com/articles/africa/2018-08-28/post-american-africa. Another example is Trump's tweet on the white nationalist cause in South Africa, in which—on the basis of one incorrect report from Fox News—he cited a "large-scale killing of farmers" over land redistribution. After a swift and angry reaction from South Africa's press and government, Trump nominated a designer of expensive handbags as US ambassador to fill a post that had been vacant for two years. Elise Viebeck, "'These Things Matter': Sen. Flake Cautions Trump on South Africa Claims," *WaPo*, August 23, 2018.

86. Nick Tulse and Sean D. Taylor, "Revealed: The U.S. Military's 36 Code-Named Operations in Africa," *Yahoo! News*, April 17, 2019, https://news.yahoo.com/revealed-the-us-militarys-36-codenamed-operations-in-africa-090000841.html. Tunisia was an exception; see Lilia Blaise, Eric Schmitt, and Carlotta Gall, "U.S. and Tunisia Are Fighting Militants Together," *NYT*, March 2, 2019.

87. One writer who investigated Somalia found that US drone strikes against Al Shabab targets tripled in 2018 compared with 2016. The CIA may also have been conducting air strikes separately from AFRICOM, but the administration refused to acknowledge them. Amanda Sperber, "Terror Out of the Blue," *The Nation*, February 25–March 4, 2019, pp. 16–20.

88. Brigety, "A Post-American Africa." Another report notes that Chinese investments between 2014 and 2018 were double those from US companies. Max Bearak, "In Strategic Djibouti, a Microcosm of China's Growing Foothold in Africa," *WaPo*, December 30, 2019.

89. Bearak, "In Strategic Djibouti." The Chinese presence there is huge: Besides the naval base, it includes underwater data transmission lines for Djibouti's neighboring countries, a port, and a railroad. These assets are said to give Chinese banks a potential hold on the equivalent of 70 percent of Djibouti's GNP.

90. Frida Ghitis, "Democracy in Latin America Is in Grave Peril, A Respected Pollster Warns," *World Politics Review*, November 15, 2018, https://www.worldpoliticsreview.com/articles/26762/democracy-in-latin-america-is-in-grave-peril-a-respected-pollster-warns.

91. Contrary to Trump's claim, various US officials actually cited cooperative aid programs with El Salvador as having succeeded in bringing down migration and crime. Kevin Sieff, "U.S. Officials Said Aid to El Salvador Helped Slow Migration," *WaPo*, April 1, 2019. The administration also turned its back on the refugees in immigration cases brought before the Inter-American Commission for Human Rights, just as Cuba, Nicaragua, and Venezuela did. Christopher Sabatini and Jimena Galindo, "How the Trump Administration Joined the Western Hemisphere's Rogue Regimes," *World Politics Review*, January 4, 2019, https://www.worldpoliticsreview.com/articles/27101/how-the-trump-administration-joined-the-western-hemisphere-s-rogue-regimes.

92. "We have many options for Venezuela including a possible military option if necessary," Trump said in public remarks in August 2017. His advisers evidently pressed him not to attack, but Trump persisted, finally abandoning the idea when it became apparent that no one supported him. Julian Borger, "Trump Repeatedly Suggested Venezuela Invasion, Stunning Top Aides—Report," *The Guardian*, July 5, 2018. But that changed once Bolton came aboard.

93. Ernest Londoño and Nicholas Casey, "Trump Administration Discussed Coup Plans with Rebel Venezuelan Officers," *NYT*, September 8, 2018.

94. John R. Bolton, "Remarks by National Security Advisor Ambassador John R. Bolton on the Administration's Policies in Latin America," November 2, 2018, https://www.whitehouse.gov/briefings-statements/remarks-national-security-advisor-ambassador-john-r-bolton-administrations-policies-latin-america.

95. U.S. Department of State, Office of the Spokesperson, "The United States Imposes Sanctions on Venezuelan Individuals and Entities," September 25, 2018, https://www.state.gov/r/pa/prs/ps/2018/09/286190.htm.

96. Trump said he rejected the meeting "because so many really horrible things have been happening in Venezuela." Aaron Blake, "Trump's Thoroughly Confused Super Bowl Interview," *WaPo*, February 4, 2019.

97. Mike Pence, "Venezuela, America Stands with You," *Wall Street Journal*, January 22, 2019; Josh Rogin, "Inside the Trump Administration's Diplomatic Intervention in Venezuela," *WaPo*, January 25, 2019.

98. The report said, "Although stronger economic sanctions could influence the Venezuelan government's behavior, they also could have negative effects and unintended consequences. Analysts are concerned that stronger sanctions could exacerbate Venezuela's difficult humanitarian situation, which has been marked by shortages of food and medicines, increased poverty, and mass migration. Many Venezuelan civil society groups oppose sanctions that could worsen humanitarian conditions." Mark P. Sullivan, "Venezuela: Overview of U.S. Sanctions," *Congressional Research Service*, November 21, 2018, https://fas.org/sgp/crs/row/IF10715.pdf.

99. Human Rights Watch, "Venezuela: Numbers Highlight Health Crisis," November 15, 2018, https://www.hrw.org/news/2018/11/15/venezuela-numbers-highlight-health-crisis; Rachelle Krygier, "After Years of Crisis, Venezuela's Maduro Might Be Ready to Accept Some Help," *WaPo*, December 12, 2018.

100. John Hudson, "Exclusive: In Secret Recording, Pompeo Opens Up about Venezuelan Opposition," *WaPo*, June 5, 2019.

101. The Trump administration imposed additional sanctions on Venezuela in February 2020, this time on the Russian oil company Rosneft, which sells about two-thirds of the country's oil exports.

102. Anatoly Kurmanaev and Isayen Herrera, "Venezuela's Capital Is Booming. Is This the End of the Revolution?," *NYT*, February 1, 2020.

103. William M. LeoGrande, a noted Latin America scholar, reported from a visit, "This unanticipated surge in political mobilization by well-organized constituencies resisting state policy, from private sector regulations to gay marriage, is remarkable. No comparable campaign has been allowed in Cuba since the early 1960s. The government's willingness to not only tolerate these organized challenges but [also] to change policies in response to them indicates a new openness to public debate." William M. LeoGrande, "Sixty Years after the Revolution, Is a 'New Cuba' Emerging?," *World Politics Review*, January 14, 2019, https://www.worldpoliticsreview.com/articles/27173/sixty-years-after-the-revolution-is-a-new-cuba-emerging.

104. Peter Kornbluh, "Is Cuba Next?," *The Nation*, February 25–March 4, 2019, pp. 6–8; and Peter Kornbluh, "Cold War on Cuba," *The Nation*, May 13, 2019, pp. 4–8. Trump reversed US policy of several predecessors by reinstating the Helms-Burton Act that permits Cuban Americans whose property was seized after the 1959 revolution to sue US and foreign companies. European companies were particularly incensed by this move, which was meant to discourage foreign investment in Cuba. Trump made one exception, encouraging US telecommunications firms, Google especially, to continue contact with the Cuban government, which would expand people's access to the Internet and social media. See Stephanie Kirchgaessner, "Google Revealed as Unlikely Go-Between to Help Trump-Cuba Relations," *The Guardian*, March 29, 2019.

105. Frances Robles, "In Nicaragua, Ortega Was on the Ropes; Now He Has Protesters on the Run," *NYT*, December 24, 2018. The investigating group was the Interdisciplinary Group of Independent Experts (GIEI, by its initials in Spanish); see its report, *Nicaragua*, December 2018, http://gieinicaragua.org/giei-content/uploads/2018/12/GIEI_INFORME_DIGITAL.pdf.

106. Reuters, "Nicaragua Releases Prisoners before Crisis Talks with Opposition," *The Guardian*, February 27, 2019.

107. Quoted in Nicole Gaouette, "Bolton Praises Brazil's Far-Right Leader, Slams Latin America's 'Troika of Tyranny,'" *The Guardian*, November 1, 2018.

108. See the portrait by Jon Lee Anderson, "Southern Strategy," *The New Yorker*, April 1, 2019, pp. 18–26, and David Miranda, "Fires Are Devouring the Amazon. And Jair Bolsonaro Is to Blame," *The Guardian*, August 26, 2019.

109. Francisco Goldman, "Jimmy Morales, a President against Democracy in Guatemala," *NYT*, January 17, 2019; Jonathan Blitzer, "The Trump Administration's Self-Defeating Policy toward the Guatemalan Elections," *The New Yorker*, May 30, 2019, https://www.newyorker.com/news/daily-comment/the-trump-administrations-self-defeating-policy-toward-the-guatemalan-elections.

110. Anthony Faiola and Karen DeYoung, "In Venezuela, Russia Pockets Key Energy Assets in Exchange for Cash Bailouts," *WaPo*, December 24, 2018.

111. Joseph S. Tulchin, "China's Rising Profile in Latin America," *The Asia-Pacific Journal*, vol. 17, no. 3 (January 15, 2019), https://apjjf.org/2019/02/Tulchin.html.

112. Brook Larmer, "What Soybean Politics Tells Us about Argentina and China," *New York Times Magazine*, January 30, 2019, https://www.nytimes.com/2019/01/30/magazine/what-soybean-politics-tell-us-about-argentina-and-china.html.

113. Pompeo threatened military intervention in response to widespread anti-Maduro protests in April and May 2019, and Trump cited (without evidence) Cuban intervention. But Trump backtracked, calling such accounts "rumors." The Russians, meanwhile, assailed US demands that Maduro step down as "a gross violation of international law." Anthony Faiola and Mariana Zuñiga, "After Uprising Falls Short, Venezuela's Guaidó Tries to Regain Momentum against Maduro," *WaPo*, May 2, 2019.

114. "Trump: Putin Not Looking to Get Involved in Venezuela," CNN, May 3, 2019, https://www.cnn.com/videos/politics/2019/05/03/trump-putin-not-looking-to-get-involved-in-venezuela-sot-nr-vpx.cnn.

7. DEALING AWAY INTERNATIONAL RESPONSIBILITY

1. Franklin D. Roosevelt, "1941 State of the Union Address 'The Four Freedoms,'" January 6, 1941, *Voices of Democracy*, https://voicesofdemocracy.umd.edu/fdr-the-four-freedoms-speech-text.

2. World Justice Project, https://worldjusticeproject.org.

3. Freedom House, https://freedomhouse.org/countries/freedom-world/scores.

4. Ed Pilkington, "US Halts Cooperation with UN on Potential Human Rights Violations," *The Guardian*, January 4, 2019, https://www.theguardian.com/law/2019/jan/04/trump-administration-un-human-rights-violations. Trump's decision not to allow UN monitors to evaluate conditions in the United States led Senator Robert Menendez of New Jersey to complain to Pompeo that the United States "risks undermining human rights globally and will be seen as empowering repressive regimes, like China and Russia, who seek to delegitimize internationally accepted human rights norms." Ed Pilkington, "Trump UN Human Rights Snub Will Buoy Repressive Regimes, Top Democrat Warns," *The Guardian*, April 30, 2019, https://www.theguardian.com/world/2019/apr/30/trump-un-human-rights-china-russia.

5. Nahal Toosi, "Trump Ambassador Blocks Scrutiny of Israel," *Politico*, June 16, 2016, https://www.politico.com/story/2018/06/16/trump-ambassador-israel-scrutiny-military-human-rights-david-friedman-650383.

6. Nicholas Kristof, "Dictators Love Trump, and He Loves Them," *New York Times*, March 14, 2018.

7. From Khashoggi's last opinion article, which discussed suppression of the news and freedom of expression by Middle East governments: see Jamal Khashoggi, "What the Arab World Needs Most Is Free Expression," *WaPo*, October 17, 2018.

8. Laura Koran, "Tillerson Skips Release of Annual Human Rights Report," CNN, March 3, 2017, https://www.cnn.com/2017/03/03/politics/rex-tillerson-state-department-human-rights-report/index.html.

9. Robbie Gramer, "Human Rights Groups Bristling at State Department Report," *Foreign Policy*, April 21, 2018, https://foreignpolicy.com/2018/04/21/human-rights-groups-bristling-at-state-human-rights-report.

10. As Secretary of State Mike Pompeo said, "The policy of this Administration is to engage with other governments, regardless of their record, if doing so will further US interests." Nicole Gaouette and Jennifer Hansler, "US Human Rights Report Notes Khashoggi Killing, Avoids Mention of Saudi Prince," CNN, March 13, 2019, https://www.cnn.com/2019/03/13/politics/human-rights-2018-state-department/index.html.

11. Edward Wong and Eileen Sullivan, "New Human Rights Panel Raises Fears of a Narrowing U.S. Advocacy," *NYT*, July 8, 2019.

12. Ernest J. Moniz and Sam Nunn, "The Return of Doomsday," *Foreign Affairs*, August 6, 2019, https://www.foreignaffairs.com/articles/russian-federation/2019-08-06/return-doomsday.

13. Johnston, *The Making of Donald Trump*, pp. xviii–xix.

14. Matthew J. Belvedere, "Trump Asks Why US Can't Use Nukes: MSNBC," CNBC, August 3, 2016, https://www.cnbc.com/2016/08/03/trump-asks-why-us-cant-use-nukes-msnbcs-joe-scarborough-reports.html.

15. Julian Borger, "US Nuclear Weapons: First Low-Yield Warheads Roll Off the Production Line," *The Guardian*, January 28, 2019, https://www.theguardian.com/world/2019/jan/28/us-nuclear-weapons-first-low-yield-warheads-roll-off-the-production-line.

16. These additional steps were discussed for the first time in the Pentagon's "nuclear posture review" for 2018. See Richard A. Clarke and Stephen Andreasen, "With Nuclear Weapons, We're Getting Too Comfortable Thinking the Unthinkable," *WaPo*, January 30, 2018.

17. Bruce G. Blair, "Loose Cannons: The President and US Nuclear Posture," *Bulletin of the Atomic Scientists*, January 13, 2020, https://thebulletin.org/2020/01/loose-cannons-the-president-and-us-nuclear-posture; Andrew Cockburn, "How to Start a Nuclear War," *Harper's Magazine*, August 2018, pp. 51–58.

18. For a thoughtful discussion that proposes additional checks on presidential authority to launch a nuclear weapon, see Richard K. Betts and Matthew C. Waxman, "The President and the Bomb," *Foreign Affairs*, vol. 97, no. 2 (March–April 2018), pp. 119–28. In February 2020, for example, the Pentagon announced deployment of a new version of a submarine-launched nuclear warhead, one with a lower yield than the previous version. But as critics pointed out, such a weapon, equivalent to one deployed by the Russians, is just as likely to increase as decrease the chance of its use in a nuclear exchange precisely because of its lower yield.

19. The total of deployed US nuclear weapons is about 1,750, of which about 900 are on submarines and 400 on land-based intercontinental ballistic missiles. The total US nuclear weapon inventory is about 5,800. See Hans M. Kristensen and Matt Korda, "United States Nuclear Forces, 2020," *Bulletin of the Atomic Scientists*, January 13, 2020, https://thebulletin.org/2020/01/united-states-nuclear-forces-2020; Lara Seligman, "Will Congress Let Trump Build More Nuclear Weapons?," *Foreign Policy*, April 11, 2019, https://foreignpolicy.com/2019/04/11/will-congress-let-trump-expand-americas-nuclear-arsenal; Michael T. Klare, "Making Nuclear Weapons Menacing Again," *The Nation*, April 8, 2019, pp. 16–19.

20. The treaty enters into force when ratified by fifty states; as of December 2018, only nineteen parties had ratified, while sixty-nine had signed. The opposition of the United States and other nuclear weapon states is based in part on the treaty's lack of a compliance mechanism, but probably more important is the challenge posed by the treaty to great-power nuclear hegemony and strategic doctrines that embrace deployment and use of nuclear weapons. An Australian NGO, the International Campaign to Abolish Nuclear Weapons (ICAN), won the 2017 Nobel Peace Prize for its efforts to bring the issue before the UN. For background on the TPNW, see the "Treaty on the Prohibition of Nuclear Weapons (TPNW)," Nuclear Threat Initiative, https://www.nti.org/learn/treaties-and-regimes/treaty-on-the-prohibition-of-nuclear-weapons. On the treaty's text and current signing status, see https://www.icanw.org.

21. Missy Ryan and John Hudson, "Trump Administration Expected to Distance Itself from Global Arms Treaty," *WaPo*, April 26, 2019.

22. George P. Shultz, William J. Perry, and Sam Nunn, "The Threat of Nuclear War Is Still with Us," *Wall Street Journal*, April 10, 2019, https://www.wsj.com/articles/the-threat-of-nuclear-war-is-still-with-us-11554936842.

23. New START caps deployed strategic nuclear warheads and bombs at 1,550 and puts limits on their delivery systems (submarines, ICBMs, and bombers).

24. Eric Schmitt and Thomas Gibbons-Neff, "Before Saudi Visit, Congress Questions U.S. Support for Yemen Campaign," *NYT*, March 18, 2018.

25. Woodward, *Fear*, p. 112.

26. Kushner failed to support Secretary of State Tillerson's efforts to settle the dispute. Qatar later did loan Kushner the $184 million he sought. Jed Handelsman Shugerman, "L'Affaire Kushner," *Slate*, March 2, 2018, https://slate.com/news-and-politics/2018/03/a-series-of-revelations-about-jared-kushner-have-added-further-credence-to-a-key-claim-of-the-steele-dossier.html.

27. The full story is in Trita Parsi's *Losing an Enemy: Obama, Iran, and the Triumph of Diplomacy.*

28. Shuaib Almosawa , Ben Hubbard, and Troy Griggs, "'It's a Slow Death': The World's Worst Humanitarian Crisis," *NYT*, August 23, 2017. Save the Children estimates 85,000 children under age five may have died of starvation in the three years of civil war in Yemen and estimates that half of Yemen's population—about fourteen million people—are at risk of starvation. "Save the Children News," November 21, 2018, https://twitter.com/SaveUKNews.

29. Erica Orden, "Saudi Disappearance Puts Spotlight on Trump's Business Ties," CNN, October 12, 2018, https://www.cnn.com/2018/10/12/politics/trump-saudi-business-ties/index.html.

30. Philip Rucker, Carol D. Leonnig, and Anne Gearan, "Two Princes: Kushner Now Faces a Reckoning for Trump's Bet on the Heir to the Saudi Throne," *WaPo*, October 14, 2018.

31. Mark Landler, Edward Wong, and Eric Schmitt, "Khashoggi's Disappearance Puts Kushner's Bet on Saudi Prince at Risk," *NYT*, October 20, 2018.

32. Nicole Gaouette and Michael Conte, "Saudi Prince Has Gone 'Full Gangster,' Says Rubio, as Lawmakers Decry Kingdom's Abuses," CNN, March 6, 2019, https://www.cnn.com/2019/03/06/politics/abizaid-us-saudi-gangster/index.html.

33. Landler, Wong, and Schmitt, "Khashoggi's Disappearance."

34. Mark Landler and Edward Wong, "Trump Says Saudi Account of Khashoggi Killing Is 'Worst Cover-Up' in History," *NYT*, October 23, 2018; Bruce Riedel, "The $110 Billion Arms Deal to Saudi Arabia Is Fake News," *Brookings* (blog), June 5, 2017, https://www.brookings.edu/blog/markaz/2017/06/05/the-110-billion-arms-deal-to-saudi-arabia-is-fake-news.

35. David Ignatius, "How the Mysteries of Khashoggi's Murder Have Rocked the U.S.-Saudi Partnership," *WaPo*, March 29, 2019. According to Ignatius, the training might have been done by the CIA or a private organization under State Department license.

36. Philip Rucker, "Trump Vows 'Severe Punishment' if U.S. Determines Saudi Arabia Killed Khashoggi," *WaPo*, October 13, 2018.

37. John Hudson, "Saudi Arabia Transfers $100 Million to U.S. amid Khashoggi Crisis," *WaPo*, October 17, 2018.

38. David D. Kirkpatrick, Malachy Browne, Ben Hubbard, and David Botti, "The Jamal Khashoggi Case: Suspects Had Ties to Saudi Crown Prince," *NYT*, October 17, 2018.

39. Josh Dawsey, John Hudson, and Anne Gearan, "Trump Doubts Saudi Account of Journalist's Death," *WaPo*, October 20, 2018.

40. That was the CIA's conclusion: Shane Harris, Greg Miller, and Josh Dawsey, "CIA Concludes Saudi Crown Prince Ordered Jamal Khashoggi's Assassination," *WaPo*, November 16, 2016.

41. In his interview with the *Washington Post* on November 27, 2018, Trump said, "Maybe he [Prince Mohammed] did and maybe he didn't. But he denies it. And people around him deny it. And the CIA did not say affirmatively he did it, either, by the way. I'm not saying that they're saying he didn't do it, but they didn't say it affirmatively." Aaron Blake, "President Trump's Full Washington Post Interview Transcript, Annotated," *WaPo*, November 27, 2018.

42. Blake, "President Trump's Full Washington Post Interview Transcript, Annotated."

43. Bolton's excuse was "I don't speak Arabic." The CIA director, Gina Haspel, was kept by the administration from appearing in closed-door testimony before the Senate even though she traveled to Turkey to hear the tape. But a UN group representing the High Commissioner for Human Rights found "credible evidence" of MBS's responsibility. Carol Morello and Kareem Fahim, "U.N. Investigator Calls for Probing Saudi Officials in Khashoggi Killing," *NYT*, June 19, 2019.

44. Donald J. Trump, "Statement from President Donald J. Trump on Standing with Saudi Arabia," November 20, 2018, https://www.whitehouse.gov/briefings-statements/statement-president-donald-j-trump-standing-saudi-arabia. Unmentioned in this statement was US interest in selling nuclear power plants to Saudi Arabia. Michael Flynn had been lining up such a deal when he joined the Trump team. Negotiations, including sharing of nuclear energy information, continued after Flynn's firing and at the time of the Khashoggi affair, despite objections from national security officials and White House lawyers and despite lack of consultation with the Nuclear Regulatory Commission. The Saudis reportedly rejected international inspection of the facilities, raising concern about their secret ambition to build an atomic bomb. See David E. Sanger and William J. Broad, "Saudis Want a U.S. Nuclear Deal," *NYT*, November 22, 2018; and Tom Hamburger, Steven Mufson, and Ellen Nakashima, "Top Trump Appointees Promoted Selling Nuclear Power Plants to Saudi Arabia," *WaPo*, February 19, 2019. Jared Kushner's apparent involvement in the nuclear deal raised a serious conflict of interest, since the purchaser of his New York high-rise for $1.1 billion was Brookfield Asset Management, owner of Westinghouse Electric, the nuclear plant construction firm.

45. David D. Kirkpatrick et al., "The Wooing of Jared Kushner: How the Saudis Got a Friend in the White House," *NYT*, December 8, 2018.

46. Michael LaForgia and Walt Bogdanich, "Trump Allows High-Tech U.S. Bomb Parts to Be Built in Saudi Arabia," *NYT*, June 7, 2019.

47. Julian Borger, "Trump Officials Approved Saudi Nuclear Permits after Khashoggi Murder," *WaPo*, June 4, 2019.

48. Ignatius, "How the Mysteries of Khashoggi's Murder Have Rocked the U.S.-Saudi Partnership."

49. A UN investigation in 2019 concluded that all sides in the Yemen war—including the United States, Britain, France, Iran, Saudi Arabia, the UAE, and the rebel Houthis—were possibly guilty of war crimes in the death of civilians. Sudersan Raghavan, "U.N. Report Says U.S., Britain, France May Be Complicit in Potential War Crimes in Yemen," *WaPo*, September 3, 2019.

8. BUSINESS FIRST

1. Adam Taylor, "U.S. Ambassador to Europe: Let's Take On China Together," *WaPo*, October 4, 2018.

2. Woodward, *Fear*, pp. 334–35.

3. In October 2018, a coalition of some one hundred industry groups, from real estate to oil, produced a study that found the new tariffs were costing consumers and businesses $1.4 billion a month. The coalition's report targeted states where these costs were being especially harmful. Ginger Gibson, "US Business Group Says Trump China Tariffs Cost $1.4 Billion per Month," Reuters, October 11, 2018, https://www.aol.com/article/finance/2018/10/11/us-business-group-says-trump-china-tariffs-cost-dollar14-billion-per-month/23558294.

4. On Trump's rocky relations with the US Chamber of Commerce, see Julie Creswell, "Trump and U.S. Chamber of Commerce Pull No Punches on Trade Policy," *NYT*, July 11, 2016. For the sharply critical comments of the American Chamber of Commerce's chief executive officer, Thomas J. Donohue, see Gardiner Harris, "Ahead of Asia Trip, Business Lobby Gives Pompeo an Earful on Trade War," *NYT*, July 30, 2018. When a new trade agreement with China was signed, James M. Zimmerman, the former chair of the American Chamber of Commerce in China, lamented, "The very fact that this is a 'phase one' deal is a reflection of

utter defeat. Nothing gained but lukewarm purchases after 18 months of a costly trade war." Heather Long, "5 Big Takeaways from Trump's 'Phase One' China Trade Deal," *WaPo*, December 13, 2019.

5. Adam S. Posen, "How Trump Is Repelling Foreign Investment," *Foreign Affairs*, July 23, 2018, https://www.foreignaffairs.com/articles/united-states/2018-07-23/how-trump-repelling-foreign-investment.

6. Kate Trafecante, "The Myth of the Manufacturing Jobs Renaissance," CNN, February 8, 2020.

7. Laura Davison and Jeff Kearns, "Trump Promised to Bring Back $4 Trillion in Offshore Cash. He Missed by $3.3 Trillion," *Bloomberg*, March 27, 2019, https://www.bloomberg.com/news/articles/2019-03-27/trump-s-offshore-cash-promise-falters-as-665-billion-returns.

8. Jesse Drucker and Jim Tankersley, "How Big Companies Won New Tax Breaks from the Trump Administration," *NYT*, December 30, 2019.

9. Jeffrey Schott, "The TPP after Trump," *Global Asia*, vol. 13, no. 2 (June 2018), pp. 32–35.

10. A Chinese commerce ministry statement quoted in Danielle Paquette, "China Says It Will Immediately Retaliate When Trump Tariffs Take Effect," *WaPo*, September 18, 2018.

11. For example, Trump's 2017 tax "reform" was an extraordinary windfall for the largest corporations. Apple, AT&T, Bank of America, Verizon, and Walmart saved $12.4 billion in taxes during the first three quarters of 2018 alone. Some, like Apple, paid no federal taxes at all that year. Adding insult to injury, many of the largest companies used those savings to cut jobs and buy back their stocks, inflating their value, rather than (as Trump predicted) investing in creating jobs at home. *The Hightower Lowdown*, February 2019.

12. See the *Public Citizen* report: Rick Claypool, Taylor Lincoln, Michael Tanglis, and Alan Zibel, "Corporate Impunity," *Public Citizen*, July 2018, https://www.citizen.org/wp-content/uploads/migration/corporate-enforcement-public-citizen-report-july-2018.pdf.

13. See Nathaniel Rich, *Losing Earth: A Recent History* (New York: Farrar, Straus and Giroux, 2019); and Bill McKibben, "How Extreme Weather Is Shrinking the Planet," *The New Yorker*, November 26, 2018, https://www.newyorker.com/magazine/2018/11/26/how-extreme-weather-is-shrinking-the-planet.

14. A report written by former officials and published by the bipartisan Brennan Center for Justice documents "the efforts of the current [Trump] administration not only to politicize scientific and technical research on a range of topics, but also, at times, to undermine the value of objective facts themselves." Brennan Center for Justice, "Proposals for Reform Volume II: National Task Force on Rule of Law & Democracy," October 3, 2019, https://www.brennancenter.org/our-work/policy-solutions/proposals-reform-volume-ii-national-task-force-rule-law-democracy.

15. Rebecca Morin, "Trump Says He Has 'Natural Instinct for Science' When It Comes to Climate Change," *Politico*, October 17, 2018, https://www.politico.com/story/2018/10/17/trump-instinct-climate-change-910004.

16. Just one of many examples: Alaska's Pebble Mine project, which Obama's EPA had judged would decimate wild salmon habitat in Bristol Bay. Under Trump, following meetings with the project's promoters, including Alaska's governor, EPA scientists were ordered to drop further work under the Clean Water Act, since the mining project would be allowed to go forward. Scott Bronstein et al., "EPA Dropped Salmon Protection after Trump Met with Alaska Governor," CNN, August 9, 2019.

17. The personal experiences of whistleblowers and other government scientists are recounted by Oliver Milman, "The Silenced: Meet the Climate Whistleblowers Muzzled by Trump," *The Guardian*, September 13, 2019. See also Robbie Gramer, "Trump's Shadow War on Climate Science," *Foreign Policy*, July 31, 2019, https://foreignpolicy.com/2019/07/31/trumps-shadow-war-on-climate-science-state-department-intelligence-analyst-resigns-white-house-muzzles-intelligence-assessment-climate-change-environment; Gabriel Popkin, "Trump Doesn't Want the Public to Know What Government Scientists Are Doing," *WaPo*, December 12, 2018. Scientists and economists at the Agriculture Department were given even worse treatment, being asked, in the guise of a budgetary reduction, to move from Washington, DC, to

Kansas City if they wanted to keep their jobs. The real reason for the move was to exile people who questioned administration policy.

18. Juliet Eilperin, "EPA's Scientific Advisers Warn Its Regulatory Rollbacks Clash with Established Science," *WaPo*, December 31, 2019.

19. In September 2019 Trump incorrectly added Alabama to an official map of states that would be hit by Hurricane Dorian. When the National Weather Service office in Birmingham contradicted Trump, the leadership at the National Oceanic and Atmospheric Administration (NOAA) jumped to Trump's defense, drawing sharp criticism from NOAA's weather experts for politicizing the forecast and undermining public confidence in NOAA's objectivity. Veronica Stracqualursi, "NOAA Emails Show Outrage and Panic Over Trump's False Claims on Hurricane Dorian," CNN, February 1, 2020.

20. Emily Holden, "How Bad Can the Climate Crisis Get if Trump Wins Again?," *The Guardian*, January 12, 2020.

21. See, for example, Lisa Friedman and Claire O'Neill, "Who Controls Trump's Environmental Policy?," *NYT*, January 14, 2020; and Juliet Eilperin, "EPA's Watchdog Is Scrutinizing Ethics Practices of Former Air Policy Chief," *WaPo*, July 22, 2019.

22. Between 2017 and 2019, the Trump administration leased nearly ten million acres of federal water and land to the oil and gas industries, far more than any previous administration. Emily Holden, "Trump 'Turns Back the Clock' by Luring Drilling Companies to Pristine Lands," *The Guardian*, February 12, 2020.

23. As of fall 2019, the *New York Times* counted eighty-four environmental regulations affecting climate that the Trump administration had succeeded in reversing or was seeking to reverse. John Schwartz, "Major Climate Change Rules the Trump Administration Is Reversing," *NYT*, August 29, 2019.

24. Brad Plumer, "Carbon Dioxide Emissions Hit a Record in 2019, Even as Coal Fades," *NYT*, December 3, 2019.

25. Text of the report, Intergovernmental Panel on Climate Change, "Global Warming of 1.5°C," October 2018, is at https://www.ipcc.ch/sr15. For background, see the Union of Concerned Scientists, "The IPCC: Who Are They and Why Do Their Climate Reports Matter?," Union of Concerned Scientists, published July 16, 2008, updated October 11, 2018, https://www.ucsusa.org/global-warming/science-and-impacts/science/ipcc-backgrounder.html.

26. Juliet Eilperin, Brady Dennis, and Chris Mooney, "Trump Administration Sees a 7-Degree Rise in Global Temperatures by 2100," *WaPo*, September 27, 2018.

27. Christopher W. Avery et al., "Chapter One: Overview," in *Impacts, Risks, and Adaptation in the United States: Fourth National Climate Assessment, Volume II*, ed. D. R. Reidmiller et al. (Washington, DC: U.S. Global Change Research Program, 2018), https://nca2018.globalchange.gov/chapter/1, emphasis in original.

28. Chris Mooney, "The Arctic Is in Even Worse Shape Than You Realize," *WaPo*, December 11, 2018.

29. J. Richter-Menge, M. L. Druckenmiller, and M. Jeffries, eds., "Arctic Report Card 2019," NOAA: Arctic Program, 2019, https://arctic.noaa.gov/Report-Card/Report-Card-2019.

30. Brad Plumer and Lisa Friedman, "Trump Team Pushes Fossil Fuels at Climate Talks," *NYT*, December 10, 2018.

31. Lisa Friedman, "'I Don't Know That It's Man-Made,' Trump Says of Climate Change. It is," *NYT*, October 15, 2018.

32. Juliet Eilperin and Brady Dennis, "New EPA Document Tells Communities to Brace for Climate Change Impacts," *WaPo*, April 27, 2019.

33. Plumer and Friedman, "Trump Team Pushes Fossil Fuels at Climate Talks."

9. RACISM AT THE BORDER

1. Robert Kuttner, "Steve Bannon, Unrepentant," *The American Prospect*, August 16, 2017, https://prospect.org/article/steve-bannon-unrepentant.

2. Trump's presidential announcement speech, June 16, 2015, quoted in Michelle Ye Hee Lee, "Donald Trump's False Comments Connecting Mexican Immigrants and Crime," *WaPo*, July 8, 2015.

3. Darran Simon, "President Trump's Other Insensitive Comments on Race and Ethnicity," CNN, January 13, 2018, https://www.cnn.com/2018/01/11/politics/president-trump-racial-comments-tweets/index.html.

4. Frum, *Trumpocracy*, pp. 128–29.

5. Julie Hirschfeld Davis and Peter Baker, "How the Border Wall Is Boxing Trump In," *NYT*, January 5, 2019.

6. Compared with 2016, the number of refugees admitted to the United States in 2019 dropped 71 percent, and Muslims, 90 percent—this, at a time of rapidly rising refugee numbers worldwide. Carol Morello, "Number of Refugees Down Sharply, Again, under Restrictions Set by Trump Administration," *WaPo*, April 2, 2019. The worldwide refugee figure is around 68 million.

7. Fred Barbash, "Wilbur Ross Broke Law, Violated Constitution in Census Decision, Judge Rules," *WaPo*, March 6, 2019. Subsequently, documents belonging to a deceased Republican Party leader who had devised the citizenship question confirmed the actual political aim behind it: to promote white Republican election interests. Michael Wines, "Deceased G.O.P. Strategist's Hard Drives Reveal New Details on the Census Citizenship Question," *NYT*, May 30, 2019.

8. Hundreds of Miller's e-mails were discovered that confirmed his white supremacist, far-right leanings. Kim Bellware, "Leaked Stephen Miller Emails Show Trump Point Man on Immigration Promoted White Nationalism, SPLC Reports," *WaPo*, November 13, 2019.

9. Tweet of July 29, 2018; Amber Phillips, "After a Tough Few Weeks, Trump Is Picking Fights That Please His Base," *WaPo*, July 29, 2018.

10. Senator Dick Durban (Democrat of Illinois) and Senator Lindsey Graham (Republican of South Carolina) put together the proposal on DACA. The White House debate is covered in Woodward, *Fear*, pp. 317–21.

11. The figure widely used in 2018 was around 2,700 separated children, but many months later the Department of Justice, under court order, disclosed the higher figure to the American Civil Liberties Union. Maria Sacchetti, "ACLU Says 1,500 More Migrant Children Were Taken from Parents by Trump Administration," *WaPo*, October 24, 2019.

12. Nielsen evidently was not hard-line enough; she was forced to resign in April 2019.

13. Jeff Merkley, "Merkley Demands Answers on Long-term Detention of Children," press release, September 4, 2019, https://www.merkley.senate.gov/news/press-releases/merkley-demands-answers-on-long-term-detention-of-children-2019.

14. Julia Jacobs, "U.S. Says It Could Take Two Years to Identify Up to Thousands of Separated Immigrant Families," *NYT*, April 6, 2019.

15. Caitlin Dickerson, Annie Correal, and Mitchell Ferman, "Federal Authorities Say They Have Met Deadline to Reunite Migrant Families," *NYT*, July 27, 2018.

16. Miriam Valverde, "Donald Trump's Executive Order Ending His Administration's Separation of Immigrant Families," *Politifact*, June 25, 2018, https://www.politifact.com/truth-o-meter/article/2018/jun/25/donald-trumps-executive-order-ending-his-administr.

17. For example, at the Trump National Golf Club in Bedminster, New Jersey. See Joshua Partlow et al., "'My Whole Town Practically Lived There,'" *WaPo*, February 8, 2019.

18. In 2019 the union representing US asylum officers joined a lawsuit *challenging* the policy, arguing that it was inhumane and contrary to US and international law. Maria Sacchetti, "U.S. Asylum Officers Say Trump's 'Remain in Mexico' Policy Is Threatening Migrants' Lives, Ask Federal Court to End It," *WaPo*, June 27, 2019.

19. Jonathan Capehart, "Trump Learned 'the Worst Lessons of History,' Says David Miliband," *WaPo*, July 10, 2018.

20. Kirstjen Nielsen's rejection of that illegal proposal was apparently one reason she was forced out. Zolan Kanno-Youngs et al., "Kirstjen Nielsen Resigns as Trump's Homeland Security Secretary," *NYT*, April 7, 2019. Interviews established that Miller was extremely upset about the failure to implement new anti-immigrant rules. See Eileen Sullivan and Michael D.

Shear, "Trump Sees an Obstacle to Getting His Way on Immigration: His Own Officials," *NYT*, April 14, 2019.

21. For those reasons the United States voted against a UN General Assembly resolution promising cooperation on migrant populations. The vote was 152–5 with twelve abstentions. "U.N. Formally Approves Global Migration Pact Opposed by U.S., Others," Thomson Reuters, December 19, 2018.

22. See the report from the western highlands of Guatemala by Jonathan Blitzer, "How Climate Change Is Fuelling the U.S. Border Crisis," *The New Yorker*, April 3, 2019, https://www.newyorker.com/news/dispatch/how-climate-change-is-fuelling-the-us-border-crisis.

23. As one study pointed out, "Despite extensive reporting to the contrary in recent years, nearly half of all Americans still believe immigration raises crime rates, although immigrants commit crimes at lower rates than the native-born population. Trump and his officials have also repeatedly warned that terrorists were infiltrating the United States through its refugee program, despite the fact that terrorist attacks by refugees are nearly nonexistent." In fact, there is room for doubt that *any* terrorists have crossed into the United States from Mexico. Marshall Cohen et al., "The Cascade of False Claims as Trump Makes His Case for a Crisis on the US-Mexico Border," CNN, January 8, 2019.

24. Nick Miroff and Maria Sacchetti, "Burgeoning Court Backlog of 850,000 Cases Undercuts Trump Immigration Agenda," *WaPo*, May 1, 2019.

25. In February 2019 both houses of Congress passed a border security bill that had been negotiated by a bipartisan group eager to avoid another government shutdown. Trump was forced to sign it even though he said he wasn't "happy" with it and would find additional money elsewhere to build his wall. The consensus estimate of the cost of the US government's partial shutdown was between $11 and $14 billion.

26. "President Trump Border Security Briefing," C-Span, January 10, 2019, https://www.c-span.org/video/?456866-1/president-trump-tours-border-mcallen-texas.

27. Ellen Nakashima, "Former Senior National Security Officials to Issue Declaration on National Emergency," *WaPo*, February 24, 2019.

28. Mary Beth Sheridan and Kevin Sieff, "Trump Plans to Cut U.S. Aid to 3 Central American Countries in Fight Over U.S.-Bound Migrants," *WaPo*, March 30, 2019.

29. Kevin Sieff, "Mexico's Migration Crackdown Overwhelms Its Shelters, Antagonizes Its Neighbors," *WaPo*, July 1, 2019. The horrific conditions in the US camps run by the border patrol were condemned by the Department of Homeland Security's own inspector general. Zolan Kanno-Youngs, "Squalid Conditions at Border Detention Centers, Government Report Finds," *NYT*, July 2, 2019.

30. "Many of these illegal aliens are living far better now than where they came from, and in far safer conditions," Trump tweeted on July 3, 2019. "Our Border Patrol people are not hospital workers, doctors, or nurses." Naturally, he blamed Democrats for the squalid conditions of the camps. https://twitter.com/realDonaldTrump/status/1146501821579583488.

10. RETREAT AND ADVANCE

1. For example, William Webster, the only person to serve as both CIA and FBI director, and under both Republican and Democratic presidents, wrote in 2019 that he had "a responsibility to speak out about a dire threat to the rule of law in the country I love. Order protects liberty, and liberty protects order. Today, the integrity of the institutions that protect our civil order are, tragically, under assault from too many people whose job it should be to protect them." William Webster, "I Headed the F.B.I. and C.I.A. There's a Dire Threat to the Country I Love," *NYT*, December 16, 2019. See also Mitt Romney's statement, "The President Shapes the Political Character of the Nation," *WaPo*, January 1, 2019.

2. As Richard Haass has written, for the United States to resuscitate its reputation requires that it "get its own house in order. . . . The United States cannot effectively promote order abroad if it is divided at home, distracted by domestic problems, and lacking in resources."

Richard Haass, "How a World Order Ends," *Foreign Affairs*, vol. 98, no. 1 (January–February 2019), p. 30 [22–30].

3. Text at Kevin Liptak, "Exclusive: Read the Inauguration Day Letter Obama Left for Trump," CNN, September 5, 2017, https://www.cnn.com/2017/09/03/politics/obama-trump-letter-inauguration-day/index.html.

4. On Trump's white nationalist appeal, see Bernard E. Harcourt, "How Trump Fuels the Fascist Right," *New York Review of Books*, November 29, 2018, https://www.nybooks.com/daily/2018/11/29/how-trump-fuels-the-fascist-right.

5. See Stephen M. Walt, "The End of Hubris," *Foreign Affairs*, vol. 98, no. 3 (May–June 2019), pp. 26–75; and Larry Diamond, "Democracy Demotion," *Foreign Affairs*, vol. 98, no. 4 (July–August 2019), pp. 17–25.

6. Though John Bolton did not testify against Trump at his Senate trial, he became the object of a major Internet conspiracy campaign to cast him as a venal, deep-state "Never Trumper." See Isaac Stanley-Becker, "Anatomy of a 'Smear': How John Bolton Became a Target of the Pro-Trump Internet," *WaPo*, January 28, 2020.

7. In July 2019, for instance, Trump hosted a "social media summit" attended by some of the most offensive and dishonest conspiracy mongers—an event barred to Facebook and other mainstream social media.

8. Jana Winter, "FBI Document Warns Conspiracy Theories Are a New Domestic Terrorism Threat," *HuffPost*, August 1, 2019, https://www.huffpost.com/entry/fbi-domestic-terrorism_n_5d430db7e4b0acb57fc91818.

9. For a fuller review, see Alexandra Schmitt, "President Trump's Alarming Human Rights Agenda at Home and Abroad," Center for American Progress, December 10, 2019, https://www.americanprogress.org/issues/security/reports/2019/12/10/478458/president-trumps-alarming-human-rights-agenda-home-abroad.

10. As just one example, consider how Trump portrayed his quickly arranged meeting with Kim Jong-un at the Korean demilitarized zone in June 2019. The event made for great theater, nothing more. Trump was able to proclaim he was the first sitting US president to step on North Korean soil. But Trump tried to make it more historic than that: "Certainly, this was a great day; this was a very legendary, very historic day." Seung Min Kim and Simon Denyer, "Trump Becomes First Sitting President to Set Foot inside North Korea," *WaPo*, June 30, 2019.

11. More likely, a bargain will be struck on the exact amount of their bill, but it will leave them with a bad taste in their mouths—and give groups in South Korea and Japan new arguments for either obtaining their own nuclear weapons, establishing closer relations with China, or removing US forces from their territory. On South Korea, for example, see Uri Friedman, "America's Alliance System Will Face One of Its Biggest Tests Yet," *The Atlantic*, May 23, 2019, https://www.theatlantic.com/politics/archive/2019/05/us-and-south-korea-gear-burden-sharing-talks/589999.

12. Robert A. Pape, "Why Economic Sanctions Do Not Work," *International Security*, vol. 22, no. 2 (Fall 1997), pp. 90–136. Pape examined 115 cases that had been investigated in a previous influential study of sanctions and found that only in five cases had economic sanctions succeeded in changing a target state's policies or caused it to make concessions. See also David S. Cohen, "Why Trump's Sanctions Aren't Working," *WaPo*, March 30, 2019. With Russia, against which Trump generally rejected sanctions, one study found that although congressional sanctions had a modest impact on the economy, they did not seem to affect Russia's external behavior. Andrew Chatzky, "Have Sanctions on Russia Changed Putin's Calculus?," Council on Foreign Relations: In Brief, May 2, 2019, https://www.cfr.org/in-brief/have-sanctions-russia-changed-putins-calculus.

13. William H. McRaven, "If Good Men Like Joe Maguire Can't Speak the Truth, We Should Be Deeply Afraid," *WaPo*, February 21, 2020. Admiral McRaven, retired commander of the US Special Operations Command from 2011 to 2014, was writing in defense of DNI Joseph Maguire, whom Trump fired in February 2020.

14. Richard Wolf, "Article II of the Constitution: Trump's 'Right to Do Whatever I Want'? Or a Roadmap for Impeachment?," *USA Today*, October 24, 2019, https://www.msn.com/en-us/news/politics/article-ii-of-the-constitution-trumps-right-to-do-whatever-i-want-or-a-roadmap-for-impeachment/ar-AAJh3bb.

15. Susan B. Glasser, "The Secretary of Trump," *The New Yorker*, August 26, 2019, p. 58, quoting a "former senior official."

16. For a good review of Trump's destructive trade policies, see Chad P. Brown and Douglas A. Irwin, "Trump's Assault on the Global Trading System," *Foreign Affairs*, September/October 2019, https://www.foreignaffairs.com/articles/asia/2019-08-12/trumps-assault-global-trading-system.

17. Robert Kagan, "Trump's America Does Not Care," *WaPo*, June 14, 2018.

18. Maria Abi-Habib, "After India Loses Dogfight to Pakistan, Questions Arise about Its 'Vintage' Military," *NYT*, March 3, 2019.

19. Even with China's rise, the United States still commands a 23 percent share of the world economy, and the US dollar remains the currency of choice for most international transactions and reserves. Ruchir Sharma, "Worried about Turkey's Economic Problems? China's Could Be Worse," *NYT*, August 15, 2018; Peter S. Goodman, "The Dollar Is Still King," *NYT*, February 22, 2019.

20. Ivo H. Daalder and James M. Lindsay, *The Empty Throne: America's Abdication of Global Leadership* (New York: PublicAffairs, 2018), pp. 119–20.

21. See Max Boot, "Trump Hasn't Ended the 'Endless Wars'; Neither Will Democrats," *WaPo*, January 22, 2020.

22. For a different view, see Daniel W. Drezner, "This Time Is Different: Why U.S. Foreign Policy Will Never Recover," *Foreign Affairs*, vol. 98, no. 3 (May–June 2019), pp. 10–17.

23. See the masterful essay by Christopher R. Browning, "The Suffocation of Democracy."

24. Shultz, Perry, and Nunn, "The Threat of Nuclear War Is Still with Us"; Madeleine Albright and Igor Lavrov, "A Plea to Save the Last Nuclear Arms Treaty," *NYT*, February 10, 2020. Albright and Lavrov, two former foreign secretaries, write, "Experts are suddenly talking less about the means for deterring nuclear conflict than about developing weapons that could be used for offensive purposes. Some have even embraced the folly that a nuclear war can be won."

25. Max Boot, "A New Poll Shows Voters Aren't Buying What Trump Is Selling," *WaPo*, September 9, 2019. Boot's article relies on polling by the Pew Research Center.

26. See, for example, Ivo H. Daalder and James Lindsay, "The Committee to Save the World Order," *Foreign Affairs*, September 30, 2018, https://www.foreignaffairs.com/articles/2018-09-30/committee-save-world-order.

27. Yasmeen Abutaleb, Josh Dawsey, Ellen Nakashima, and Greg Miller, "The U.S. Was Beset by Denial and Dysfunction as the Coronavirus Raged," *WaPo*, April 4, 2020.

28. The court case involved the sentencing of Roger Stone, Trump's convicted longtime adviser. When the Justice Department's prosecutors urged a lengthy sentence, Trump tweeted that the sentence was unfair, and Barr followed in lockstep by overriding his own lawyers and urging leniency. All four prosecutors resigned in protest. The fired witnesses were Lieutenant Colonel Vindman and Ambassador Sondland. Trump went so far as to suggest "disciplinary action" against Vindman. The likely sell-off of public lands was reported by Emily Holden, "Trump 'Turns Back the Clock' by Luring Drilling Companies to Pristine Lands," *The Guardian*, February 12, 2020.

29. Timothy Naftali, "The Wounded Presidency, Part One," *Foreign Affairs*, January 28, 2020, https://www.foreignaffairs.com/articles/united-states/impeachment_nixon_wounded_presidency_part_one.

30. Trump said that "China will do everything they can to have me lose this race" for president. The reverse is clearly true: China has benefited enormously from Trump's retreat from Asia. Pete Buttigieg makes the case in "China Wants Four More Years of Trump," *WaPo*, May 1, 2020.

31. See, for example, Joseph R. Biden, Jr., "Why America Must Lead Again," *Foreign Affairs*, January 23, 2020, https://www.foreignaffairs.com/articles/united-states/2020-01-23/why-america-must-lead-again.

32. On Russia policy, for example, the liberal position of confronting Putin promises a resumption of the kind of "patient" containment first evoked by George Kennan in the 1950s. Today the strategy is called "selective cooperation," but it flows from essential mistrust of Russia's intentions. See Michael McFaul, "Russia as It Is: A Grand Strategy for Confronting

Putin," *Foreign Affairs*, vol. 97, no. 4 (July–August 2018), pp. 82–91. As for China, we should keep in mind that key Democratic congressional members supported Trump's trade war and other economic pressures. Liberal Democrats like Biden also seem to be in agreement with Trump that China is a greater threat than Russia to US national security.

33. Joe Biden ("Why America Must Lead Again"), however, promised a departure from the Middle East wars, writing, "As I have long argued, we should bring the vast majority of our troops home from the wars in Afghanistan and the Middle East and narrowly define our mission as defeating al Qaeda and the Islamic State (or ISIS). We should also end our support for the Saudi-led war in Yemen."

34. Two examples are Bernie Sanders, "Sanders Speech at SAIS: Building a Global Democratic Movement to Counter Authoritarianism," Speech at the School of Advanced International Studies, Johns Hopkins University, Washington, DC, October 9, 2018, https://www.sanders.senate.gov/newsroom/press-releases/sanders-speech-at-sais-building-a-global-democratic-movement-to-counter-authoritarianism; and Elizabeth Warren, "A Foreign Policy for All: Strengthening Democracy—At Home and Abroad," *Foreign Policy*, vol. 98, no. 1 (January–February 2019), pp. 50–61.

35. As Bruce Blair writes ("Loose Cannons," p. 2), the "bad choices" available to any president in a nuclear crisis are such that "the only completely satisfactory, permanent solution . . . is to completely eliminate nuclear weapons." The process of bringing the treaty to the UN General Assembly is notable in several respects, including the key role played by civil society groups in many countries. See Tilman Ruff, "Negotiating the UN Treaty on the Prohibition of Nuclear Weapons and the Role of ICAN," *Global Change, Peace & Security*, April 30, 2018, https://doi.org/10.1080/14781158.2018.1465908.

36. See the proposals of the Geneva Initiative (genevainitiative.org), which brings Israelis and Palestinians together on joint peace projects.

37. See my *Engaging Adversaries* for specific ideas on US relations with all these countries.

38. On both the difficulties and the occasional triumphs in promoting human rights during the Obama administration, see Samantha Power, *The Education of an Idealist: A Memoir* (New York: William Morrow, 2019).

39. Thomas Wright ("Democrats Need to Place China at the Center of Their Foreign Policy," *Brookings* (blog), May 15, 2019, https://www.brookings.edu/blog/order-from-chaos/2019/05/15/democrats-need-to-place-china-at-the-center-of-their-foreign-policy) points out that the three main Democratic challengers to Trump—Joe Biden, Bernie Sanders, and Elizabeth Warren—all took hard-line positions on China during their campaigns, though Sanders did say that as president he would still hope to work with China rather than be in a cold war with it. In fact, most members of the liberal establishment—in Congress, the media, journals, and think tanks—agreed with the Trump administration that China was a growing threat to US national security, though they disagreed as to whether the threat was primarily ideological and military or technological and political. See Gurtov and Selden, "The Dangerous New US Consensus on China and the Future of US-China Relations."

40. For some excellent charts displaying these differences, see Brian F. Schaffner, "These 5 Charts Explain Who Voted How in the 2018 Midterm Election," *WaPo*, November 10, 2018.

41. George Packer, "A Hole in the Center," *The New Yorker*, November 12, 2018, pp. 52–61.

42. See Stephen M. Walt, "Global Warming Is Setting Fire to American Leadership," *Foreign Policy*, December 3, 2018, https://foreignpolicy.com/2018/12/03/global-warming-will-set-fire-to-american-leadership.

43. A "Green New Deal Resolution" was introduced in the US Congress by Representative Alexandria Ocasio-Cortez and Senator Ed Markey in 2019, https://apps.npr.org/documents/document.html?id=5731829-Ocasio-Cortez-Green-New-Deal-Resolution. The resolution cited the IPCC report of 2018 in calling for a "ten-year national mobilization" to bring carbon emissions down to zero via a combination of renewable energy, infrastructure repairs, and community-level projects. On the many benefits of a green economy, see Alison Smith, *The Climate Bonus: Co-benefits of Climate Policy* (London: Routledge/Earthscan, 2013).

44. See Chris Hedges, "The Coming Collapse," *Common Dreams*, May 21, 2018, https://www.commondreams.org/views/2018/05/21/coming-collapse?amp. Hedges blames the "Dem-

ocratic mandarins" as much as Trump for America's predicament and makes the case for grassroots local organizing as the only way to achieve progressive goals such as universal health care and an end to government surveillance.

45. Brett McGurk, who resigned in protest after having served in the Trump administration as special envoy on ISIS, said, "The imagery of a head of state [Trump] in a call with other governing officials saying, 'Dominate the streets, dominate the battlespace'—these are iconic images that will define America for some time. It makes it much more difficult for us to distinguish ourselves from other countries we are trying to contest." See Greg Miller, "CIA Veterans Who Monitored Crackdowns Abroad See Troubling Parallels to Trump's Handling of Protests," *WaPo*, June 2, 2020. General Mattis broke his silence on Trump to denounce his lack of "mature leadership," saying, "Donald Trump is the first president in my lifetime who does not try to unite the American people—does not even pretend to try. Instead he tries to divide us." On calling up the military, Mattis said: "We must reject any thinking of our cities as a 'battlespace' that our uniformed military is called upon to 'dominate.' At home, we should use our military only when requested to do so, on very rare occasions, by state governors. Militarizing our response, as we witnessed in Washington, D.C., sets up a conflict—a false conflict—between the military and civilian society." Barbara Starr and Paul LeBlanc, "Mattis Tears into Trump: 'We Are Witnessing the Consequences of Three Years without Mature Leadership,'" CNN, June 3, 2020.

Bibliography

Books

Abramson, Seth. *Proof of Collusion: How Trump Betrayed America*. New York: Simon & Schuster, 2018.

Allison, Graham. *Destined for War: Can America and China Escape Thucydides's Trap?* New York: Houghton Mifflin Harcourt, 2017.

Blackwill, Robert D., and Philip H. Gordon. *Containing Russia: How to Respond to Moscow's Intervention in U.S. Democracy and Growing Geopolitical Challenge*, Council Special Report No. 80. New York: Council on Foreign Affairs, January 2018.

Coll, Steve. *Directorate S: The C.I.A. and America's Secret Wars in Afghanistan and Pakistan*. New York: Penguin Press, 2018.

Comey, James. *A Higher Loyalty*. New York: Macmillan, 2018.

Daalder, Ivo H., and James M. Lindsay. *The Empty Throne: America's Abdication of Global Leadership*. New York: PublicAffairs, 2018.

Enrich, David. *Dark Towers: Deutsche Bank, Donald Trump, and the Epic Tale of Destruction*. New York: HarperCollins, 2020.

Farrow, Ronan. *War on Peace: The End of Diplomacy and the Decline of American Influence*. New York: W. W. Norton, 2018.

Frum, David. *Trumpocracy: The Corruption of the American Republic*. New York: HarperCollins, 2018.

Gurtov, Mel. *Engaging Adversaries: Peacemaking and Diplomacy in the Human Interest*. Lanham, MD: Rowman & Littlefield, 2018.

Hofstadter, Richard. *The Paranoid Style in American Politics and Other Essays*. New York: Vintage Books, 1967.

Isikoff, Michael, and David Corn. *Russian Roulette: The Inside Story of Putin's War on America and the Election of Donald Trump*. New York: Twelve, 2018.

Johnston, David Cay. *The Making of Donald Trump*. New York: Melville House, 2017.

Kranish, Michael, and Marc Fisher. *Trump Revealed: The Definitive Biography of the 45th President*. New York: Scribner, 2016.

Lee, Bandy X., and Robert Jay Lifton, eds. *The Dangerous Case of Donald Trump: 27 Psychiatrists and Mental Health Experts Assess a President*. New York: Macmillan, 2017.

Parsi, Trita. *Losing an Enemy: Obama, Iran, and the Triumph of Diplomacy*. New Haven, CT: Yale University Press, 2017.

Power, Samantha. *The Education of an Idealist: A Memoir*. New York: William Morrow, 2019.

Rich, Nathaniel. *Losing Earth: A Recent History*. New York: Farrar, Straus and Giroux, 2019.

Ritter, Scott. *Dealbreaker: Donald Trump and the Unmaking of the Iran Nuclear Deal.* Atlanta, GA: Clarity Press, 2018.

Rucker, Philip, and Carol D. Leonnig. *A Very Stable Genius: Donald J. Trump's Testing of America.* New York: Penguin, 2020.

Sims, Cliff. *Team of Vipers: My 500 Extraordinary Days in the White House.* New York: Thomas Dunne Books, 2019.

Smith, Alison. *The Climate Bonus: Co-benefits of Climate Policy.* London: Routledge/Earthscan, 2013.

Woodward, Bob. *Fear: Trump in the White House.* New York: Simon & Schuster, 2018.

Working Group on Chinese Influence Activities in the United States, *Chinese Influence & American Interests: Promoting Constructive Vigilance.* Stanford, CA: Hoover Institution Press, 2018, https://www.hoover.org/sites/default/files/research/docs/chineseinfluence_ americaninterests_fullreport_web.pdf.

Articles

Abrams, Elliott. "Trump Versus the Government," *Foreign Affairs*, vol. 98, no. 1 (January–February 2019), pp. 129–37.

Alexander, Dan, and Chase Peterson-Withorn. "How Trump Is Trying—and Failing—to Get Rich Off His Presidency," *Forbes*, October 2, 2018, https://www.forbes.com/sites/danalexander/2018/10/02/how-trump-is-tryingand-failingto-get-rich-off-his-presidency.

Anderson, Jon Lee. "Behind the Wall," *The New Yorker*, May 28, 2018, pp. 24–30.

Appelbaum, Yoni. "Impeach Trump," *The Atlantic*, March 2019, https://www.theatlantic.com/magazine/archive/2019/03/impeachment-trump/580468.

Åslund, Anders. "How the United States Can Combat Russia's Kleptocracy," Atlantic Council, July 2018, https://www.atlanticcouncil.org/in-depth-research-reports/issue-brief/how-the-united-states-can-combat-russia-s-kleptocracy.

———. "In Ukraine It's No Longer about Little Green Men," *Politico*, November 27, 2018, https://www.politico.eu/article/in-ukraine-its-no-longer-about-little-green-men-russia-agression-azov-sea-kerch-strait.

Beinart, Peter. "The New Authoritarians Are Waging War on Women," *The Atlantic*, January–February 2019, https://www.theatlantic.com/magazine/archive/2019/01/authoritarian-sexism-trump-duterte/576382.

Béraud-Sudreau, Lucie. "Global Defence Spending: The United States Widens the Gap," International Institute for Strategic Studies: *Military Balance Blog*, February 14, 2020, https://www.iiss.org/blogs/military-balance/2020/02/global-defence-spending.

Bertrand, Natasha. "Trump's Top Targets in the Russia Probe Are Experts in Organized Crime," *The Atlantic*, August 30, 2018, https://www.theatlantic.com/politics/archive/2018/08/trumps-top-targets-in-the-russia-probe-are-experts-in-organized-crime/569056.

Betts, Richard K., and Matthew C. Waxman. "The President and the Bomb," *Foreign Affairs*, vol. 97, no. 2 (March–April 2018), pp. 119–28.

Biden, Joseph R., Jr. "Why America Must Lead Again," *Foreign Affairs*, January 23, 2020, https://www.foreignaffairs.com/articles/united-states/2020-01-23/why-america-must-lead-again.

Blair, Bruce G. "Loose Cannons: The President and US Nuclear Posture," *Bulletin of the Atomic Scientists*, January 13, 2020, https://thebulletin.org/2020/01/loose-cannons-the-president-and-us-nuclear-posture.

Blank, Stephen. "The North Korean Factor in the Sino-Russian Alliance," *Joint U.S.-Korea Academic Studies Journal* (2019), http://keia.org/publication/north-korean-factor-sino-russian-alliance.

Blitzer, Jonathan. "How Climate Change Is Fuelling the U.S. Border Crisis," *The New Yorker*, April 3, 2019, https://www.newyorker.com/news/dispatch/how-climate-change-is-fuelling-the-us-border-crisis.

———. "The Trump Administration's Self-Defeating Policy toward the Guatemalan Elections," *The New Yorker*, May 30, 2019, https://www.newyorker.com/news/daily-comment/the-trump-administrations-self-defeating-policy-toward-the-guatemalan-elections.

Bolton, John R. "How to Get Out of the Iran Nuclear Deal," *National Review*, August 28, 2017, https://www.nationalreview.com/2017/08/iran-nuclear-deal-exit-strategy-john-bolton-memo-trump.

Brennan Center for Justice. "Proposals for Reform Volume II: National Task Force on Rule of Law & Democracy," October 3, 2019, https://www.brennancenter.org/our-work/policy-solutions/proposals-reform-volume-ii-national-task-force-rule-law-democracy.

Brigety, Reuben. "A Post-American Africa," *Foreign Affairs*, August 28, 2018, https://www.foreignaffairs.com/articles/africa/2018-08-28/post-american-africa.

Brown, Chad P., and Douglas A. Irwin. "Trump's Assault on the Global Trading System," *Foreign Affairs*, September/October 2019, https://www.foreignaffairs.com/articles/asia/2019-08-12/trumps-assault-global-trading-system.

Browning, Christopher R. "The Suffocation of Democracy," *New York Review of Books*, October 25, 2018, https://www.nybooks.com/articles/2018/10/25/suffocation-of-democracy.

Burns, William J. "How the U.S.-Russian Relationship Went Bad," *The Atlantic*, April 2019, https://www.theatlantic.com/magazine/archive/2019/04/william-j-burns-putin-russia/583255.

———. "The Lost Art of American Diplomacy," *Foreign Affairs*, vol. 98, no. 3 (May–June 2019), pp. 98–107.

Campbell, Kurt, and Eli Ratner. "The China Reckoning," *Foreign Affairs*, vol. 97, no. 1 (March–April 2018), pp. 60–70.

Chait, Jonathan. "Will Trump Be Meeting with His Counterpart—Or His Handler?" *New York Magazine*, July 2018, http://nymag.com/daily/intelligencer/2018/07/trump-putin-russia-collusion.html.

Chatzky, Andrew. "Have Sanctions on Russia Changed Putin's Calculus?" Council on Foreign Relations: In Brief, May 2, 2019, https://www.cfr.org/in-brief/have-sanctions-russia-changed-putins-calculus.

Cho Seong Ryoul. "Accomplishments of Korea's Special-Envoy Diplomacy and Future Tasks," *ROK Angle*, no. 76 (April 6, 2018).

Claypool, Rick, Taylor Lincoln, Michael Tanglis, and Alan Zibel. "Corporate Impunity," *Public Citizen*, July 2018, https://www.citizen.org/wp-content/uploads/migration/corporate-enforcement-public-citizen-report-july-2018.pdf.

Cockburn, Andrew. "How to Start a Nuclear War," *Harper's Magazine*, August 2018, pp. 51–58.

Cohen, Michael A. "Mitch McConnell, Republican Nihilist," *New York Review of Books*, February 28, 2019, https://www.nybooks.com/daily/2019/02/25/mitch-mcconnell-republican-nihilist.

Cohen, Raphael S., and Andrew Radin. *Russia's Hostile Measures in Europe: Understanding the Threat*. Santa Monica, CA: RAND Corporation, 2019, https://www.rand.org/pubs/research_reports/RR1793.html.

Daalder, Ivo H., and James M. Lindsay. "The Committee to Save the World Order," *Foreign Affairs*, September 30, 2018, https://www.foreignaffairs.com/articles/2018-09-30/committee-save-world-order.

Davidson, Adam. "Is Fraud Part of the Trump Organization's Business Model?" *The New Yorker*, October 17, 2018, https://www.newyorker.com/news/swamp-chronicles/is-fraud-part-of-the-trump-organizations-business-model.

Diamond, Larry. "Democracy Demotion," *Foreign Affairs*, vol. 98, no. 4 (July–August 2019), pp. 17–25.

Drezner, Daniel W. "This Time Is Different: Why U.S. Foreign Policy Will Never Recover," *Foreign Affairs*, vol. 98, no. 3 (May–June 2019), pp. 10–17.

Engdahl, F. William. "Unintended Consequences: Did Trump Just Give the Middle East to China and Russia?" *Global Research*, January 15, 2020, https://www.globalresearch.ca/did-trump-just-give-middle-east-china-russia/5700660.

Entous, Adam. "Donald Trump's New World Order," *The New Yorker*, June 18, 2018, https://www.newyorker.com/magazine/2018/06/18/donald-trumps-new-world-order.

Falk, Richard. "Wider Consequences of U.S. Withdrawal from the UN Human Rights Council," *Global Justice in the 21st Century* (blog), June 21, 2018, https://richardfalk.wordpress.com/2018/07/07/wider-consequences-of-u-s-withdrawal-from-the-un-human-rights-council.

Filkins, Dexter. "On the Warpath," *The New Yorker*, May 6, 2019, pp. 32–45.

Fitzgerald, Mary, and Claire Provost. "Revealed: Trump-Linked US Christian 'Fundamentalists' Pour Millions of 'Dark Money' into Europe, Boosting the Far Right," *Open Democracy*, March 27, 2019, http://www.opendemocracy.net/en/5050/revealed-trump-linked-us-christian-fundamentalists-pour-millions-of-dark-money-into-europe-boosting-the-far-right.

Foer, Franklin. "The Kremlin Inches Closer to the Biden Plot," *The Atlantic*, January 18, 2010, https://www.theatlantic.com/ideas/archive/2020/01/firtash-kremlin-biden/605188.

Fox, Emily Jane. "Michael Cohen Says Trump Repeatedly Used Racist Language before His Presidency," *Vanity Fair*, November 2, 2018, https://www.vanityfair.com/news/2018/11/michael-cohen-trump-racist-language.

Friedman, Uri. "America's Alliance System Will Face One of Its Biggest Tests Yet," *The Atlantic*, May 23, 2019, https://www.theatlantic.com/politics/archive/2019/05/us-and-south-korea-gear-burden-sharing-talks/589999.

Fuchs, Michael. "The North Korea Deal: Why Diplomacy Is Still the Best Option," *Foreign Affairs*, December 21, 2017, https://www.foreignaffairs.com/authors/michael-fuchs.

Glass, Charles. "'Tell Me How This Ends,'" *Harper's*, February 2019, pp. 51–61.

Glasser, Susan B. "The Secretary of Trump," *The New Yorker*, August 26, 2019, pp. 50–59.

Ghitis, Frida. "Democracy in Latin America Is in Grave Peril, A Respected Pollster Warns," *World Politics Review*, November 15, 2018, www.worldpoliticsreview.com/articles/26762/democracy-in-latin-america-is-in-grave-peril-a-respected-pollster-warns.

———. "Grumbling Grows from Guyana to Australia Over China's 'Debt Trap Diplomacy,'" *World Politics Review*, November 8, 2018, www.worldpoliticsreview.com/articles/26694/grumbling-grows-from-guyana-to-australia-over-china-s-debt-trap-diplomacy.

Glueck, Katie. "Donald Trump's Man on Israel," *Politico*, August 4, 2016, https://www.politico.com/story/2016/08/donald-trump-israel-jason-greenblatt-226651.

Gramer, Robbie. "Human Rights Groups Bristling at State Department Report," *Foreign Policy*, April 21, 2018, https://foreignpolicy.com/2018/04/21/human-rights-groups-bristling-at-state-human-rights-report.

———. "Trump's Shadow War on Climate Science," *Foreign Policy*, July 31, 2019, https://foreignpolicy.com/2019/07/31/trumps-shadow-war-on-climate-science-state-department-intelligence-analyst-resigns-white-house-muzzles-intelligence-assessment-climate-change-environment.

Gurtov, Mel. "The China Conundrum," *China-US Focus*, September 26, 2018, https://www.chinausfocus.com/foreign-policy/the-china-conundrum.

———. "The Coronavirus and China-U.S. Relations," *Foreign Policy In Focus*, March 31, 2020, https://fpif.org/the-coronavirus-and-china-u-s-relations.

———. "Summit Misdirection: Trump's North Korea Ploy to Tackle Iran," *Global Asia*, September 21, 2018, https://globalasia.org/v13no3/focus/summit-misdirection-trumps-north-korea-ploy-to-tackle-iran_mel-gurtov.

Gurtov, Mel, and Carla Freeman. "Unpacking a US Decision to Engage North Korea: What It Entails and What It Could Achieve," *38 North* Special Report, April 2018, https://www.38north.org/reports/2018/04/cfreemanmgurtov041618.

Gurtov, Mel, and Mark Selden. "The Dangerous New US Consensus on China and the Future of US-China Relations," *The Asia-Pacific Journal*, vol. 17, no. 5 (July 21, 2019), https://apjjf.org/2019/15/Gurtov-Selden.html.

Haass, Richard. "How a World Order Ends," *Foreign Affairs*, vol. 98, no. 1 (January–February 2019), pp. 22–30.

Harcourt, Bernard E. "How Trump Fuels the Fascist Right," *New York Review of Books*, November 29, 2018, https://www.nybooks.com/daily/2018/11/29/how-trump-fuels-the-fascist-right.

Harp, Seth. "Is the Trump Administration Pivoting the Fight in Syria toward War with Iran?" *The New Yorker*, November 26, 2018, www.newyorker.com/news/dispatch/is-the-trump-administration-pivoting-the-fight-in-syria-toward-a-war-with-iran.

Hedges, Chris. "The Coming Collapse," *Common Dreams*, May 21, 2018, http://www.commondreams.org/views/2018/05/21/coming-collapse.

Holden, Emily. "Trump 'Turns Back the Clock' by Luring Drilling Companies to Pristine Lands," *The Guardian*, February 12, 2020.

Human Rights Watch. "Venezuela: Numbers Highlight Health Crisis," November 15, 2018, http://www.hrw.org/news/2018/11/15/venezuela-numbers-highlight-health-crisis.

Inglehart, Ronald. "The Age of Insecurity," *Foreign Affairs*, vol. 97, no. 3 (May–June 2018), pp. 20–28.

Kalmbacher, Colin. "Trump Adviser Admits He Got Background Info on Hunter Biden, Then Tells Falsehood on Air about It," *Law & Crime*, October 10, 2019, https://lawandcrime.com/high-profile/trump-advisor-admitted-he-got-background-info-on-hunter-biden-from-china-then-lied-on-air-about-it.

Kertscher, Tom. "Donald Trump's Racial Comments about Hispanic Judge in Trump University Case," *Politifact*, June 8, 2016, http://www.politifact.com/wisconsin/article/2016/jun/08/donald-trumps-racial-comments-about-judge-trump-un.

Khalidi, Rashid. "The Neocolonial Arrogance of the Kushner Plan," *New York Review of Books*, June 12, 2019, http://www.nybooks.com/daily/2019/06/12/the-neocolonial-arrogance-of-the-kushner-plan.

Klare, Michael T. "Making Nuclear Weapons Menacing Again," *The Nation*, April 8, 2019, pp. 16–19.

Kornbluh, Peter. "Cold War on Cuba," *The Nation*, May 13, 2019, pp. 4–8.

———. "Is Cuba Next?" *The Nation*, February 25–March 4, 2019, pp. 6–8.

Kristensen, Hans M., and Matt Korda. "United States Nuclear Forces, 2020," *Bulletin of the Atomic Scientists*, January 13, 2020, https://thebulletin.org/2020/01/united-states-nuclear-forces-2020.

Kuttner, Robert. "Steve Bannon, Unrepentant," *The American Prospect*, August 16, 2017, https://prospect.org/article/steve-bannon-unrepentant.

Lagarda, Helena. "China Rhetoric Meets Reality: Beijing Caught Out by the Iran Crisis," *International Institute for Security Studies*, no. 6 (July–September 2019), https://www.iiss.org/blogs/research-paper/2020/02/china-security-tracker-n6.

Larmer, Brook. "What Soybean Politics Tells Us about Argentina and China," *New York Times Magazine*, January 30, 2019, https://www.nytimes.com/2019/01/30/magazine/what-soybean-politics-tell-us-about-argentina-and-china.html.

Lankov, Andrei. "Kim Jong Un Is a Survivor, Not a Madman," *Foreign Policy*, April 26, 2017, http://foreignpolicy.com/2017/04/26/kim-jong-un-is-a-survivor-not-a-madman.

Layne, Christopher, and Benjamin Schwarz. "American Hegemony—Without an Enemy," *Foreign Policy*, no. 92 (Fall 1993), pp. 1–8.

LeoGrande, William M. "Sixty Years after the Revolution, Is a 'New Cuba' Emerging?" *World Politics Review*, January 14, 2019, http://www.worldpoliticsreview.com/articles/27173/sixty-years-after-the-revolution-is-a-new-cuba-emerging.

Lynch, Colum. "Trump's 'Unbridled, Egotistical Narcissism Defines White House Summits," *Foreign Policy*, July 20, 2018, https://foreignpolicy.com/2018/07/20/trumps-unbridled-egotistical-narcissism-thomas-pickering_helsinki-summit-putin-u-s-russiadefines-white-house-summits.

Maddow, Rachel. "Rachel Maddow Interviews Lev Parnas," parts 1 and 2, MSNBC, January 15, 2020, https://www.youtube.com/watch?v=DVnZVuhOycs (part 1) and https://www.youtube.com/watch?v=Xj-4V5ui8H4 (part 2).

Mansourov, Alexandre Y. "Kim Jong Un's Nuclear Doctrine and Strategy: What Everyone Needs to Know," Nautilus Institute: NAPSNet paper, December 16, 2014, https://nautilus.org/napsnet/napsnet-special-reports/kim-jong-uns-nuclear-doctrine-and-strategy-what-everyone-needs-to-know.

Mastro, Oriana Skylar. "The Stealth Superpower: How China Hid Its Global Ambitions," *Foreign Affairs*, vol. 98, no. 1 (January–February 2019), pp. 31–39.

Mathews, John A., and Mark Selden. "China: The Emergence of the Petroyuan and the Challenge to US Dollar Hegemony," *The Asia-Pacific Journal*, vol. 16, no. 3 (November 10, 2018), https://apjjf.org/2018/22/Mathews.html.

Mazarr, Michael J. "The Real History of the Liberal Order: Neither Myth nor Accident," *Foreign Affairs*, August 7, 2018, http://www.foreignaffairs.com/articles/2018-08-07/real-history-liberal-order.

———. "Summary of the Building a Sustainable International Order Project," RAND Corporation, 2018, http://www.rand.org/pubs/research_reports/RR2397.html.

McAdams, Dan P. "The Mind of Donald Trump," *The Atlantic*, June 2016, http://www.theatlantic.com/magazine/archive/2016/06/the-mind-of-donald-trump/480771.

McKibben, Bill. "How Extreme Weather Is Shrinking the Planet," *The New Yorker*, November 26, 2018, http://www.newyorker.com/magazine/2018/11/26/how-extreme-weather-is-shrinking-the-planet.

McFaul, Michael. "Russia as It Is: A Grand Strategy for Confronting Putin," *Foreign Affairs*, vol. 97, no. 4 (July–August 2018), pp. 82–91.

Metz, Steven. "Trump Seems to Be Writing Off African Security, but Will It Matter to the U.S.?" *World Politics Review*, September 7, 2018, http://www.worldpoliticsreview.com/articles/25794/trump-seems-to-be-writing-off-african-security-but-will-it-matter-to-the-u-s.

Miller, Jennifer M. "Let's Not Be Laughed at Anymore: Donald Trump and Japan from the 1980s to the Present," *Journal of American-East Asian Relations*, vol. 25 (2018), pp. 138–68.

Mogelson, Luke. "The Afghan Way of Death," *The New Yorker*, October 28, 2019, pp. 32–53.

Moniz, Ernest J., and Sam Nunn. "The Return of Doomsday," *Foreign Affairs*, August 6, 2019, http://www.foreignaffairs.com/articles/russian-federation/2019-08-06/return-doomsday.

Morin, Rebecca. "Trump Says He Has 'Natural Instinct for Science' When It Comes to Climate Change," *Politico*, October 17, 2018, http://www.politico.com/story/2018/10/17/trump-instinct-climate-change-910004.

Mounk, Yascha, and Roberto Stefan Foa. "The End of the Democratic Century," *Foreign Affairs*, vol. 97, no. 3 (May–June 2018), pp. 29–36.

Müller, Jan-Werner. "False Flags: The Myth of the Nationalist Resurgence," *Foreign Affairs*, vol. 98, no. 2 (March–April 2019), pp. 35–41.

Naftali, Timothy. "The Wounded Presidency, Part One," *Foreign Affairs*, January 28, 2020, http://www.foreignaffairs.com/articles/united-states/impeachment_nixon_wounded_presidency_part_one.

Nathan, Andrew J. "How China Really Sees the Trade War," *Foreign Affairs*, June 27, 2019, http://www.foreignaffairs.com/articles/china/2019-06-27/how-china-really-sees-trade-war.

Nguyen, Tina. "Leaked Documents Confirm the Worst-Kept Secret of Trump's Presidency," *Vanity Fair*, February 4, 2019, http://www.vanityfair.com/news/2019/02/the-worst-kept-secret-of-trumps-presidency.

———. "Steve Bannon's Populist Media Empire Is Funded with Offshore Cash," *Vanity Fair*, November 7, 2017, http://www.vanityfair.com/news/2017/11/steve-bannon-paradise-papers-offshore-cash.

Osnos, Evan. "Fight Fight, Talk Talk," *The New Yorker*, January 13, 2020, pp. 32–45.

———. "On the Brink," *The New Yorker*, September 18, 2017, pp. 36–53.

Packer, George. "A Hole in the Center," *The New Yorker*, November 12, 2018, pp. 52–61.

Pape, Robert A. "Why Economic Sanctions Do Not Work," *International Security*, vol. 22, no. 2 (Fall 1997), pp. 90–136.

Pieraccini, Federico. "The Deeper Story behind the Assassination of Soleimani," *Strategic Culture*, January 8, 2020, http://www.strategic-culture.org/news/2020/01/08/the-deeper-story-behind-the-assassination-of-soleimani.

Plaskin, Glenn. "The Playboy Interview with Donald Trump," *Playboy*, March 1, 1990, https://www.playboy.com/read/playboy-interview-donald-trump-1990.

Pompeo, Michael R. "After the Deal: A New Iran Strategy," U.S. Department of State, May 21, 2018, https://www.state.gov/after-the-deal-a-new-iran-strategy.

———. "Confronting Iran: The Trump Administration's Strategy," *Foreign Affairs*, vol. 97, no. 6 (November–December 2018), pp. 60–70.

———. "Transcript: Secretary of State Mike Pompeo on 'Face the Nation,'" interview by Margaret Brennan, CBS News, September 22, 2019, https://www.cbsnews.com/news/transcript-secretary-of-state-mike-pompeo-on-face-the-nation-september-22-2019.

Posen, Adam S. "How Trump Is Repelling Foreign Investment," *Foreign Affairs*, July 23, 2018, https://www.foreignaffairs.com/articles/united-states/2018-07-23/how-trump-repelling-foreign-investment.

Riedel, Bruce. "The $110 Billion Arms Deal to Saudi Arabia Is Fake News," *Brookings* (blog), June 5, 2017, https://www.brookings.edu/blog/markaz/2017/06/05/the-110-billion-arms-deal-to-saudi-arabia-is-fake-news.

Roth, David. "The Man Who Was Upset: Making Sense of Donald Trump's Petulant Reign," *The New Republic*, June 12, 2019, https://newrepublic.com/article/154100/making-sense-donald-trump-petulant-presidency.

Sigal, Leon V. "Premature Epitaphs for Nuclear Diplomacy with North Korea," *38 North*, January 9, 2020, http://www.38north.org/2020/01/lsigal200109.

Ruff, Tilman. "Negotiating the UN Treaty on the Prohibition of Nuclear Weapons and the Role of ICAN," *Global Change, Peace & Security*, April 30, 2018, https://doi.org/10.1080/14781158.2018.1465908.

Sabatini, Christopher, and Jimena Galindo. "How the Trump Administration Joined the Western Hemisphere's Rogue Regimes," *World Politics Review*, January 4, 2019, http://www.worldpoliticsreview.com/articles/27101/how-the-trump-administration-joined-the-western-hemisphere-s-rogue-regimes.

Sanders, Bernie. "Sanders Speech at SAIS: Building a Global Democratic Movement to Counter Authoritarianism," Speech at the School of Advanced International Studies, Johns Hopkins University, Washington, DC, October 9, 2018, http://www.sanders.senate.gov/newsroom/press-releases/sanders-speech-at-sais-building-a-global-democratic-movement-to-counter-authoritarianism.

Schmitt, Alexandra. "President Trump's Alarming Human Rights Agenda at Home and Abroad," Center for American Progress, December 10, 2019, http://www.americanprogress.org/issues/security/reports/2019/12/10/478458/president-trumps-alarming-human-rights-agenda-home-abroad.

Schott, Jeffrey. "The TPP after Trump," *Global Asia*, vol. 13, no. 2 (June 2018), pp. 32–35.

Seligman, Lara. "Will Congress Let Trump Build More Nuclear Weapons?" *Foreign Policy*, April 11, 2019, https://foreignpolicy.com/2019/04/11/will-congress-let-trump-expand-americas-nuclear-arsenal.

Scoville, Ryan. "Troubling Trends in Ambassadorial Appointments: 1980 to the Present," *Lawfare*, February 20, 2019, http://www.lawfareblog.com/troubling-trends-ambassadorial-appointments-1980-present.

Shambaugh, David. "All Xi, All the Time: Can China's President Live Up to His Own Top Billing?" *Global Asia*, vol. 13, no. 3 (September 2018), pp. 14–19.

———. "U.S.-China Decoupling: How Feasible, How Desirable?" *China-US Focus Digest*, vol. 24 (December 2019), pp. 18–22.

Shany, Yuval. "Israel's New Plan to Annex the West Bank: What Happens Next?" *Lawfare*, May 6, 2019, http://www.lawfareblog.com/israels-new-plan-annex-west-bank-what-happens-next.

Shugerman, Jed Handelsman. "L'Affaire Kushner," *Slate*, March 2, 2018, https://slate.com/news-and-politics/2018/03/a-series-of-revelations-about-jared-kushner-have-added-further-credence-to-a-key-claim-of-the-steele-dossier.html.

Simon, Steven. "The Middle East: Trump Blunders In," *New York Review of Books*, February 13, 2020, https://www.nybooks.com/articles/2020/02/13/middle-east-trump-blunders-in.

Simon, Steven, and Jonathan Stevenson. "Iran: The Case against War," *New York Review of Books*, August 15, 2019, http://www.nybooks.com/articles/2019/08/15/iran-case-against-war.

"SMA TRADOC White Paper—Russian Strategic Intentions," NSI, May 2019, https://nsiteam.com/sma-white-paper-russian-strategic-intentions.

Smith, Sheila A. "Seoul and Tokyo: No Longer on the Same Side," Council on Foreign Relations: *Asia Unbound* (blog), July 1, 2019, http://www.cfr.org/blog/seoul-and-tokyo-no-longer-same-side.

Snodgrass, Guy. "Inside Trump's First Pentagon Briefing," *Politico*, October 21, 2019, http://www.politico.com/magazine/story/2019/10/21/inside-trumps-first-pentagon-briefing-229865.

Sperber, Amanda. "Terror Out of the Blue," *The Nation*, February 25–March 4, 2019, pp. 16–20.

Sullivan, Mark P. "Venezuela: Overview of U.S. Sanctions," *Congressional Research Service*, November 21, 2018, https://fas.org/sgp/crs/row/IF10715.pdf.

Swan, Jonathan, and Jim VandeHei, "Exclusive: Trump Says His Supporters Demand Red-Hot Rhetoric," *Axios*, November 1, 2018, http://www.axios.com/trump-axios-hbo-media-enemy-of-the-people-441ae349-3670-4f7d-b5d5-04d339a15f68.html.

Toobin, Jeffrey. "Roger Stone's and Jerome Corsi's Time in the Barrel," *The New Yorker*, February 18, 2019, http://www.newyorker.com/magazine/2019/02/18/roger-stones-and-jerome-corsis-time-in-the-barrel.

Toosi, Nahal. "Trump Ambassador Blocks Scrutiny of Israel," *Politico*, June 16, 2016, https://www.politico.com/story/2018/06/16/trump-ambassador-israel-scrutiny-military-human-rights-david-friedman-650383.

Trump, Donald. "President Trump on Christine Blasey Ford, His Relationships with Vladimir Putin and Kim Jong Un and More," interview by Lesley Stahl, *60 Minutes*, October 15, 2018, https://www.cbsnews.com/news/donald-trump-full-interview-60-minutes-transcript-lesley-stahl-2018-10-14.

"The Trump Trademarks: The 'America First' President's Truly Global IP Portfolio Revealed," *World Trademark Review*, October 24, 2019.

Tulchin, Joseph S. "China's Rising Profile in Latin America," *The Asia-Pacific Journal*, vol. 17, no. 3 (January 15, 2019), https://apjjf.org/2019/02/Tulchin.html.

Turner, Fred. "Machine Politics," *Harper's*, January 2019, pp. 25–33.

Union of Concerned Scientists. "The IPCC: Who Are They and Why Do Their Climate Reports Matter?" October 11, 2018, https://www.ucsusa.org/global-warming/science-and-impacts/science/ipcc-backgrounder.html.

Valverde, Miriam. "Donald Trump's Executive Order Ending His Administration's Separation of Immigrant Families," *Politifact*, June 25, 2018, https://www.politifact.com/truth-o-meter/article/2018/jun/25/donald-trumps-executive-order-ending-his-administr.

Vatanka, Alex. "China's Great Game in Iran," *Foreign Policy*, September 5, 2019, https://foreignpolicy.com/2019/09/05/chinas-great-game-in-iran.

Waas, Murray. "The Flynn Tapes: A New Tell," *New York Review of Books*, August 29, 2018, http://www.nybooks.com/daily/2018/08/29/the-flynn-tapes-a-new-tell.

Walt, Stephen M. "The End of Hubris," *Foreign Affairs*, vol. 98, no. 3 (May–June 2019), pp. 26–75.

———. "Global Warming Is Setting Fire to American Leadership," *Foreign Policy*, December 3, 2018, https://foreignpolicy.com/2018/12/03/global-warming-will-set-fire-to-american-leadership.

Wang Jisi, "Did America Get China Wrong?" *Foreign Affairs*, vol. 97, no. 4 (July–August 2018), pp. 183–84.

Warren, Elizabeth. "A Foreign Policy for All: Strengthening Democracy—At Home and Abroad," *Foreign Policy*, vol. 98, no. 1 (January–February 2019), pp. 50–61.

Weiner, Tim. "The 'Witch Hunters,'" *New York Review of Books*, August 16, 2018.

Wise, Justin. "Senate Intel Found No Evidence of 2016 Ukraine Interference: Report," *The Hill*, December 2, 2019, https://thehill.com/homenews/senate/472721-senate-intel-committee-found-no-evidence-of-top-down-ukraine-interference.

Wit, Joel S. "You Can Negotiate Anything—Even North Korea," *Foreign Affairs*, April 27, 2016, http://foreignpolicy.com/2016/04/27/north_korea_negotiations_kim_jong_un_agreed_framework.

Woon, Darren. "Deutsche Bank Whistleblower: Russian State-Owned Bank Underwrote Trump's Loans," *The Intellectualist*, January 3, 2020, https://mavenroundtable.io/theintellectualist/news/deutsche-bank-whistleblower-russian-state-owned-bank-underwrote-trump-s-loans-8aSkypIDCUOWj7AKxwASAA.

Wright, Thomas. "Democrats Need to Place China at the Center of Their Foreign Policy," Brookings, May 15, 2019, http://www.brookings.edu/blog/order-from-chaos/2019/05/15/democrats-need-to-place-china-at-the-center-of-their-foreign-policy.

Yan Xuetong, "The Age of Uneasy Peace: Chinese Power in a Divided World," *Foreign Affairs*, vol. 98, no. 1 (January–February 2019), pp. 40–46.

Zessoules, Daniella. "China Tariff Costs by Congressional District," Center for American Progress, August 29, 2019, http://www.americanprogress.org/issues/economy/news/2019/08/29/473895/china-tariff-costs-congressional-district.

Zhang Tuosheng, "Developing a New Type of Major Power Relationship with the U.S.," *China-US Focus*, January 4, 2013, http://www.chinausfocus.com/foreign-policy/developing-a-new-type-of-major-power-relationship-between-china-and-the-u-s.

Zunes, Stephen. "U.S. Recognition of Israel's Golan Annexation a Threat to World Order," *The Progressive*, March 25, 2019, https://progressive.org/dispatches/us-recognition-golan-annexation-a-threat-to-world-order-zunes-190325.

Reports and Documents

Bolton, John R. "Remarks by National Security Advisor Ambassador John R. Bolton on the Administration's Policies in Latin America," November 2, 2018, https://www.whitehouse.gov/briefings-statements/remarks-national-security-advisor-ambassador-john-r-bolton-administrations-policies-latin-america.

———. "Remarks by National Security Advisor Ambassador John R. Bolton on the Trump Administration's New Africa Strategy," December 13, 2018, http://www.whitehouse.gov/briefings-statements/remarks-national-security-advisor-ambassador-john-r-bolton-trump-administrations-new-africa-strategy.

Brown University: Watson Institute for International and PublicAffairs. Costs of War Project, https://watson.brown.edu/costsofwar.

Coats, Daniel R. *Worldwide Threat Assessment of the US Intelligence Community*, Senate Select Committee on Intelligence, January 29, 2019, https://www.dni.gov/files/ODNI/documents/2019-ATA-SFR---SSCI.pdf.

Finn, Peter, ed. *The Mueller Report*. New York: Scribner, 2019.

Freedom House. https://freedomhouse.org/countries/freedom-world/scores.

Fund for Peace. "Fragile States Index, 2018," http://www.fundforpeace.org/fsi/2018/04/24/fragile-states-index-2018-annual-report.

Geneva Initiative. "Two-State Index, December 26," 2019, via TSI@genevainitiative.org.

House Permanent Select Committee on Intelligence. *The Trump-Ukraine Impeachment Report*, U.S. House of Representatives, 2019, https://www.documentcloud.org/documents/6566093-House-impeachment-report-PDF.html.

Interdisciplinary Group of Independent Experts. *Nicaragua*, December 2018, http://gieinicaragua.org/giei-content/uploads/2018/12/GIEI_INFORME_DIGITAL.pdf.

Intergovernmental Panel on Climate Change. "Global Warming of 1.5°C," October 2018, http://www.ipcc.ch/sr15.

International Campaign to Abolish Nuclear Weapons. http://www.icanw.org.

"Joint Statement of President Donald J. Trump of the United States of America and Chairman Kim Jong Un of the Democratic People's Republic of Korea at the Singapore Summit," June 12, 2018, https://www.whitehouse.gov/briefings-statements/joint-statement-president-donald-j-trump-united-states-america-chairman-kim-jong-un-democratic-peoples-republic-korea-singapore-summit.

Kim Jong-un. "Report on 5th Plenary Meeting of 7th C.C. [Central Committee], WPK [Korean Workers Party]," January 1, 2020, https://kcnawatch.org/newstream/1577829999-473709661/report-on-5th-plenary-meeting-of-7th-c-c-wpk.

Ocasio-Cortez, Alexandria, and Ed Markey. "Green New Deal Resolution," 2019, https://apps.npr.org/documents/document.html?id=5731829-Ocasio-Cortez-Green-New-Deal-Resolution.

Pence, Mike. "Remarks by Vice President Pence on the Administration's Policy toward China," October 4, 2018, http://www.whitehouse.gov/briefings-statements/remarks-vice-president-pence-administrations-policy-toward-china.

Reidmiller, D. R., C. W. Avery, D. R. Easterling, K. E. Kunkel, K. L. M. Lewis, T. K. Maycock, and B. C. Stewart, eds. *Impacts, Risks, and Adaptation in the United States: Fourth National Climate Assessment, Volume II*, Washington, DC: U.S. Global Change Research Program, 2018, https://doi.org/10.7930/NCA4.2018.

Richter-Menge, J., M. L. Druckenmiller, and M. Jeffries, eds. "Arctic Report Card 2019," NOAA: Arctic Program, 2019, https://arctic.noaa.gov/Report-Card/Report-Card-2019.

Ruston, Lynn, and Richard Johnson. *Building Security through Cooperation: Report of the NTI Working Group on Cooperative Threat Reduction with North Korea*, Nuclear Threat Initiative, 2019, https://media.nti.org/documents/NTI_DPRK2019_RPT_FNL.pdf.

"Statement by Former Federal Prosecutors," May 6, 2019, https://medium.com/@dojalumni/statement-by-former-federal-prosecutors-8ab7691c2aa1.

Taylor, William B. "Opening Statement of Ambassador William B. Taylor, October 22, 2019," October 23, 2019, http://www.washingtonpost.com/context/opening-statement-of-ambassador-william-b-taylor/6b3a6edf-f976-4081-ba7f-bce45468a3ff.

Trump, Donald J. *National Security Strategy of the United States of America*, December 2017, https://www.whitehouse.gov/wp-content/uploads/2017/12/NSS-Final-12-18-2017-0905-2.pdf.

———. "Remarks by President Trump after Meeting with Vice Chairman Kim Yong Chol of the Democratic People's Republic of Korea," June 1, 2018, https://www.whitehouse.gov/briefings-statements/remarks-president-trump-meeting-vice-chairman-kim-yong-chol-democratic-peoples-republic-korea.

———. "Remarks by President Trump to the 74th Session of the United Nations General Assembly," September 29, 2019, https://www.whitehouse.gov/briefings-statements/remarks-president-trump-74th-session-united-nations-general-assembly.

———. "Statement from President Donald J. Trump on Standing with Saudi Arabia," November 20, 2018, https://www.whitehouse.gov/briefings-statements/statement-president-donald-j-trump-standing-saudi-arabia.

Union of Concerned Scientists. "The IPCC: Who Are They and Why Do Their Climate Reports Matter?," October 11, 2018, https://www.ucsusa.org/global-warming/science-and-impacts/science/ipcc-backgrounder.html.

United Nations Human Rights, Office of the High Commissioner. "North Korea: UN Expert Calls for Engagement Amid Continuing Rights Violations," October 24, 2019, https://www.ohchr.org/en/NewsEvents/Pages/DisplayNews.aspx?NewsID=25199&LangID=E.

United Nations Security Council. "Report of the Panel of Experts Established Pursuant to Resolution 1874 (2009)," S/2019/691, August 30, 2019, https://undocs.org/s/2019/691.

U.S. Department of State, Office of the Spokesperson. "The United States Imposes Sanctions on Venezuelan Individuals and Entities," September 25, 2018, https://www.state.gov/r/pa/prs/ps/2018/09/286190.htm.

U.S. Senate Select Committee on Intelligence. *Report of the Select Committee on Intelligence on Russian Active Measures Campaigns and Interference in the 2016 U.S. Election, Volume 2: Russia's Use of Social Media with Additional Views*, 2019, https://www.intelligence.senate.gov/sites/default/files/documents/Report_Volume2.pdf.

World Justice Project. https://worldjusticeproject.org.

Yovanovitch, Marie L. "Opening Statement of Marie L. Yovanovitch to the House of Representatives Permanent Select Committee on Intelligence, Committee on Foreign Affairs, and Committee on Oversight and Reform," October 11, 2019, https://int.nyt.com/data/documenthelper/6456-yovanovitch-opening-statement-ukraine/45caf98f358647f0a796/optimized/full.pdf#page=1.

Media

Note: News articles and opinion pieces may be found in the notes section of each chapter.

AOL News
Bloomberg
Buzzfeed News
CBS News
CNBC
CNN
DW.com
Financial Times (London)
Fox News
The Guardian (US edition)
Huffpost
The Korea Times (Seoul)
Los Angeles Times
Military Times
MSNBC
NBC News
The New York Times
Reuters
The Sun (London)
The Telegraph (London)
The Times (London)
The Times of Israel
The Wall Street Journal
The Washington Post
Yahoo! News
Zeit Online

Index

US bases, increased danger to, 81; waivers on oil sanctions as revoked, 83
Johnson, Boris, 62, 63, 151n23
Joint Comprehensive Plan of Action (JCPOA), 81, 84
Jones, Alex, 50–51

Kagan, Robert, 122
Kasich, John, 10–11
Kelly, John, 22, 43, 60, 136n9, 136n12
Keystone XL pipeline, 54
Khamenei, Ayatollah Ali, 84, 85
Khashoggi, Jamal, 95, 96, 100, 101
Kim Dae-jung, 77, 78
Kim Jong-un: at 2018 nuclear summit, 13, 16, 18, 75; as an authoritarian leader, 26; Hanoi summit, ending without agreement, 79; human rights record, 95; missile tests, sanctioning, 76, 78, 80–81; nuclear weapons, reliance on, 76–77, 124; Trump, diplomatic relations with, 38, 39, 77. *See also* North Korea
Kissinger, Henry, 125
Koch, Charles, 13, 40
Kudlow, Larry, 25
Kurdish forces, 45, 86, 120, 145n40
Kushner, Jared: Israeli-Palestinian conflict, plans to resolve, 30, 31; as a real estate owner, 56; Saudi monarchy, ties to, 17, 34, 98–99, 100–101, 142n84; security clearance issues, 34, 48, 136n9; as a Trump advisor, 22, 25, 26, 33, 121, 141n74; as a Trump surrogate, 59

Lankov, Andrei, 76–77
Latin America, 24, 73, 88–92
Le Pen, Marine, 62–63
Lewandowski, Corey, 49–50
Libya, 17, 26, 79
Lighthizer, Robert, 25

Macron, Emmanuel, 37
Maduro, Nicolás, 89–91, 92, 120, 166n113
Make American Great Again (MAGA), 39–40
Manafort, Paul, 27–28, 33, 62
market socialism, 68

Mattis, James: as a former NATO commander, 18; globalist view, representing, 25, 119; NATO leaders, intervening with, 61; Pyongyang, diplomatic relations with, 78; resignation of, 14, 60, 86; as a Trump appointee, 43, 60, 98
May, Theresa, 49, 62, 63
MBS. *See* Salman, Mohammed bin
McCabe, Andrew, 54, 148n89
McCain, John, 10, 42, 60, 129, 133n6, 147n77
McChrystal, Stanley, 60
McDonnell, Mitch, 54, 121
McFarland, K. T., 33
McKinley, Michael, 29, 140n57
McMaster, H. R., 25, 37, 60, 119, 137n31
McRaven, William, 60, 120, 174n13
Mercer, Robert, 62
Merkel, Angela, 49, 63, 151n21
Merkley, Jeff, 114
Mexico. *See* US-Mexico border
Middle East. *See* Afghanistan; Iran; Iraq; Israel; Saudi Arabia; Syria; Turkey; Yemen
Miliband, David, 114
Miller, Stephen, 25, 113, 114, 144n30, 172n8, 172n20
Mnuchin, Steve, 25
Moon Jae-in, 39, 76, 77, 80
Morales, Jimmy, 91–92
Mueller, Robert S., III, 10, 14, 34, 35, 50, 65
Mueller Report: Barr, interference with, 15, 53, 140n60; coup, investigators accused of trying to carry out, 12; Mafioso, making Trump sound like, 16, 154n57; Republicans, failing to vote for protection of investigation, 67; Russian assistance to Trump team, revealing, 30, 33, 34, 64, 142n80, 142n89; Sessions, as criticized for not undermining investigation, 13, 133n4
Mullen, Mike, 14
Mulvaney, Mick, 22–23, 43–44, 136n12, 138n45
Murdoch, Rupert, 50
Muslims: Chinese Muslims of Xinjiang, 71; cultural threat, Trump, portraying

122–124; North Korea, maximum pressure approach to, 75–81; obstruction of justice, engaging in, 34, 120, 142n91, 148n89; political enemies, attacks on, 10, 11–13, 14–15, 22–23, 46, 118; Russia connection, 64–68; Saudi-Trump relations, 93, 98–101; tariffs, imposing, 77–78, 103–106; tribalism, accelerating the triumph of, 129; Trump rallies, 12, 46, 147n70; Ukraine funds, withholding, 14, 29, 65, 120. *See also* Trump administration advisers; Trump character traits; Trump threats and attacks; Trump tweets

Trump, Donald, Jr. (Don), 6, 22, 32, 33, 55

Trump, Eric, 6, 55, 67

Trump, Fred, 5, 48

Trump, Ivanka, 22, 33, 48, 56, 136n9

Trump, Melania, 88

Trump administration advisers: attempts to reign in or sway Trump, 52, 75; border wall, as the idea of a political adviser, 111–112; coronavirus, Trump not listening to advisers on, 125; creative explanations, as known for, 49–50; disconnect with policy advisers, 65, 66; informal and civilian advisers, 43, 50, 59, 97; internationalists and globalists, 3, 104, 117, 119; Jared Kushner, senior adviser, 22, 25, 30, 33, 98–99; John Bolton, national security adviser, 14, 25, 26, 29; Kim Jong-un, advisers worried over exchanges with, 76; Kurdish forces, Trump defying advice on, 45, 86; lawlessness of, 16, 120; Michael Flynn, national security adviser, 15; Middle East advisers, 23, 80, 84; NATO, Trump complaining about to advisers, 61; Omarosa M. Newman, firing of, 13–14, 46; Roger Stone, longtime adviser, 33, 53, 144n28, 175n28; South America, right-leaning advisers on, 89, 164n92; tight circle of advisers, Trump maintaining, 5; unpredictability of Trump, contending with, 38; Vladimir Putin, Trump believing over advisers, 92

Trump character traits: corruption, 6, 16, 34, 55–57, 94, 117, 125; ethics, lack of,

12, 24, 48; ignorance, vii, 23, 53, 108, 120; incendiary language use, 6, 47, 111, 119, 149n109; insensitivity, 19, 117, 148n80; intolerance, 16, 58, 117; lies, engaging in, 1, 5, 6, 11, 13, 33, 34, 46, 47–50, 54, 55, 57, 113, 120–121; loyalty, demanding, 5, 10, 15, 21, 43, 44, 46, 120–121, 125; official secrets, inability to safeguard, 59, 121; self-aggrandizement, 9; unpredictability, 22, 38, 117

Trump Organization, 5, 30, 55, 131n2, 154n55

Trump threats and attacks: allies and friends, Trump threatening, 2; concessions, threats as a method of achieving, 119; congressional bill, Trump threatening to veto, 115; enemies, attacking through Twitter, 11; European allies, threatening with auto tariffs, 84; government, threatening to shut down over immigration, 113; Hillary Clinton, attacking through tweets, 11; Iraq, threats to incite mass protests in, 87; Kim Jong-un, trading threats with, 76, 95; Mexico, threatening with escalating tariffs, 25; military, Trump threatening to use, 7; NATO, threatening withdrawal from, 62, 124; North Korea, threatening war with, 38, 75, 96–97; sanctions, Trump imposing, 26, 95, 120, 123; security clearances, threatening to remove, 23–24; threatening tweets, Trump sending, 12; Trumpism, costs of, 118–120; Turkey, threatening economic devastation on, 45; US-Mexico border, threats to close, 49

Trump Tower, 6, 32, 38, 49, 67, 68

Trump tweets: disdainful messaging of, 12, 14, 161n48; excessive use of, 12, 22, 23; far-right worldview, support for, 51, 119; media reporting on, 51–52; Muslim travelers, tweets directed at, 112; North Korea, tweets on, 18, 61, 76, 80–81; tariffs, tweets in support of, 103; women, insulting via, 47

Trump University, 47, 55, 56, 113

About the Author

Mel Gurtov is professor emeritus of political science at Portland State University and senior editor of *Asian Perspective*. Dr. Gurtov's graduate education was at Columbia University's School of International Affairs and the University of California Los Angeles. He has published twenty-five books on international affairs, US foreign policy, and East Asia, among them Engaging Adversaries: Peacemaking and Diplomacy in the Human Interest (2018); *Will This Be China's Century? A Skeptic's View* (2013); *Global Politics in the Human Interest* (5th ed., 2007); *Superpower on Crusade: The Bush Doctrine in US Foreign Policy* (2006); and *Pacific Asia? Prospects for Security and Cooperation in East Asia* (2001). A former senior Fulbright scholar, RAND Corporation analyst, and an author of the *Pentagon Papers*, he now lives in Deadwood, Oregon. His blog, *In the Human Interest*, can be found at https://melgurtov.com.

WORLD SOCIAL CHANGE

Series Editor: Mark Selden

www.ingramcontent.com/pod-product-compliance
Lightning Source LLC
Chambersburg PA
CBHW030649270326
41929CB00007B/284